An Anthology of British Neo-Latin Literature

BLOOMSBURY NEO-LATIN SERIES

Series editors: William M. Barton, Stephen Harrison, Gesine Manuwald and
Bobby Xinyue

Early Modern Texts and Anthologies
Edited by Stephen Harrison and Gesine Manuwald

The 'Early Modern Texts and Anthologies' strand of the *Bloomsbury Neo-Latin Series* presents editions of texts with English translations, introductions and notes. Volumes include complete editions of longer single texts and themed anthologies bringing together texts from particular genres, periods or countries and the like.

These editions are primarily aimed at students and scholars and intended to be suitable for use in university teaching, with introductions that give authoritative but not exhaustive accounts of the relevant texts and authors, and commentaries that provide sufficient help for the modern reader in noting links with classical Latin texts and bringing out the cultural context of writing.

Alongside the series' 'Studies in Early Modern Latin Literature' strand, it is hoped that these editions will help to bring important and interesting Neo-Latin texts of the period from 1350 to 1800 to greater prominence in study and scholarship, and make them available for a wider range of academic disciplines as well as for the rapidly growing study of Neo-Latin itself.

An Anthology of British Neo-Latin Literature

Edited by L. B. T. Houghton,
Gesine Manuwald and Lucy R. Nicholas

BLOOMSBURY ACADEMIC
LONDON • NEW YORK • OXFORD • NEW DELHI • SYDNEY

BLOOMSBURY ACADEMIC
Bloomsbury Publishing Plc
50 Bedford Square, London, WC1B 3DP, UK
1385 Broadway, New York, NY 10018, USA

BLOOMSBURY, BLOOMSBURY ACADEMIC and the Diana logo are trademarks
of Bloomsbury Publishing Plc

First published in Great Britain 2020

Cover design: Terry Woodley
Cover image: Elizabeth I when a Princess c.1546, attributed to William Scrots.
Royal Collection Trust / © Her Majesty Queen Elizabeth II 2019

A catalogue record for this book is available from the British Library.

A catalog record for this book is available from the Library of Congress.

ISBN: HB: 978-1-3500-9888-6
PB: 978-1-3500-9889-3
ePDF: 978-1-3500-9891-6
eBook: 978-1-3500-9890-9

Series: Bloomsbury Neo-Latin Series: Early Modern Texts and Anthologies

Typeset by RefineCatch Limited, Bungay, Suffolk

To find out more about our authors and books visit www.bloomsbury.com and
sign up for our newsletters.

To the memory of Professor Ann Moss,
first President of the Society for Neo-Latin Studies (SNLS)
and tireless champion of the study of Neo-Latin language, literature
and culture.

Contents

List of Illustrations

List of Contributors

William M. Barton is Key Researcher at the Ludwig Boltzmann Institute for Neo-Latin Studies, Innsbruck, Austria. His research focuses primarily on engagements with the natural environment and landscape in Latin literature. Within this broad field, his interests have centred on the shifting attitudes towards the mountain in early modern Latin literature, the representation of nature's creative power in the post-classical period and the depiction of the natural world in early descriptions of *la Nouvelle-France*. Barton's more recent published work in these fields includes the monograph *Mountain Aesthetics in Early Modern Latin Literature* (2016) and a critical edition with introduction, translation and commentary of the late-antique *Pervigilium Veneris* (2018).

Jacqueline Glomski is Honorary Senior Research Associate in the Centre for Editing Lives and Letters at University College London (UCL). Her present work focuses on seventeenth-century Neo-Latin prose writing. She is a contributor to and the co-editor of *Acta Conventus Neo-Latini Monasteriensis: Proceedings of the Fifteenth International Congress of Neo-Latin Studies* (with A. Steiner-Weber, K. A. E. Enenkel et al.; 2015) and *Seventeenth-Century Fiction: Text and Transmission* (with Isabelle Moreau, 2016), and has also contributed to *Der neulateinische Roman als Medium seiner Zeit / The Neo-Latin Novel in its Time* (2013) and *A Guide to Neo-Latin Literature* (2017). Jacqueline Glomski is a fellow of the Royal Historical Society and a fellow of the Society of Antiquaries.

Daniel Hadas is Lecturer in Medieval Latin at King's College London (KCL). He has published an edition and commentary of St Augustine's *Epistulae ad Romanos Inchoata Expositio* (*Augustin d'Hippone: Commencement de Commentaire sur l'épître aux Romains*, 2019).

Stephen Harrison is Professor of Latin Literature at the University of Oxford and Extraordinary Professor at the University of Stellenbosch. He has published extensively on Virgil, Horace, Apuleius and their reception, is engaged in an international project to edit the works of George Buchanan and is co-editor of the texts and anthologies strand of Bloomsbury's Neo-Latin Series.

L. B. T. Houghton teaches Classics at Rugby School and is an honorary research fellow of the Department of Greek and Latin at University College

London (UCL). His publications include *Virgil's Fourth Eclogue in the Italian Renaissance* (2019) and numerous chapters and articles on Latin and Neo-Latin literature and the iconography of classical authors. He has edited *Perceptions of Horace* (with Maria Wyke, 2009), *Neo-Latin Poetry in the British Isles* (with Gesine Manuwald, 2012) and *Virgil and Renaissance Culture* (with Marco Sgarbi, 2018).

Sarah Knight is Professor of Renaissance Literature in the School of Arts at the University of Leicester. She has published widely on the association between literary composition and educational experience, and on works written at or about early modern institutions of learning (schools, colleges, universities, Inns of Court). She has translated and co-edited Leon Battista Alberti's *Momus* for the I Tatti Renaissance Library (2003) and the accounts of Elizabeth I's visits to Oxford and several other texts for the new multi-authored critical edition of John Nichols' *The Progresses and Public Processions of Queen Elizabeth I* (5 volumes, 2014). She has co-edited three essay collections related to her research and teaching interests: *The Oxford Handbook of Neo-Latin* (2015), *The Cultural and Intellectual World of the Early Modern Inns of Court* (2011) and *The Progresses, Pageants, and Entertainments of Queen Elizabeth I* (2007).

Gesine Manuwald is Professor of Latin at University College London (UCL) and President of the Society for Neo-Latin Studies (SNLS). She has published widely on classical Latin authors (including Cicero, Ennius and Valerius Flaccus) as well as on Neo-Latin literature. Publications in the latter field include several articles on Thomas Campion as well as the edited collection *Neo-Latin Poetry in the British Isles* (with L. B. T. Houghton, 2012). She is co-editor of the texts and anthologies strand of Bloomsbury's Neo-Latin Series.

David McOmish is an honorary research fellow at the University of Glasgow. His main fields of research are Scottish Neo-Latin literature and culture as well as Latinate scientific literature and culture more widely. He has published numerous articles on early scientific writings in Latin and was the chief contributor to *Selections from the Delitiae Poetarum Scotorum: An Electronic Edition* (2015; http://www.dps.gla.ac.uk/).

Victoria Moul is Associate Professor of Early Modern Latin and English at University College London (UCL). She works on the bilingualism of early modern English literary culture, as well as more generally on classical and early modern poetry, and has published widely in these fields. Her publications include *Jonson, Horace and the Classical Tradition* (2010) and the edited volume, *A Guide to Neo-Latin Literature* (2017). A new monograph on the relationship between English and Latin poetry in early modern England is forthcoming.

Lucy R. Nicholas teaches in the Classics department at King's College London (KCL) and at the Warburg Institute. She works primarily on Neo-Latin literature of the sixteenth century and is particularly interested in the relationship between humanism and the Reformation. She has published extensively on the mid-Tudor humanist Roger Ascham and is currently co-editing a volume entitled *Roger Ascham and his Sixteenth-Century World* (forthcoming). She has also written on Thomas More, and her chapter on the Latin *Utopias* of the early modern period will soon be available in the forthcoming *Oxford Handbook of Thomas More's Utopia* (eds. C. Shrank and P. Withington). The Latin works of Walter Haddon represent the focus of her current research.

George Pounder has been a school teacher since 2001. He has taught at Ardvreck School in Perthshire, and Rugby School in Warwickshire. He currently teaches at Glenalmond College in Perthshire, where he went to school as a boy. Before becoming Head of Classics, he was Housemaster of his old boarding house. Teaching Latin, Greek, Classical Civilization and Ancient History up to A Level currently takes up most of his time, but he also tries to pursue his research interests in British Neo-Latin literature.

Andrew W. Taylor is Fellow, Senior Lecturer and Director of Studies in English at Churchill College, Cambridge. He has published widely on sixteenth-century English humanism, the transmission and reception of the writings of Christian antiquity and the Bible, literary translation (including, with Sarah Annes Brown, *Ovid in English, 1480–1625* [2013]), and the interplay between Latin and the vernacular in French and English poetry. He has also edited essay collections on *Neo-Latin and Translation in the Renaissance* (2014) and, with Philip Ford, on *Neo-Latin and the Pastoral* (2006) and *The Early Modern Cultures of Neo-Latin Drama* (2013).

Preface

This volume is designed to provide a taster and a representative selection of the rich resources of literature produced in Latin in Britain during the early modern period. Such writing is an integral part of the literary output of Britain over several centuries, but much of this literature is not as widely read as it once was, mainly owing to difficulties of access and the fact that it is written in Latin. Many works of Neo-Latin literature still remain *terra incognita* despite their obvious significance and quality. This book presents a wide-ranging selection of both popular items and less well-known gems, covering a range of periods, literary genres, styles and themes. The excerpts have been prepared by a team of scholars based in Britain, who have approached them from different backgrounds and with a variety of interests, thereby illustrating the interdisciplinary nature of the field of 'Neo-Latin literature' and the various kinds of questions that may be asked.

In line with the book's character as an introductory volume, each entry offers a translation, contextual information and guidance concerning literary and linguistic details, while the notes are primarily intended to assist those with less experience of Neo-Latin literature. It is thus hoped that the texts will be accessible to a wide range of readers, especially interested laypeople and advanced school pupils and university students, but they might also have something to offer to scholars. Those new to reading Neo-Latin texts might find the selection from John Owen's epigrams (Text 9), the epitaphs by Elizabeth Cooke Hoby Russell (Text 6) or the scene from Ruggle's *Ignoramus* (Text 10) congenial starting points for their explorations.

This Anthology is the first volume in the new Bloomsbury Neo-Latin Series, to be followed by similar volumes. In this context, it was natural to use the term 'Neo-Latin', which has become established for Latin writings of the early modern period. This label is not entirely satisfactory, since its definition is vague, and elsewhere terms such as 'early modern Latin' or 'Renaissance Latin' are preferred. However, what seemed most important here was the presentation of Latin texts rather than a fastidious concern for terminological precision, and perhaps the more important point is that the Latin of this era, which is generally classicizing, may be distinguished from medieval Latin, which is generally not.

Most of the contributors to this volume are members of the Society for Neo-Latin Studies (SNLS), the subject organization representing and bringing together people interested in Neo-Latin literature from all over the UK (https://warwick.ac.uk/fac/arts/ren/snls/). SNLS has long had a teaching anthology on its website (https://warwick.ac.uk/fac/arts/ren/snls/snls_ teaching_anthology/), and in some respects this volume is an extension of the Society's long-standing aim to spread knowledge of Neo-Latin literature and to offer another point of entry. It is hoped that this book will represent a first step in achieving such an aim on a larger scale.

The editors would like to thank all the contributors for their enthusiastic support from the beginning of this project and for their cooperation and flexibility throughout the editorial process. Heartfelt thanks are also owed to Bloomsbury, and especially to Alice Wright, for their early adoption of the plan, their eagerness to take on such a project and the energy they have devoted to realizing it.

L. B. T. H. / G. M. / L. R. N.

London, June 2019

Introduction

L. B. T. Houghton, Gesine Manuwald and Lucy R. Nicholas

Neo-Latin as a literary medium

The composition of works in Latin prose and verse formed a major part of literary production in Britain between the sixteenth and the eighteenth centuries; the number of works written in Latin during this period should not be underestimated, though it is difficult to provide precise figures as these works are now spread across the world and are not always easily accessible. The authors of this vast body of material include some of the most celebrated names in English literature, for instance Sir Thomas More, Francis Bacon, John Milton and George Herbert, as well as a host of lesser-known figures. No serious study of literary culture in Britain during this period can afford to neglect the Latin output of poets, prose-writers and playwrights, much of which is accomplished and enjoyable literature in its own right. This volume aims to give an impression of the range and quality of British Neo-Latin writing over the course of these centuries, by presenting a selection of examples that, between them, encompass a variety of literary genres, many different subjects and an assortment of local and historical circumstances.

Why did British authors choose to express themselves and to address their readers in a language and in literary forms inherited from ancient Rome, rather than (or as well as) in other forms of expression available to them? There are several reasons, any number of which may have been applicable in any particular instance. One is a desire for durability: for much of this period, the triumph of the vernacular, which with hindsight may seem so inevitable, must have appeared far from a foregone conclusion. Literary ventures in English, French and Italian, for example, however distinguished, had yet to stand the test of time, whereas the creative achievements of classical antiquity had already endured for a millennium and a half, seemingly offering a ringing endorsement of Horace's claim to have produced 'a monument more lasting than bronze' (*monumentum aere perennius*, Odes 3.30.1), of Virgil's promise to confer poetic immortality on the subjects of his epic (*Aeneid* 9.446–9) and of Ovid's defiant prediction of his continuing survival despite the ravages of time, violent destruction and the wrath of Jupiter (*Metamorphoses* 15.871–9). Not only had these ancient masterpieces proved their perennial staying power; they continued to form the principal element in the education of the literate élite in Britain and elsewhere, shaping their notions of literary value and decorum. To what higher goal could authors aspire than to fashion works that might stand alongside the classics which had provided the bulk of their schooling and which, in consequence, had probably given them the initial inspiration to try their hand at literary composition? Moreover, Latin remained the language of learning throughout Europe and beyond, and the literary forms practised by Roman authors commanded universal recognition within the republic of letters irrespective of political and confessional allegiances, meaning that those who sought to reach an audience beyond the shores of their native land had a strong incentive to adopt this international medium. This helps to explain the production of works in both Latin and vernacular editions and the appearance of translations of English works into Latin, as writers endeavoured to gain for their works and ideas the widest possible diffusion.

At a distance of several centuries, the corpus of classical Latin literature may have been felt to possess a certain monumental timelessness, attractive to Neo-Latin authors hoping to win for themselves a comparable literary immortality. The practice of *imitatio* was a fundamental precondition of much of the Neo-Latin literature of the time, and manuals offering guidance on the best authors to emulate proliferated during the period. Even so, early modern readers of the Classics knew that these ancient works had been produced in response to specific contemporary circumstances, and they saw that the techniques and forms employed by writers such as Cicero, Virgil, Horace and Tacitus to address the pressing concerns of their time could likewise be drafted into service to comment on their own societies and situations. The adoption of Latin forms of expression conferred cultural prestige on the undertakings (and, not least importantly, the patrons) of the present day, inviting comparison with the past glories of the ancients and asserting an equivalent historical significance. This could have led – and in some cases did lead – to artistic sterility and stagnation, a frigid, backward-looking replication of inert and obsolete cultural forms. Yet the would-be successors of the canonical authors of antiquity were keenly aware of the challenge posed by their recycling of the terminology and literary templates of their predecessors: for both early modern writers and their audiences, part of the appeal of producing works in the language and generic forms of ancient Rome lay precisely in the opportunity it extended to reshape these venerable models into something new and specifically relevant to their own time. It was through recognition of the changes wrought on patterns inherited from an earlier age and directed towards a different civilization that the originality and ingenuity of the Neo-Latin writers could best be appreciated. For the most talented authors, the evocation of classical literature not only appropriated for their own era something of the grandeur that was Rome, but was also a jumping-off point, a springboard for innovative forays in directions never imagined by their ancient forerunners.

The historical and literary importance of some Neo-Latin works (Thomas More's *Utopia*, for instance [Text 1]) has never been in doubt. In other cases, illuminating and attractive items have suffered serious neglect, surviving only in manuscript form or lurking unnoticed in early printed editions or rarely perused anthologies. The study of Neo-Latin literature and culture therefore presents exciting opportunities for pioneering work on overlooked but potentially rewarding material. It also embraces a range of different academic disciplines, comprising classical and later Latin and vernacular languages; ancient, medieval and early modern literatures; social, political, cultural and intellectual history; history of art and of science; religious and philosophical studies; and manuscript studies and book history (this list is by no means exhaustive). Neo-Latin writing spread to every corner of Europe, and through conquest, colonialism and evangelization to the East and the New World, making it – by the standards of the time – a truly global phenomenon. It was practised by Catholics, Protestants and sceptics; by men, women and children; and by religious mystics, calculating diplomats and experimental scientists. It was used to celebrate births, marriages, accessions, coronations, military victories, peace treaties and revolutions, and to mourn deaths, defeats, natural disasters, original sin and broken hearts. Its subjects could be taken from the past, the present or the future; from the animal, vegetable and mineral kingdoms; from the principles of mathematics or the discoveries of medicine (Girolamo Fracastoro's poem *Syphilis* gave its name to the disease). Literature in Latin could be harnessed to convey the full spectrum of human emotions; it could be deployed on almost any occasion, for intimate communications and personal exchanges as well as for public pronouncements; and it could be wielded to attack vested interests and subvert political and religious authority, as well as to entrench distinctions of class and status. This versatility, combined with the unprecedented proliferation granted to early modern books by the printing press, only served to amplify the enormous quantity of Neo-Latin material now awaiting attention from students in the many branches of learning on which it touches.

In recent years scholarship in this field has been put on a much firmer footing by the publication of three fundamental reference works: *Brill's Encyclopaedia of the Neo-Latin World* (Ford, Bloemendal and Fantazzi 2014),

The Oxford Handbook of Neo-Latin (Knight and Tilg 2015) and *A Guide to Neo-Latin Literature* (Moul 2017). There is also a new single-volume history of Neo-Latin literature (Korenjak 2016), as well as a number of series dedicated to various aspects of Neo-Latin studies (the *I Tatti Renaissance Library*, for example, makes available texts and translations of Latin works by authors of the Italian Renaissance, while *Noctes Neolatinae* and *Officina Neolatina* publish texts by writers from a wider range of backgrounds; the *NeoLatina* series features collections of essays on the Latin productions of particular authors). Two journals, *Humanistica Lovaniensia* and *Neulateinisches Jahrbuch*, are exclusively devoted to presenting research on Neo-Latin topics, and the many volumes of *Acta* from the conferences of the International Association for Neo-Latin Studies (IANLS) contain a wealth of relevant material. Among older works, Jozef IJsewijn's *Companion to Neo-Latin Studies* (originally published in 1977; revised edition, IJsewijn and Sacré 1990–8) and W. Leonard Grant's *Neo-Latin Literature and the Pastoral* (Grant 1965) remain valuable, as do the anthologies edited by Laurens and Balavoine (1975), Perosa and Sparrow (1979), Nichols (1979) and McFarlane (1980). Newer anthologies, differing from the present volume in scope, approach and emphasis, include Riley (2016) and Minkova (2017).

British Neo-Latin literature

The very notion of a British Neo-Latin literature immediately prompts several questions. The first is a most basic one: what counts as 'Britain'? Then, too, what exactly did British Neo-Latin involve? Given the international coordinates of Latin as a language and a form of expression, is it even possible to treat British Neo-Latin as a discrete phenomenon? How did individuals in Britain access Latin? What was its relationship with the vernaculars of the British Isles? Was the production of Neo-Latin across the regions of Britain the same or different? Such issues are in part addressed here, and they can productively be considered afresh by readers when going through the individual sections of this anthology.

The nomenclature of the areas comprising the British Isles is surprisingly complicated. In this book 'Britain' is used as a geographical term devoid of any political baggage. However, since some of the entries in this volume relate expressly to the history of the British Isles or parts of it, some description of the relationships between the various regions through the early modern period may be helpful. At the start of the sixteenth century the number of states in the largest part, 'Great Britain', stood at two: the Kingdom of England (including Wales) and the Kingdom of Scotland. The once independent

Principality of Wales had come under the control of English monarchs during the thirteenth century. The accession of James VI of Scotland to the English Crown (as James I) in 1603 brought about a personal union between the kingdoms of England, Scotland and Ireland, but a full political union was only achieved a century later through an Act of Parliament in 1707. The Kingdom of Ireland was gradually brought under English control between 1541 and 1691, with a formal union between the Kingdom of Great Britain and Ireland being effected in 1801. There were then many cultural and political points of intersection between 'Britain' and Ireland throughout the period covered by this volume, the modern Republic of Ireland being declared independent and separate only in the twentieth century. This notwithstanding, this anthology does not include examples of Irish Neo-Latin; a helpful series of studies is already available in *Making Ireland Roman: Irish Neo-Latin Writers and the Republic of Letters*, edited by J. Harris and K. Sidwell (2009).

There exists a long tradition of Latin writing in the British Isles. A fair-sized corpus of Latin texts from the Anglo-Saxon era survives, and considerably more from the twelfth to the fifteenth centuries. Much of this material can be accounted for by the fact that Latin was the medium in which universal, transnational Christendom operated. By the time of the early modern period Latin composition in Britain was not something new, but in style it was quite different from the late medieval Latin that immediately preceded it. The important change of approach came in Britain around 1530–40, when the Latin language increasingly ceased to exemplify its medieval configuration and interests and instead adopted a more classical linguistic register. While scholars are careful to avoid suggesting an overly linear development from medieval or scholastic Latin to Renaissance Latin, there was an appreciable surge in British Neo-Latin that embraced a stylistically more ambitious and self-consciously classical form.

The practice of Neo-Latin writing was established in Britain by many of the same stimuli that had powered a cultural transformation across Europe, most crucially Renaissance humanism, and ideas about linguistic methodology and the perfection of Latin were often informed by contact with the Continent. Neo-Latin writers from the British Isles frequently travelled to mainland Europe as part of their education or career: for example, George Buchanan (Text 3) and John Leland (Text 2) spent time in France, and John Milton (Text 13) and Thomas Gray (Text 18) in Italy. There was further cross-pollination when celebrated European scholars were invited to the British Isles, where they could disseminate their ideas more effectively, the most important example being Desiderius Erasmus of Rotterdam. Many of the Latin texts of England, Scotland, Ireland and Wales were produced by the same forces as in mainland Europe: hopes for patronage, geographical discoveries, the Protestant and Counter-Reformations and the scientific revolution. In many ways it is legitimate to understand the Neo-Latin showcased in this anthology as a microcosm of European Neo-Latin: this is surely how the authors featured in this volume would have viewed their use of the language. Yet, with the benefit of hindsight, it is also valid to regard British Neo-Latin texts as a distinct category, one that fused European and national, ancient and modern thought, that interacted with the English language and that was rooted in an inter-cultural exchange between the four areas of the British Isles. A good proportion of the Neo-Latin works were, moreover, shaped by historical, political and social circumstances and events that were peculiar to the British Isles or to specific parts of them.

When reading the extracts in this book, one should be mindful of the fact that Latin composition was not an arcane activity involving a niche language for the very few. It is true that the British Isles were late participants in the Renaissance, but in the early sixteenth century pioneering figures like the enormously influential Thomas More (Text 1) paved the way for the reception and assimilation of new learning on the shores of Britain. This was followed by an expansion of schools organized around a rigorously schematized Latin pedagogy and the concurrent development of Latin textbooks written by English schoolmasters and educationalists like John Colet and William Lily, both of St Paul's School in London. Latin, the *lingua franca* of Europe, came to be deeply embedded in many parts of the British educational system. Most students would have their first encounter with the language around the age of six or seven, though some theorists believed that the learning of Latin should start in the cradle. Instruction in the language was certainly the single most significant component of secondary education, with several hours a day tending to be devoted to Latin and lessons often delivered in the ancient tongue. School turned young boys into readers and translators of Latin, but students were also exposed throughout their schooling to a constant diet of ancient literature. Not all students followed the Latin cursus within the formal system of secondary education, and a limited number (male and less commonly female) were educated via, for example, private tutors. Whatever the educational route pursued, the substance of these classical texts was formative and helped shaped the contours of young imaginations.

The universities of England, Scotland and Ireland were the main hubs for continued education in Latin, and they provided a venue where the language enjoyed a particular prominence. Latin had been a long-standing feature of higher education, but curriculum changes during the sixteenth century, ushered in by the demands of the Renaissance and Reformation and supported by successive regimes, placed even greater emphasis on classical

Latin and its literature. New posts in Latin and Greek were established. An Arts curriculum termed the *studia humanitatis*, which focused on grammar, rhetoric, poetry, ancient history and moral philosophy, became a compulsory part of a university degree course. The thinking behind these innovations was that an education centred on Latin would not only help nurture reason and eloquence, but also prepare students for a profession in education, the Church, law, politics or medicine. Although the primary function of universities was not the production of Neo-Latin literature, universities were nonetheless important venues for facilitating it. University libraries held many of the classical works that gave shape to British Neo-Latin composition; they also fostered and reinforced an affinity for the Latin tongue and sponsored occasional productions in the ancient language. At universities in the British Isles, Latin was the language of instruction, examination and even conversation. A significant portion of the Neo-Latin corpus was composed by authors when they were still students.

As a result of all this, Latin, based on classical models, came to be used across the British Isles as a matter of course, in a range of fields and by a broad spectrum of people. There are even examples of merchants (in Scotland) in the seventeenth century writing quantities of competent Latin. Women are less conspicuous in the production of Latin, mainly because of their exclusion from the education system, and the fact that female spheres were often associated with the vernacular rather than the Latin language. However, there are a number of important exceptions. Female royals were given the same education as their male counterparts. Princess Elizabeth, for example (later Queen Elizabeth I: Text 5), was instructed in advanced Latin and Greek composition. Other women, including the noblewoman Elizabeth Hoby (Text 6), attained a proficiency at least comparable to some of the more talented males of the period.

Latin was so integral to British literature that one might reasonably ask, not why people of the British Isles wrote in Latin, but why people would choose to write in English, Welsh, Gaelic or Scots. Indeed, certain writers featured here (for example, Walter Haddon: Text 4) only wrote in Latin and were openly adamant that serious works ought to be put into Latin. On the other hand, authors such as Thomas More (Text 1), John Milton (Text 13) and George Herbert wrote sometimes in Latin and sometimes in English. Some texts, such as George Ruggle's *Ignoramus* (Text 10), even combined more than one language. Early modern Britain, like mainland Europe, enjoyed a bilingualism whereby individuals would use Latin in addition to their own native tongue (e.g. Text 11). Modern scholarship is only just beginning to appreciate the complex interaction between Latin and the vernacular. It is increasingly demonstrating that Latin culture co-existed with the vernacular in vibrant ways and could even enhance the vernacular tongues. It seems probable that most periods and remits of early modern thought had to continuously reformulate their position relative to the cultural matrix of Neo-Latin and the vernacular.

The sixteenth to eighteenth centuries in Britain can boast some of the finest works of Neo-Latin literature in Europe. The production of Neo-Latin, however, was not necessarily uniform across the British Isles. English authors produced much of the Neo-Latin that survives. This was to a large degree owing to the pre-eminence of England's leading schools, such as Eton, Westminster, St Paul's and Winchester, and its twin bastions of classical learning, the universities of Oxford and Cambridge. But Scotland too stands out for its Latinity. In 1500 Scotland could boast three universities – St Andrews, Glasgow and Aberdeen – as compared with two in England and none in Ireland or Wales. A highly cultivated Scottish Court also had an impact. It is generally misleading to suggest that, following the Reformation, Latin was the preserve of either Protestants or Catholics, but it does appear that the vast majority of the accomplished Neo-Latinists from Scotland (George Buchanan [Text 3] and Andrew Melville, for example) belong to the Protestant camp; the Catholic Adam King (Text 8) is an exception. Welsh Neo-Latin is less well represented: Wales lacked the great power-houses of education, and it is noteworthy that John Owen, the Welsh epigrammatist, was educated at Winchester and Oxford in England (Text 9). Conversely, Neo-Latin writing in Ireland was more common, Latin being one of its principal languages. This was despite the fact that it was competing with a deep-rooted Irish literary culture, where law and medicine were based more heavily on Irish Gaelic than Latin or Greek. The Neo-Latin of early modern Ireland was outward-looking and made fundamental contributions, for instance, to the European Counter-Reformation.

Overview of Neo-Latin literary genres

The Neo-Latin writers of the early modern period selected and blended elements from earlier works, and from their own contemporaries, to create innovative and sophisticated forms. Consequently, a wide range of literary genres is on display in this anthology. The process of identifying a literary category to which a work belongs may to modern eyes seem a rather artificial or pedantic exercise. Yet, for the early moderns, generic distinctions and categories, each of which implied and necessitated certain techniques, aesthetics and etiquette, were of primary concern. In verse the choice of metre was of vital importance, and in prose an author's particular style, lexicon and formal arrangement could signal to the reader a set of expectations about the type of text on offer. This generic preoccupation and the full nature and range of genres cannot be properly comprehended if we only take account of early modern works in the vernacular. Neo-Latin works offer a much more diverse picture, often also augmenting and compounding the generic classifications that were established in the ancient canon. The full range of Neo-Latin production of this period defies exhaustive summary, for there was a profusion of writings in every field of Latin, experimentation with every known literary genre and the development of new ones. This anthology can offer only a small fraction of the broader picture and outline some of the genres readers will encounter within Neo-Latin literature.

Under the broad headings of verse and prose, there was a myriad of sometimes overlapping sub-divisions. In the area of verse, some of the sections of this anthology exhibit what is often called 'occasional' poetry. This term is used to designate verse produced for a specific occasion. Such pieces were often rooted in a special set of social experiences, such as royal births, anniversaries, bereavement and so on. While such 'occasional' poetry does not constitute a genre *per se*, several established genres originated as occasional works, including *epithalamia* (wedding songs) and victory odes. Walter Haddon's verse marking the coronation of Elizabeth I in 1559 (Text 4) represents a type of occasional poetry, one that also drew on the classical model of panegyric. Likewise, Elizabeth Hoby's epitaphic poetry, which she composed upon the death of close friends and family, fell within the popular and extensive genre of funerary verse or elegy (Text 6). Certain historical events also generated such strong emotions that a whole raft of poems might be composed on a single theme. The Gunpowder Plot of 1605, for instance, motivated John Milton's *In Quintum Novembris* (Text 13). While this is an extraordinary composition and deserves special attention, it nevertheless counts as just one poem of many (including several others by Milton himself) that commemorated deliverance from Catholic conspiracy. Other events might equally stimulate Latin verse, including the delightful hexameter composition by William Baker about a frost fair on the river Thames during England's Little Ice Age (Text 14).

A more classically anchored genre was lyric. Indebted to the lyric poets of ancient Greece, and developed in Latin most notably by Horace, the genre is marked by its range of complex metres. On display in Text 11 are two Latin versions of the same poem on the precariousness of human power, in different metres: Alcaics and Sapphics. Complicating the issue of genre further here is the fact that the Neo-Latin poems constitute a *translation* of a work in the vernacular, namely an English lyric poem 'Dazel'd thus with height of place' by Sir Henry Wotton.

Another important poetic genre was the epigram. Epigrams are short, pithy poems characterized primarily by their witty turn of thought. This genre found precedent in the classical world, but experienced a spectacular development and growth in the early modern period (see de Beer et al. 2009). A huge range of epigrams, tightly related to the world of things, people, places and events, was produced; they might be used to satirize, praise, commemorate and describe. John Leland's Anglo-Latin epigrams offer a good example of the staggering diversity possible within this genre. Many of his epigrams stem from his profound antiquarian interests, as does a longer poem on the hot springs at Bath (Text 2). Epigrams are ubiquitous in the early modern period, and many of the big names in Renaissance poetry engaged with the form. Thomas More's *Epigrammata* initially brought him more attention than his *Utopia* (Text 1). The genre of epigram is exemplified by the Welsh poet John Owen (Text 9), who mastered the form and whose books of epigrams became some of the most famous and widely imitated Latin verse produced in the period.

If the epigram championed the small-scale, epic represented the large-scale. Epic was the most prestigious and most serious genre of the classical hierarchy, traditionally associated with themes of war and national prowess. Some of the best examples of British Neo-Latin epic were not produced until the seventeenth century and emerged from Scotland. One of them, James Philp's *Grameid* (Text 17), harnessed the epic form as the appropriate mode to chart the 1689 uprising against the Dutch Protestant William of Orange.

Other longer verse forms included verse drama, one of the finest examples of which is Ruggle's aforementioned *Ignoramus*. There was a very lively culture of Neo-Latin verse drama in early modern Britain, supported, in particular, by the public schools and universities. Ruggle's play (Text 10) falls within the genre of comedy, a form that began to dominate dramatic production at the start of the seventeenth century. The satiric focus of this play is an ignorant lawyer, and it is therefore even possible to situate the *Ignoramus* within a yet more specific genre of legal satire, which became fashionable in this period. The satiric spark is likewise in evidence in another of the entries: a biting satire in free verse on the Bishop of Salisbury (Text 16). Although evidence points to the authorship of one seventeenth-century Thomas Brown, it is perhaps no surprise that this anticlerical broadside originally circulated anonymously.

It is sometimes not sufficiently stressed that much of the scientific, philosophical and mathematical scholarship of the early modern period found expression in Latin and even in verse. Didactic poetry seems to have functioned as a generic continuum through the sixteenth, seventeenth and eighteenth centuries. Authors had recourse to this genre as a means to expound or refute contemporary scientific viewpoints, which they would package in such a way that it combined both profit and pleasure. This anthology contains several examples of didactic verse. George Buchanan's *De sphaera* (Text 3) was a poetic defence of the geocentric view of the universe against the new heliocentric view, in addition to being a means to encourage students to engage with cosmology. Adam King's *Genethliacon Iesu Christi* (Text 8) provides a good illustration of the interrelated pursuits of science and religion. This poem, whose primary focus is the life of Christ, was also the vehicle for astronomical instruction. The penchant for Neo-Latin astronomical didacticism is arguably reflected in Thomas Gray's poem *Luna habitabilis* (Text 18), which advanced an imaginative (and playful or even satirical) vision of life on the moon and its future relations with Earth. His verse also effectively epitomizes how scientific invention could be mirrored by generic inventiveness on the part of the Latin poet.

Scientific theories were often explored in prose as well as verse, a prime example being Thomas Burnet's *Telluris theoria sacra* (Text 15), one of the best-known geological works of the seventeenth century, which was probably influenced by the philosophy of René Descartes. There was a vast amount of writing in Latin in fields such as science, philosophy, historiography, biography, law and theology, including, for instance, works by Isaac Newton and William Harvey.

Another prose work, chronologically the earliest in this volume and arguably one of the best-known works of Neo-Latin, Thomas More's *Utopia* (Text 1), is an interesting case generically. Although structured, at least in part, as a philosophical dialogue, it is nowadays sometimes loosely referred to as 'fiction', but when More first composed this work, it did not fall into an immediately recognizable 'genre'. Rather, this work was so influential that it inaugurated a whole new genre of utopian writing that would continue to flourish through the following centuries and includes Francis Bacon's *Nova Atlantis*, published more than a century later, in 1624. The early modern period also witnessed the development of Neo-Latin novels, the most accomplished author of such prose fiction being John Barclay. His *Argenis* (Text 12) was one of the best-selling novels of the seventeenth century in any language.

A genre of considerable significance since classical times was oratory. The discovery of many of its key texts injected a new impetus into the art of rhetoric in the early modern period. Three modes of rhetoric that had been delineated in ancient handbooks were often on display, namely deliberative (persuasive/advisory), judicial (legal/forensic) and epideictic (praise/blame), the last of these being by far the most important in early modern times. Rhetoric was in many ways the beating heart of the Renaissance. It was harnessed in a range of media, most obviously in sermons and orations, though all the literary forms included in this volume draw much of their theoretical basis from rhetoric, and rhetorical skill might be as much on display in poetry as in prose. Oratory as a discipline became associated with morality and notions of citizenship, inspired to a great degree by the classical ideal of the orator as *vir bonus dicendi peritus* ('a good man skilled in speaking'; see Quintilian, *Inst.* 12.1.1), which might explain the high number of epideictic speeches. Text 5 provides a good example of rhetorical proficiency in action: it exhibits two rousing and highly polished speeches by Queen Elizabeth I, which she delivered at the University of Oxford. These orations breathe the classical spirit, and Elizabeth self-consciously roots her words in an established rhetorical framework of motifs and techniques.

Another important channel for the transmission of rhetoric was the epistle or letter. Writing letters had been an art form since antiquity, but as with the epigram, the letter form became a booming business in early modern literary production and was absolutely central to an international community of learned men and women, often termed the 'Republic of Letters', while also being used as a merely literary vehicle. The letter selected here serves as the preface to William Camden's work on British history and chorography, *Britannia*, and is therefore addressed to the reader (Text 7).

Although the entries in this volume present individual authors producing specific forms and genres of Neo-Latin literature, the vast majority of these figures were responsible for works in a multiplicity of different genres. The strictly delineated academic disciplines and subject divisions of today's schools and universities were then largely absent. Neo-Latinists of the early modern period were people of considerable breadth, Renaissance polymaths, who often composed numerous Latin works on a whole variety of scholarly subjects. Neo-Latin writers usually had more in common with each other than with writers in the vernacular, even when operating in the same genre. For example, those who wrote Neo-Latin drama were primarily not dramatists who happened to write in Latin, but intellectuals who happened to write plays. George Buchanan (Text 3), who articulated his theories of the universe in Latin, also wrote Neo-Latin tragedies, political treatises and history, and men of science were often perfectly at home in the realm of classical literature, the conventions of poetry and religious thought. It was only in the late eighteenth century and during the nineteenth century that a more rigid academic specialization began to emerge, and this development was accompanied by the beginnings of a decline of Latin in British education and public life.

Aims and coverage of this volume

Out of the wealth of material produced in Latin throughout the British Isles between about 1500 and 1800, this volume can only offer a small selection. This selection has not been made at random. Rather, it has been designed in such a way as to offer a rich and diverse medley of texts and to represent the immense variety of literature available, in terms of chronological and geographical distribution as well as literary genres and themes, although, of course, not every possible variety of British Neo-Latin literature can be represented in a volume of this size. This anthology is intended to act as a spur to further exploration of these works of literature and the questions raised by them. Consequently, where possible and appropriate, sections provide references to complete editions and translations of the excerpted texts as well as to secondary literature.

The selected texts are arranged in chronological order, so as to sketch out the development of Neo-Latin literature over time and also to illustrate the way in which this literature engages with contemporary developments. The sequence starts with one of the earliest texts (from the early sixteenth century) that can be regarded as British Neo-Latin literature, on account of its literary ambitions and its reliance on classical literature as a basis (as opposed to, for instance, medieval chronicles). The final entry is a product of the mid-eighteenth century and marks the end of the period in which writing in Latin was an unquestionably important literary medium. While Latin would continue to be used after 1800, it no longer had the same currency or dominance.

The selection includes writers from England, Scotland and Wales, men and women, as well as texts in poetry and prose, both well-known and forgotten. It features literary genres such as epic, epyllion, drama, elegy, epigram, oratory, letters and technical writing. Some of these authors composed pieces in Latin and in English (some also including references to ancient Greek, Scots, Welsh or French), and some had their Latin works published in contemporary English translations. In these cases, comparisons are drawn with their writings in English, or well-known contemporary English translations are printed or referenced.

The accomplished classicism achieved on a stylistic level by many of the authors can run the risk of obscuring how contemporary Neo-Latin literature is. The authors included in this volume were writing about, influenced by and indeed influencing the political and religious controversies, major events and scientific developments of their time. A number of the pieces refer to the most significant and pressing matters of the day, such as the opposition between Protestants and Catholics, the succession of kings and queens in

Britain, the political union between different parts of Britain and the plot to blow up Parliament at Westminster on 5 November 1605. Writing in Latin was a prominent feature of public discourse during this period and, as far as these authors were concerned, the most obvious, appropriate and potent medium to present their accounts.

The entries for the various authors can be read in their chronological sequence; at the same time, they are all self-contained and may be studied selectively and individually, depending on the interests of readers. Each entry opens with an introduction offering the necessary background on the biography of the writer, the context of the work in question and important features of the selected passage. This is followed by the original Latin text accompanied by a modern English translation and attached commentary notes (keyed to line numbers for verse passages and to numerical references within the text in the case of prose texts). Where relevant, a contemporary English translation or other comparative material is also given. Beyond this standard structure, details vary between entries according to what is most appropriate for each author and text, and also what contributors, approaching these texts from different angles, have chosen to highlight as important. These differences of approach are integral to one of the overriding aims of this book, which is to introduce readers not simply to a broad range of texts, but also to the broad spread of possible ways to engage with the study of Neo-Latin. Further considerations such as genre, period and level of difficulty in the Latin add to these permutations.

In order to offer passages that are of intrinsic interest and make sense in themselves, the excerpts provided are of differing lengths, while they are all just tasters and sufficiently short to be read through in one go.

Latin texts: sources and conventions

The beauty of working with early modern texts is that it is possible to consult 'original editions'. Thus, some of the Latin texts in this book have been taken directly from early modern manuscripts or early printed books; some of the popular ones were printed so frequently in the early modern period that a decision had to be made as to which edition should be used for reference. In the case of some entries new modern editions could be adduced, and their versions of the texts have then been compared with the original editions or with manuscripts. The basis for the text given is identified in each instance.

Despite the standardization generally adopted here, the early modern layout of these texts is not unimportant to the study of Neo-Latin. Since the original authors often liaised closely with the printers, the arrangement of the words on the page, the use of illustrated initials, the choice of typeface or the decision to employ particular abbreviations have to be regarded as potentially meaningful details of a composition.

Early modern practices regarding the presentation of Latin texts can initially seem quite confusing. For the convenience of readers, the majority of texts included in this book have been slightly adjusted and standardized according to modern conventions (often following modern editions of these texts where they exist). For instance, the medial 's', *ʃ*, has been replaced by *s*, and *ij* by *ii*; ligatures such as *æ* and *œ* have been written as two letters *ae* and *oe*, and abbreviations have been resolved. The accentuation of words (diacritics), which was another common feature of the early modern presentation of Latin, has for the most part similarly not been reproduced. Capitalization has also been standardized. On the other hand, some early modern peculiarities of spelling have been retained, since changing these would have meant too much interference with the original text. In all cases where these conventions might affect understanding, explanations are provided in the commentary notes. Moreover, readers of Neo-Latin cannot escape some byzantine (to modern eyes) uses of punctuation. For example, commas were often used (sometimes in order to assist with oral delivery) where they would not be in a modern text, and authors/printers would use an exclamation mark where we would use a question mark. The editors made a conscious decision to let individual contributors determine their own policy on this front to some extent. An idea of the original presentation of a Neo-Latin text can be gained from Text 5, the speeches of Elizabeth I, which presents a basically faithful transcription of the manuscript. The notes on this text aim to help readers to navigate their way around this transcription.

Neo-Latin texts often comprised more than the main text itself. Editions might include elaborate prefaces and dedicatory letters or poems (so-called 'paratexts'), which can offer intriguing information about the contemporary cultural and intellectual background. A good example is William Camden's letter that prefaced his monumental history, *Britannia* (Text 7).

As for the Latin texts, the contributors to this volume have sought to produce felicitous renderings into English, but ones that remain very faithful to the Latin. The translations are meant to be helpful, but not definitive. This volume does not provide a word list or a glossed vocabulary; so, for the purposes of independent interpretations, other lexicographical resources might be necessary (for an overview of Neo-Latin reference works and tools see Knight and Tilg 2015: 575–9). Lewis and Short's *Latin Dictionary* should, for the most part, be sufficient, not least because of the classical configuration of so much of the Latin in the passages provided. 'Lewis and Short', given the broader scope of its coverage of Latin usage, can yield more helpful results than the *Oxford Latin Dictionary* with regard to post-classical Latin texts and their sources. For later Latin coinages and for early modern linguistic nuances, additional sources of information are available, such as Johann Ramminger's *Neulateinische Wortliste* (http://ramminger.userweb.mwn.de). A number of Latin dictionaries useful for reading Neo-Latin texts, including 'Lewis and Short', are available via the Logeion website (http://logeion. uchicago.edu).

Now, in the words of William Camden (Text 7): *Vale, fave, et fruere.*

Further reading

Binns, J. W. (ed.) (1974), *The Latin Poetry of English Poets*, London.

Binns, J. W. (1990), *Intellectual Culture in Elizabethan and Jacobean England: The Latin Writings of the Age*, Leeds.

Bradner, L. (1940), *Musae Anglicanae: A History of Anglo-Latin Poetry 1500–1925*, New York and London.

Churchill, L. J., P. R. Brown and J. E. Jeffrey (eds) (2002), *Women Writing Latin: From Roman Antiquity to Early Modern Europe*, 3 vols, New York and London.

Davies, C. (1981), *Latin Writers of the Renaissance (Writers of Wales)*, Cardiff.

de Beer, S., K. A. E. Enenkel and D. Rijser (eds) (2009), *The Neo-Latin Epigram: A Learned and Witty Genre*, Leuven.

De Smet, I. A. R. (1999), 'Not for Classicists? The State of Neo-Latin Studies', *Journal of Roman Studies*, 89: 205–9.

Ford, P., J. Bloemendal and C. Fantazzi (eds) (2014), *Brill's Encyclopaedia of the Neo-Latin World*, 2 vols, Leiden.

Grant, W. L. (1954), 'European Vernacular Works in Latin Translation', *Studies in the Renaissance*, 1: 120–56.

Grant, W. L. (1965), *Neo-Latin Literature and the Pastoral*, Chapel Hill.

Harris, J. and K. Sidwell (eds) (2009), *Making Ireland Roman: Irish Neo-Latin Writers and the Republic of Letters*, Cork.

Helander, H. (2001), 'Neo-Latin Studies: Significance and Prospects', *Symbolae Osloenses*, 76: 5–102.

Hosington, B. M. (2009), ' "Minerva and the Muses": Women Writers of Latin in Renaissance England', *Humanistica Lovaniensia*, 58: 1–43.

Houghton, L. B. T. and G. Manuwald (eds) (2012), *Neo-Latin Poetry in the British Isles*, London.

IJsewijn, J. and D. Sacré (1990–8), *Companion to Neo-Latin Studies*, 2 vols, Leuven.

Knight, S. and S. Tilg (eds) (2015), *The Oxford Handbook of Neo-Latin*, Oxford and New York.

Korenjak, M. (2016), *Geschichte der neulateinischen Literatur: Vom Humanismus bis zur Gegenwart*, Munich.

Laurens, P. and C. Balavoine (eds) (1975), *Musae Reduces: Anthologie de la poésie latine dans l'Europe de la Renaissance*, Leiden.

McFarlane, I. D. (ed.) (1980), *Renaissance Latin Poetry*, Manchester.

Minkova, M. (ed.) (2017), *Florilegium recentioris Latinitatis*, Leuven.

Money, D. K. (1998), *The English Horace: Anthony Alsop and the Tradition of British Latin Verse*, Oxford.

Moul, V. (ed.) (2017), *A Guide to Neo-Latin Literature*, Cambridge.

Nichols, F. J. (ed.) (1979), *An Anthology of Neo-Latin Poetry*, New Haven.

Perosa, A. and J. Sparrow (eds) (1979), *Renaissance Latin Verse: An Anthology*, London.

Reid, S. J. and D. McOmish (eds) (2017), *Neo-Latin Literature and Literary Culture in Early Modern Scotland*, Leiden.

Riley, M. (ed.) (2016), *The Neo-Latin Reader: Selections from Petrarch to Rimbaud* [s.l.].

Ryan, L. V. (1977), 'The Shorter Latin Poem in Tudor England', *Humanistica Lovaniensia*, 26: 101–31.

Sparrow, J. (1960), 'Latin Verse of the High Renaissance', in E. F. Jacob (ed.), *Italian Renaissance Studies*, 354–90, London.

Spitzer, L. (1955), 'The Problem of Latin Renaissance Poetry', *Studies in the Renaissance*, 2: 118–38.

Stevenson, J. (2005), *Women Latin Poets: Language, Gender, and Authority, from Antiquity to the Eighteenth Century*, Oxford.

van der Poel, M. (ed.) (2014), *Neo-Latin Philology: Old Tradition, New Approaches*, Leuven.

1

Utopia: Elsewhere and Nowhere

Thomas More (1478–1535), Extracts from *Utopia*

Lucy R. Nicholas

Introduction

Thomas More (1478–1535) is a towering figure in English history. He was a genuine Renaissance man who was active and flourished in so many areas of life: one of the greatest lawyers of the day, London undersheriff, and eventually Lord Chancellor, an author of history, social philosophy and poetry, and a fervent Catholic. He is perhaps best known for his premature end, his execution in 1535 on the orders of one whom he had once so loyally served, King Henry VIII. Locked in a clash of principles between faith and royal will following Henry's break with Rome, More lost his life, but quickly enjoyed a rich afterlife, not just as a martyr and subsequently saint of the Catholic Church, but also through his written works. More is a complex figure who carries much freight, but the Latin he left behind can be fruitfully used to help cut through the myth-making and to understand the man and the world in which he operated.

More composed many works during his lifetime, in both Latin and English. This section is devoted to his *Utopia* of 1516. This highly enigmatic but endlessly engrossing work comprises two books. The first centres on a dialogue between characters both fictional and real, including More himself, and an invented character, a traveller called Raphael Hythlodaeus (Hythloday). The second and longer book is given over to a detailed description by Raphael of *Utopia*, a fantasy place, possibly inspired by the various discoveries during that period of the New World. Raphael outlines every dimension of Utopian life from its social organization and communal ownership of everything, to its simplicity, moral order and ideology. As regards its interpretation, many grand claims have been advanced over the centuries about this work: a cursory internet search reveals a multiplicity of assertions about its purpose as a Catholic tract, communist manifesto or expression of political idealism.

The text has also been, and still is being, translated into a myriad of modern tongues from Spanish to Chinese and from Russian to Arabic. Yet it may be that somewhere along the line *Utopia* has been lost in translation. In fact, many nowadays do not realize that *Utopia* was originally written in Latin. However, it is by returning to the Latin that we are perhaps able to appreciate aspects of the work that have been sidelined. It is in the Latin itself that the original spirit of the work is most effectively captured.

The conscious choice by More to write *Utopia* in Latin is significant and not without its symbolism. To begin with, Latin was an international language, the only truly 'European' tongue of the time. A practised Latin style might win credit for the author beyond his/her place of origin. Indeed, *Utopia* was a cross-border project involving a group of European humanists, all of whom shared the common bond of Latin. This included not just More himself and his friend from the Netherlands, Peter Gillis, but also the Dutch Desiderius Erasmus who pushed to disseminate the work, the English Thomas Lupset, the French Guillaume Budé and the Dutch Hieronymus Busleyden, who wrote supporting letters that appeared as paratexts in the published text; alongside these must also be included the various humanist printers in Louvain, Paris and Basel. The use of Latin also carried subtler connotations: by casting his work in Latin, a matrix of classical learning could be established and a deeper dialogue with the classical world facilitated. *Utopia* is crammed with learned allusions to a variety of ancient authors, a feature evident particularly in the first extracts. Perhaps more crucially, the Latin of *Utopia* functioned as a conduit for specifically Greek language and ideas. The very title 'Utopia' immediately entails a degree of linguistic negotiation, for there is an ambiguity about whether the '*u*' before the Greek word '*topos*' ('place') is the Greek word '*ou*' (meaning 'not') or '*eu*' (meaning 'good'), raising the question: is this about 'no place' or 'the best place'? The same is true of the main protagonist's name, 'Hythlodaeus', a term derived from the Greek for 'speaker of nonsense'. The work is also predicated to a high degree on Lucianic jesting and Greco-Roman philosophy and rhetoric. All such features make it clear that More's *Utopia* confounds straightforward assessments, and its readers are perhaps well advised to think of it less as a treatise of instruction or dogma and more as an early modern vehicle to think with.

Utopia went through four editions in More's lifetime alone and enjoyed many more thereafter. Its influence, though difficult now to gauge with any real precision, was evidently immense. This work spawned an entire literary genre of utopian and dystopian fiction which features ideal societies or perfect cities, or their opposite. Early works influenced by *Utopia* included *New Atlantis* by Francis Bacon, *Erewhon* by Samuel Butler and *Candide* by

Voltaire. Its impact may still be felt in modern science fiction. It is, of course, helpful to appreciate the work's importance through history, but by reading the sections below, you may return *ad fontes*, to a sixteenth-century world of erudite winks and in-jokes, power politics, and the social and intellectual ferment of the time, without which this deliciously ambiguous composition could not have been produced.

Bibliography

Cave, T. (ed.) (2008), *Thomas More's Utopia in Early Modern Europe: Paratexts and Contexts*, Manchester.

Logan, G. M. (ed.) (2011), *The Cambridge Companion to Thomas More*, Cambridge.

McCutcheon, E. (1977), 'Denying the Contrary: More's Use of Litotes in the *Utopia*', in R. S. Sylvester and G. P. Marc'hardour (eds), *Essential Articles for the Study of Thomas More*, 163–74, Hamden.

McCutcheon, E. (1983), *My Dear Peter: the Ars Poetica and Hermeneutics for More's Utopia*, Angers.

Monsuez, R. (1966), 'Le Latin de Thomas More dans *Utopia*', *Annales publiées par la Faculté des Lettres et Sciences Humaines de Toulouse*: 35–78.

Nelson, E. (2004), *The Greek Tradition in Republican Thought*, Cambridge.

Nicholas, L.R. (forthcoming), 'The Latin Utopias', in C. Shrank and P. Withington (eds), *The Oxford Handbook of Thomas More's Utopia*, Oxford.

Surtz, E. (1967), 'Aspects of More's Latin Style in *Utopia*', *Studies in the Renaissance*, 14: 93–109.

Surtz, E. and J. H. Hexter (eds) (1965), *The Complete Works of St. Thomas More*, Vol. 4, New Haven and London.

Taylor, A. (2014), 'Thomas More', in P. Ford, J. Bloemendal and C. Fantazzi (eds.), *Brill's Encyclopaedia of the Neo-Latin World*, 1047, Leiden.

The Yale Edition of the Complete Works of St. Thomas More, New Haven 1963–1997.

Source of the Latin text

The Latin text is taken from the November 1518 edition (the last edition More was involved in): *De Optimo Reip. Statu, Deque nova insula Utopia, libellus aureus, nec minus salutaris quam festivus clarissimi disertissimique viri Thomae Mori inclytae civitatis. Londiniensis civis & Vicecomitis*, Basel 1518. The text has been checked against the standard modern edition, Surtz and Hexter (1965), though their edition uses the March 1518 text and does not include inverted commas.

Latin text

Passage 1: Book 1

at Petrus[1] ubi me conspexit, adit ac salutat. respondere conantem seducit paululum, et 'vides' inquit 'hunc?' (simul designabat eum cum quo loquentem videram) 'eum' inquit 'iam hinc ad te recta parabam ducere.' 'venisset' inquam 'pergratus mihi tua causa.' 'imo',[2] inquit 'ille, si nosses[3] hominem sua.[4] nam nemo vivit hodie mortalium omnium, qui tantam tibi hominum, terrarumque incognitarum[5] narrare possit historiam,[6] quarum rerum audiendarum scio avidissimum esse te'. 'ergo' inquam 'non pessime coniectavi. nam primo aspectu protinus sensi hominem esse nauclerum'. 'atque' inquit 'aberrasti[7] longissime – navigavit quidem non ut Palinurus,[8] sed ut Ulysses[9]; imo velut nempe Plato.[10] nempe Raphael[11] iste, sic enim vocatur gentilicio nomine Hythlodaeus, et Latinae linguae non indoctus, et Graecae doctissimus[12] (cuius ideo studiosior quam Romanae fuit, quoniam totum se addixerat philosophiae; qua in re nihil quod alicuius momenti[13] sit, praeter Senecae[14] quaedam, ac Ciceronis[15] extare[16] Latine cognovit) relicto fratribus patrimonio, quod ei domi fuerat – est enim Lusitanus – orbis terrarum contemplandi[17] studio Americo Vespucio[18] se adiunxit.'

English translation

Passage 1: Book 1

But when Peter[1] caught sight of me, he bounded up and greeted me. And just as I was trying to respond, he drew me a little further away and said, 'Do you see this fellow?' At the same time he began to point out the man to whom I had seen him speaking, and he said, 'I was just now planning to bring him straight to you.' 'He would have been very welcome to me, on your account', I answered. 'On his own account,[4] rather,[2] if you knew[3] the man', he replied, 'for there is no person alive today that can give so rich an exposition[6] of unknown[5] peoples and countries; I know you're very eager to hear such information.' 'In that case', I said, 'my conjecture was not very wide of the mark, for at first glance I immediately surmised that he was a ship's captain.' 'But you are very wide of the mark,[7] he replied, 'for he has sailed not as a Palinurus,[8] but as an Odysseus,[9] or rather, to be sure, as a Plato.[10] Indeed, this Raphael[11] – for so he is called, and his family name is Hythloday – is not unversed in the Latin tongue, but he's especially knowledgeable in Greek.[12] He was more inclined to study the Greek language than that of the Romans since he had applied himself completely to philosophy and he recognized that in that field there is extant[16] nothing of value[13] in Latin except certain works of Seneca[14] and Cicero.[15] Being eager to see[17] the world, he left behind to his brothers his inheritance which he had at home (he is Portuguese) and joined up with Amerigo Vespucci.'[18]

Passage 2: Book 2

sed ad convictum civium revertor. Antiquissimus[19] – ut dixi – praeest[20] familiae. ministri sunt uxores maritis, et liberi parentibus, atque in summa minores natu maioribus. civitas omnis in quattuor aequales partes dividitur. in medio cuiusque partis forum est omnium rerum. eo in certas domos opera cuiusque familiae convehuntur, atque in horrea singulae seorsum species distributae sunt. ab his quilibet paterfamilias quibus ipse suique opus[21] habent, petit, ac sine pecunia, sine omni prorsus hostimento quicquid petierit,[22] aufert. quare enim negetur quicquam cum et omnium rerum abunde satis sit nec timor ullus subsit, ne quisquam plusquam sit opus, flagitare velit?[23] nam cur supervacua petiturus putetur is, qui certum habeat,[24] nihil sibi umquam defuturum?[25] nempe avidum ac rapacem, aut timor carendi facit, in omni animantum[26] genere, aut in homine sola reddit[27] superbia, quae gloriae[28] sibi ducit, superflua rerum ostentatione ceteros antecellere, quod vitii genus in Utopiensium institutis nullum omnino locum habet.

Passage 2: Book 2

But I return to the community of its citizens: the oldest[19] male, as I have said, is the head[20] of the household; wives are attendant upon their husbands, and children upon their parents, and in the final place, the younger upon their elders. Every city-state is divided into four equal quarters, and in the middle of each quarter there is a shopping centre for every type of commodity. There the goods of each household are conveyed into designated depots, and then each type of commodity is distributed among various stores. From these, any head of a household looks for whatever he himself and his family need[21] and, without paying for it and without making any compensation whatsoever in respect of what he has looked for,[22] carries it off. For why would anything be denied to him, since there is more than enough of everything, and there is no reason to fear that anyone may be motivated to demand more than he needs?[23] And why would anyone be thought to be bent on seeking more than what is necessary when he knows for certain[24] that he'll never go short?[25] It is surely fear of want that makes anyone in the entire race of living creatures[26] greedy or acquisitive; and in man only, it is pride, which he considers can bring him glory,[28] that drives[27] a man to surpass others in an excessive display of ownership; but in the institutions of the Utopians, this type of foible has no place at all.

Passage 3: Book 2

in ea philosophiae parte qua de moribus agitur, eadem illis disputantur quae nobis, de bonis animi quaerunt et corporis, et externis, tum utrum boni nomen omnibus his, an solis animi dotibus conveniat.[29] de virtute disserunt, ac voluptate,[30] sed omnium prima est ac princeps controversia, quanam in re, una pluribusve sitam hominis felicitatem putent. at hac in re propensiores aequo[31] videntur in factionem voluptatis assertricem,[32] ut qua[33] vel totam, vel potissimam felicitatis humanae partem definiant. et quo magis mireris ab religione quoque – quae gravis et severa est fereque tristis et rigida – petunt tamen sententiae tam delicatae patrocinium. neque enim de felicitate disceptant umquam, quin principia quaedam ex religione[34] deprompta, tum[35] philosophia quae rationibus utitur coniungant, sine quibus ad verae felicitatis investigationem mancam, atque imbecillam per se rationem putant.[36]

Passage 3: Book 2

In that area of philosophy which centres on morals, the same questions are explored by them as by us. They enquire into goods of the mind, of the body and into external goods, and then into whether the name 'good' is appropriate for all of them or for gifts of the mind only.[29] They examine virtue and pleasure,[30] but their first and chief argument of all is on what factor, one or more, they consider that human happiness depends. But in this regard, they seem too much inclined[31] to the position that champions pleasure,[32] with the result that they locate the whole or the greatest part of human happiness there.[33] And you may be yet more astonished at the fact that they also seek support for this self-indulgent viewpoint from their religion, which is serious and strict and you might say cheerless and inflexible. For they do not ever debate about happiness without first joining certain first principles of religion[34] with[35] philosophy which rests on reason. Without this, they think that reason by itself is deficient and defective for any investigation into true happiness.[36]

Commentary

Passage 1

This first passage comes very near the start of Book 1. The book opens with this light-hearted scene in Bruges, and it is here that Raphael Hythloday is first introduced to the reader (*Utopia* 1518: 27–8). In addition to the characters of Peter Gillis (a real person) and Raphael Hythloday (a fictional actor), More writes himself into the narrative – he is the first-person speaker at this point. From the very start of this perplexing work, then, we are confronted with a tension between fact and fabrication.

1 *Petrus*: a reference to Peter Gillis (or Giles), More's friend and fellow humanist from the Netherlands.

2 *imo = immo.*

3 *nosses = novisses* (pluperfect subjunctive from *nosco*).

4 *sua*: re-supply *venisset pergratus . . . causa.*

5 Although this adjective technically agrees with *terrarum*, it is valid to understand it as qualifying *hominum* too. More and his circle were very interested in the exploration of the globe that was seriously underway in the sixteenth century; see also n. 18 below.

6 *tantam tibi . . . historiam*: More possibly has Homer, *Odyssey* 1.3 in mind ('Many were the men whose cities he saw and whose minds he learned ..?'), especially given the comparison to Odysseus shortly afterwards.

7 *aberrasti = aberravisti.*

8 Palinurus was the helmsman of Aeneas' ship in Virgil's *Aeneid*, but while he was singled out there as an exceptionally skilled navigator, he also fell asleep at the helm and plunged into the sea (*Aen.* 5.833–61 and 6.337–83). The point seems to be that Hythloday was, by contrast, very wide awake.

9 *Ulysses*: Odysseus of Greek mythology, whose long and difficult journey home following the Trojan War is described in Homer's *Odyssey*.

10 Gillis, the speaker here, perhaps has in mind Plato's metaphor of the 'Ship of State', outlined in *Republic* 6.488a–9d, which likens the governance of the state to the command of a ship that should be manned by the philosopher kings.

11 Raphael is Hythloday's first name. It is a Hebrew name meaning 'God has healed'. The Greek origins of the surname Hythloday are discussed in the Introduction. It may also have been an apposite name to use as Flemish

merchants had a ship called 'Raphael' which took part in a voyage ten years earlier.

12 *graecae doctissimus*: quite a claim, as very few people in Europe knew Greek at the start of the sixteenth century. More was one exception, and many of the references in *Utopia* depend on a reader knowing Greek in order to grasp them fully. Indeed those with no Greek seem to constitute one of the many potential targets of satire in this work.

13 *alicuius momenti*: a genitive of value.

14–15 Seneca and Cicero are the only Latin authors approved by name in *Utopia*. The emphasis on Greek, especially in the realm of philosophy, was very much a feature of the humanists' campaign at the time and a point stressed elsewhere by More himself.

16 *extare = exstare*.

17 *contemplandi*: genitive of the gerundive, agreeing with *orbis* and following *studio*.

18 *Americo Vespucio*: Amerigo Vespucci was an Italian explorer and part of an expedition that reached South America at the end of the fifteenth century; he gave his name to America.

Passage 2

This passage appears a little way into Book 2, which is considerably longer than Book 1 and essentially comprises a monologue delivered by Raphael concerning the condition of Utopia. His description is divided up into sections, including a review of the cities of Utopia, their governance, travel within and beyond Utopia, their use of slaves, military practice and religious observance. In this section about social relations, Raphael outlines certain social structures in Utopia and how goods are shared communally (*Utopia* 1518: 87–8). This is one of the passages of *Utopia* that seems (for some) to capture an early blueprint for communism. However, through this extract the reader should be constantly asking how all this is to be construed: are we meant to interpret it as aspirational, prescriptive or absurd?

19 *Antiquissimus* and what follows seems to reflect a patriarchal outlook which More himself may well have shared. The father and husband's authority rested upon Scripture, but also had pagan precedents (for example, Aristotle, *Pol.* 1.5.1–2, 1259a–b).

20 *praesum* takes the dative, explaining the dative form of *familiae*.

21 *opus*, when it means 'there is need of', takes the ablative of the thing needed, hence *quibus*.

22 *petierit = petiverit*. The repetition of the verb *peto* helps to reinforce the surprising nature of such transactions.

23 *velit*: a present subjunctive in a fearing clause introduced by *timor ullus subsit ne . . . .*

24 *habeat*: a present subjunctive following *qui* in a generic sense and ushering in an indirect statement ('has it as certain that . . .').

25 *defuturum*: understand *esse*.

26 *animantum*: a present participle in the genitive plural, from the verb *animo, -are*.

27 *reddit* followed by an infinitive (*antecellere*), similarly used with *do, dare*, means literally 'to give a person to . . .'.

28 *gloriae*: a predicative dative.

Passage 3

This final passage is from the middle of Book 2 in a discursive section on the philosophy of the Utopians. Here Raphael addresses the approach of the Utopians from the perspective of moral philosophy. He also touches on the nature of their religion, which he elaborates on in more detail later in the book (*Utopia* 1518: 102–3).

29 *conveniat*: a present subjunctive in an indirect question after *utrum . . . an*.

30 *de virtute disserunt, ac voluptate*: these words almost constitute a description of Cicero's *De Finibus*, an exposition of the philosophical precepts of the Epicureans and the Stoics. More may also here be engaging with Aristotle's discussion of pleasure in his *Nicomachean Ethics*. The Utopians seem to be in agreement that all men seek happiness, but the point at issue is what constitutes the object of this happiness, and this seems in essence to pivot on a contest between the virtue of the Stoics and the pleasure of the Epicureans. This was a live debate in the early modern period and addressed *inter alia* by Erasmus.

31 *aequo* plus a comparative tends to mean 'too . . .'. More (or the speaker) seems to lodge his disapproval here.

32 *assertrix* is not a common Latin word, but appears to be the feminine equivalent of *assertor* on the grounds that *factio* is feminine. The Utopians

seem to champion an Epicurean philosophy, asserting the primacy of *voluptas* ('pleasure'), but the description of their unbending religion seems more Stoic in character. The apparent incompatibility of these two strands is remarked by Raphael (*et quo magis mireris . . .*). More generally, Utopian ethics comprise a strange fusion of Stoicism and Epicureanism.

33 'there', viz. in pleasure.

34 *religione*: used in contrast to philosophy here, the latter employing reason.

35 *tum*: in the 1516 edition of Utopia appears as *cum* ('with').

36 The implication is that the object of true happiness constitutes something that surpasses the natural powers of human reason: reason has to borrow certain truths from religion.

2

An Early Tudor Antiquarian at Bath

John Leland (*c.* 1503–1552), *De thermis Britannicis*

Andrew W. Taylor

Introduction

John Leland was among the first educated at St Paul's School in London, founded by Dean Colet in 1509. He progressed to Christ's College, Cambridge (admitted BA 1522), and then, after a stint as tutor to Lord Thomas Howard, sixth son of the Duke of Norfolk, to Oxford, where he may have been associated with All Souls College. His Paris sojourn from 1526 to 1529, facilitated by Cardinal Wolsey and a royal exhibition, shaped his aspirations as a Latin poet and humanist antiquarian. Although Leland wrote a great deal in both veins, much of his work failed to reach the presses either in his lifetime or shortly thereafter (see James Carley's full survey in Leland 2010: xxxvi–li). This may reflect a reluctance or inability to conclude large-scale works as well as the want of patronage of which Leland complained, matters that may have contributed to his psychological disintegration around the time of Henry VIII's death on 28 January 1547.

Leland wrote what we may think of as epigrammatic poetry throughout his literary career. His *De thermis Britannicis* was composed in the period when, as he later stated, he had passed from youthful years consumed by poetic ardour to the more sober work on the bibliographical, and then topographical, enterprises through which he sought to record and preserve the national heritage. Many poems in the collection that has survived, though occasional in nature, are difficult to date, but some, devoted to the departures and returns of peregrinating academics and diplomats, can be placed relatively securely (Taylor 2012). In the dedication to Henry VIII of his river poem, *Cygnea cantio* (1545), Leland could look back at some kind of three-book arrangement of supposed *iuvenilia* or youthful works: *Encomiasticon, Sales* and *Epikedion* (Leland 1545, fol. Aii^v) – poems of praise, wit and mourning. Yet towards the close of 1546 he composed perhaps his last short poem, on the marriage of the ascendant statesman William Cecil. The occasion to finalize the collection for publication seems ever to have eluded him.

Some epigrams capture a sense of Leland's connectedness to the learned and influential in England, others point towards an overlapping literary cosmopolitanism involving humanists and Latin poets across the Channel (see Sutton n.d.: 'Introduction'). Some Neo-Latin poets he may have met, like the Frenchmen Jean Salmon Macrin and Nicolas Bourbon; some, like the Italian Giovanni Gioviano Pontano and his friend and pupil Michael Marullus, were Quattrocento figures; but all, including the German Helius Eobanus Hessus, seem to have been read by Leland. Moreover, his epigrams *Commigratio bonarum litterarum in Britanniam* (*Carmen* VI) and *Instauratio bonarum litterarum* (*Carmen* CXCVII) give Latin voice to a literary and scholarly nationalism asserted as rivalling foreign achievements and salute his native learned contemporaries and their recent forebears who had initiated the transfer or migration of learning (*translatio studii*) from Italy to Britain.

Whether by art or otherwise, collections of epigrams can appear to lack an organizing principle, and so it is with the corpus of Leland's short poems preserved in near-contemporary manuscripts and the resulting printed edition of 1589, *Principum, ac illustrium aliquot et eruditorum in Anglia virorum, Encomia, Trophaea, Genethliaca, et Epithalamia* (see below). The poem featured here, *De thermis Britannicis* (*Carmen* XXXVII), is placed among those addressing Thomas Lupset, Nicholas Udall, a noble youth, and Christopher Smyth, rather than arguably more aptly in the shadow of his epigram celebrating the vertical sundial erected by the astronomer Nicholas Kratzer at Oxford in 1520 (*Carmen* LII). If a three-part manuscript, as mentioned by Leland in 1545, ever existed – perhaps that organization was a projected work –, it seems not to have survived. In 1576, some 24 years after Leland's death, John Stow copied out Leland's *Collectanea, Itinerary* and poetry (now MS Oxford, Bodleian Library, Tanner 464, i–v), presumably from poorly preserved originals in the possession of Henry Cheke, the son of John Cheke (Harris 2005: 471–4). Stow's fourth volume, the poetry, served as the copy text for Thomas Newton's 1589 edition of Leland's epigrams. However, the nature of the discrepancies in the number, order, titles and texts of poems between Stow's manuscript and Newton's edition, implies that Newton was able to refer to another, probably superior copy, which could have been that which may have passed from Leland to John Bale or another, fair copy of it (see Leland 2010: xlvi–xlviii; Sutton n.d.: 'Introduction').

De thermis Britannicis stands interestingly at the intersection of Leland's poetic, antiquarian and topographical investments. In early June 1533 he set out from London, almost certainly alone, on the first of his laborious journeys, riding westward through Surrey, Hampshire, Wiltshire, and between Dorset, Somerset and Devon, before heading to the Benedictine house at Glastonbury, the location of Arthur's tomb and a library rich in ancient manuscripts. After the short hop from Glastonbury to Wells and its cathedral library, he made his way to Bath, where he visited the Benedictine cathedral priory. When he returned to Somerset in 1542, he recorded in his *Itinerary* that he had been at Bath 'an 9 yere sins' (Leland 1907: 143). In the *Itinerary* Leland recalls his entry to Bath, how he passed through 'a great gate with a stone arche at the entre of the bridge' – the South Gate – having traversed 'a longe streate as a suburbe', containing the 'chapelle of S. Mary Magdalen' (Leland 1907: 139). From the South Gate to the West, and from there to the North Gate, he saw 'divers notable antiquitees engravid in stone … yn the walles', including 'an antique hed of a man made al flat and having great lokkes of here as I have in a coine of C. Antius' (Leland 1907: 140). Could this have been the 'Gorgon's head', much debated by modern archaeologists, which was discovered in 1790? And was the coin instead one minted by the moneyer Plautius Plancus (the heavily worn legend 'LAVTIVS' misread as 'CANTIUS'), who issued denarii bearing the flattened face or mask of the Medusa in 47 BCE? The Bath Gorgon's original position was at the apex of the pediment of the late-Neronian or early Flavian temple to Sulis Minerva, and it was probably the work of first-century sculptors from Gaul. Leland's description also fits the image of Oceanus on the great silver dish found at Mildenhall, while other interpretations see it as a representation of Bladud, a legendary king of the Britons thought to have been the discoverer of the springs' healing properties (see below).

Leland's commemoration of the hot springs at Bath in his *De thermis Britannicis* stands closer to the antiquarian discourse of his *Itinerary* than to poetic representations that he would have known involving baths. So it is that he tends to stand an onlooker in this poem. There is no intimation that he immersed himself either in the 'reeking' *fontes* or in the ancient poetic sources of *thermae* and *balnea*.[1] Leland knew his Martial (see *Carmen* CXLVIII), yet the vitality and vicissitudes of the Roman poet's social world of bathing (see Fagan 1999: ch. 1) – the soliciting of dinner invitations (and the avoidance of those pestering for them), anxiety over deposited clothing, and the various liquid pleasures on tap – seem far away.

Martial's bathing epigrams exploit Baiae's reputation for both luxury and licence, a *locus* developed with relish by Pontano, the Quattrocento poet Leland praises to the stars, and not merely for the hexameters of his astronomical *Urania* (see *De quibusdam nostri saeculi poetis* [*Carmen* CXCIII]; Taylor 2012: 26–7). Pontano's *Opera*, available in 1505 from Aldine presses in Venice, as well as those of his adoptive Naples, and soon reprinted, includes his neo-Catullan *Hendecasyllaborum sive Baiarum libri duo*, where the baths are playgrounds for wanton games. Yet in his epigram *Castos esse decet poetas* ('Poets should be chaste', *Carmen* CCXXXVII) Leland distanced himself from those ancient pagan singers of amorous affairs imitated by Pontano who were ignorant of the better life: *Talia molliculi cantabant carmina vates | Ignari vitae qui melioris erant* (lines 13–14).

Lacking the warmth of baths and bodies, the verses of *De thermis Britannicis* express, as befits the latitude and religious climate, cooler antiquarian desires and claims to poetic chastity. The boys offer their services, then solicit for coins. The simple irony that these impecunious divers evidently failed to dredge deeply enough to discover any of the twelve thousand coins, the largest votive hoard in Britain, cast in by ancient visitors, is one compounded by that ancient coin brought to Leland's mind in the *Itinerary* as he contemplates the iconography of fragments of masonry embedded in the medieval walls. Nor does it seem that the lead and pewter Latin curse tablets of the second to fourth centuries, mostly vengeful imprecations to the goddess Sulis Minerva and likewise lying in the sludge, were known to him.[2]

For Leland's poem, the *thermae* are instead where two streams of history converge. The Celts had dedicated the springs to the goddess Sulis long before the advent of the Romans, who adopted the name for Bath, Aquae Sulis, associating the local deity with Minerva; *Sulis* may have been derived from *Sol* and the association of heat.[3] In the *Commentarii in Cygneam Cantionem* Leland appended to his river poem, he remarks that, although Bath (*Balnea . . . urbs*) was called Cair Badune by the Britons, the association with baths was inappropriate, as those were artificially heated (*industria incalescant*); Leland approves of Ptolemy's Greek name θερμή (*thermē*), 'for hot springs are heated by nature' (*Thermae etenim natura calent*). Leland's testing preoccupation with place names leads him, also in the *Commentarii*, first to commend Bede's pertinent drawing upon the fourth homily of Basil the Great's *Hexaemeron*, where the Greek Father discusses hot springs heated by subterranean fire, then to frown at Bede's inappropriate use of the term 'baths' for hot springs.

Leland's toponomastics subtly inform *De thermis Britannicis*. The entry on Bath in the *Commentarii in Cygneam Cantionem* finally points to *thermae* elsewhere in Britain, specifically the cooler springs at Buxton in Derbyshire. However, *De thermis Britannicis* not only restricts itself to the hot springs at Bath, but assiduously avoids both the terms 'Badune' and *balnea*: antonomasia is instead employed for Bath (*urbs thermarum*), and the baths are *thermae* or *fontes*. So, although Leland in the *Itinerary* is content to name 'The Kinges Bathe', the Latin poem finesses that: *Tres numero fontes (memini si rectius) extant, | Regius inter quos nobile nomen habet* (9–10: translation below).

In the unpublished *De viris illustribus* Leland treats these topics more expansively in the entry for the figure of Bladud or Bladudus (cap. 6; Leland 2010: 14–19), presenting him as the first to indicate the benefits of the thermal waters for the Britons. In the *Commentarii* Leland castigates Geoffrey of Monmouth's *Historia regum Britanniae* ('*History of the Kings of Britain*') for figuring Bladud as the necromantic discoverer of the *thermae*; the eleventh-century William of Malmesbury, in his *Gesta pontificum Anglicorum* ('*Deeds of the Bishops of England*'), is, in Leland's eyes, little better for believing that Julius Caesar discovered the springs: *Ut crediderint, certè ego non credo* ('Though they may have believed it, I certainly do not believe it'), Leland snaps. In the *De viris illustribus* he credits Bladud with the building of a temple to Minerva containing an eternal flame, but also censures him for having come to believe in the sham necromantic powers he peddled to cow the common folk. Bladud, Leland records, seems ultimately to have crashed to an Icarus-like death in 'Trenovantum' (London), fittingly onto a temple to Apollo. He rounds off his treatment of Bladud by invoking William of Malmesbury, now an 'unimpeachable authority', who offered Leland a bathetic parallel to Bladud's end in Olivarius, a monk, who, having raised himself on artificial wings, fell, maiming himself.

Hactenus Lelandus. We know that the Temple of Sulis Minerva was built to enclose the sacred spring from which waters flowed into the baths themselves. The temple complex seems to have been in gentle decline during the fourth century and, like the baths, abandoned by the end of the fifth. A century or so later the barrel-vaulted roof had collapsed, and it seems that masonry from the temple and elsewhere was repurposed, in particular for the maintenance of the stone pavement, in which fragments of temple columns have been found. Although much was lost to reuse in the immediate vicinity or carried further afield, other fragments sank into the mud and were preserved. In the twelfth century a new structure was raised over the extant lower walls, including the King's Baths, which included niches for bathers to sit or shelter in. This process of reclamation and rebuilding chimes with Leland's observations about the setting of antique works in the walls he saw. At his death, Leland's treatment of the *thermae* at Bath in this epigram and his *De viris illustribus* remained in manuscript, apparently unknown to the physician William Turner; although in print, Leland's *Cygnea cantio* and accompanying *Commentarii* (1545) seem not to have been brought to his attention. Edward Seymour, Duke of Somerset and Lord Protector to the young King Edward VI between 1547 and 1549, at that time granted Turner permission to visit 'Baeth' with some 'diseased persones' to test the hot springs' efficacy. Sadly, Leland's name is not to be found in Turner's list of learned sources that informed the resulting treatise. Of Bath, Turner stated,

'Wherof that I wote of noman hath writen one word, that ever I could rede' (1562: fols A.ii^r–A.iii^v).

Metre: elegiac couplets

Notes

1   On *thermae* and *balnea*, see Martial 9.75: Tucca has constructed not just a *balneum* of wood resembling a boat, but also costly (and artificially heated) *thermae* in a variety of marbles. Martial's final quip is that, as firewood is lacking for the hot baths, the *balneum* should fuel the *thermae* (*sed ligna desunt: subice balneum thermis*).
2   See Fagan (1999: 37). Most of the 130 curse tablets are a response to theft. See Martial 12.70.2 for Aper's bringing of a one-eyed woman to watch over his shabby robe, and 12.87, where the baths may have been where Cotta twice loses his sandals prior to turning up barefoot at dinner.
3   Leland then adds that Antoninus (Marcus Aurelius) called them 'waters of the sun', where *Aquarum solis* seems a corruption of *sulis*.

Bibliography

Leland's epigrams are numbered according to Dana Sutton's hypertext edition.

Binns, J. W. (1990), *Intellectual Culture in Elizabethan and Jacobean England: The Latin Writings of the Age*, Leeds.

Bradner, L. (1956), 'Some Unpublished Poems by John Leland', *Proceedings of the Modern Language Association*, 71: 827–36.

Cunliffe, B. W. (1984), *Roman Bath Rediscovered*, rev. edn, London.

Fagan, G. G. (1999), *Bathing in Public in the Roman World*, Ann Arbor.

Harris, O. (2005), 'Motheaten, Mouldye, and Rotten: The Early Custodial History and Dissemination of John Leland's Manuscript Remains', *Bodleian Library Record*, 18: 460–501.

Leland, J. (1545), *Cygnea cantio* and *Commentarii in Cygneam Cantionem indices Britannicae antiquitatis locupletissimi*, London.

Leland, J. (1907), *The Itinerary of John Leland in or about the Years 1535–1543 in England and Wales*, ed. L. Toulmin Smith, vol. 1, London.

Leland, J. (2010), *De viris illustribus / On Famous Men*, ed. J. P. Carley, Toronto and London.

Pontano, G. G. (1505), *Pontani opera* [...] *hendecasyllaborum libri duo*, Venice.

Pontano, G. G. (2006), *Baiae*, transl. R. G. Dennis, Cambridge (MA) and London (I Tatti Renaissance Library 22).

Sutton, D. (n.d.), Hypertext edition of Leland's *Epigrammata*: http://www.philological.bham.ac.uk/lelandpoems/.

Taylor, A. (2012), 'John Leland's communities of the epigram', in L. B. T. Houghton and G. Manuwald (eds), *Neo-Latin Poetry in the British Isles*, 15–35, London.

Turner, W. (1562), *A Booke of the natures and properties, as well of the bathes in England as of the other bathes in Germany and Italy, very necessary for all seik persones that can not be healed without the helpe of natural bathes*, Cologne.

Source of the Latin text

The copy text is from *Principum, ac illustrium aliquot et eruditorum in Anglia virorum, Encomia, Trophaea, Genethliaca, et Epithalamia* (London: Thomas Ortwin, 1589: 12–13). See Bradner 1956: 827 and Sutton's (n.d.) 'Introduction' for a discussion of the relationship between this edition, edited by Thomas Newton, and John Stow's manuscript, now MS Oxford, Bodleian Library, Tanner 464, iv, fols 9^v–10^r.

Variants in *MS Tanner* include: 4 *aqua*, 7 *quidem* for *latex*, 9 *meministi* for *memini si*, 11 *muro forti* (introducing a seventh foot), 15–16 *Urinatores pueri stant margine fontis* | *Et lucrum sperant officiosa cohors*, 17 *Talia cantantes*, 21 *Hac*, 30 *scilicet atque catum*.

Latin text

De thermis Britannicis

Nota Murotrigum calidis stat gloria thermis,
    Quo nitet eximium flumen Avona loco.
Hic natura potens tepidos (miracula) fontes
    Excitat, et quaedam vis salientis aquae est.
5 Crediderim venas vicinas sulphuris esse,
    Nascitur unde latens perpetuusque tepor.
Et si quando latex ebulliat auctior, ater
    Consurgit fumus, foetor et inde gravis.
Tres numero fontes (memini si rectius) extant,
10   Regius inter quos nobile nomen habet.
Cinguntur muro: sedes quoque regius offert
    Excisas saxis sedulitate pia.
Colluit in medicis undis numerosa caterva,
    Fracta salutifero et membra calore fovet.
15 Hic urinantum puerorum in margine fontis
    Sperat denarios officiosa cohors,
Talia decantans: *Visne, hospes candide, nostra*
    Uti nunc opera? Turba parata sumus.
Dives, et es largus, tua nunc patet atque crumena,
20   *Promittens nobis praemia laeta macris;*
Haec eadem poscunt fontes de more salubres,
    Hospitis extollunt munificamque manum.
De meliore nota paucos nunc proiice nummos,
    Undas in medias subsideantque graves.
25 *Nos tamen insultu facto scrutabimur ima:*
    Desine mirari, nos referemus opes.
Hactenus et pueri: doctorum turba virorum
    Undique decertant quae sit origo loci.
Somnia Cambrorum Bladudum ad sydera tollunt,
30   Inventorem operis scilicet eximii.
Maildulphusque sui decus admirabile saecli,
    Caesaris hic curas officiumque probat.
Territa quaesitis ostendit terga Britannis
    Caesar: et officium praestitit ille? logi.

English translation

On the hot springs of Britain

The acknowledged glory of the Murotriges lies in hot *thermae*, at the place
where the excellent river Avon glitters. Here mighty nature rouses up warm
sources (real wonders), and there is particular power in the bounding water. 5
I could believe that nearby there are veins of sulphur, from which hidden and
everlasting warmth is born. Indeed, whenever the liquid boils up more
abundantly, black vapours arise, with a grievous stink. Three in number are
the springs, if I rightly recall; among them the King's bears the noble name. 10
They are enclosed by a wall; the King's offers seats too, carved from the rocks
with dutiful care. A great crowd wash deeply in the healing streams, and
warm their broken limbs with health-bringing heat. Here at the spring's edge 15
a group of diving boys hope attentively for coins, repeatedly calling out such
things as, 'Do you wish, fair guest, to employ our efforts now? We're a ready
crew. You are rich and generous as well, now your purse lies open, pouring 20
forth rich pickings for us lean lads. According to custom, these wholesome
springs urge the same things, they praise the liberal hand of the guest. Now
throw in a few pieces of the better class, and let them sink down heavily in the
middle streams. Yet leaping in, we'll scour the depths: stop wondering, we'll 25
bring back your treasure'. Thus far the boys. A throng of learned men
everywhere contest the origin of the place. The day-dreams of the Welsh raise
Bladud to the skies, the inventor, doubtless, of this distinguished work. And 30
then Maildulphus, that wonderful glory of his age, approves here the care and
dutifulness of Caesar. To the Britons he had pursued, Caesar showed his

35 Induperatores alii, Romanaque virtus
        Urbem Thermarum percoluere suam,
    Moenibus inque ipsis retinet monumenta Quiritum
        Antiquae clarum nobilitatis opus.
    Gloria Thermarum sic luceat inclyta semper,
40   Tantum sint memores hospitis usque mei.

terrified back – and that man performed his duty? Piffle! Other emperors and 35
Roman virtue adorned their city of *Thermae*, and in the very walls it preserves
the monuments of the Quirites, illustrious work of noble antiquity. So may
the famed glory of the *Thermae* always shine, as long as they remember me, 40
their guest.

Commentary

1–2 Note the hyperbaton of the first line, compared with the fitting syntactic flow and repeated 'm' and 'n' sounds of the second.

1 *Murotriges*: A Celtic tribe inhabiting modern Dorset, south Wiltshire, south Somerset and Devon east of the River Axe. Prior to the Roman invasion, they were more often referred to as Durotriges. Leland calls Somerset men Murotriges in his *Naeniae in mortem Thomae Viati equitis incomparabilis* (1542) for fellow poet and friend Sir Thomas Wyatt (d. 1542): *Hinc Murotriges crudelia fata vocare | Non cessant, subito quae subtraxere Viatum.* ('The men of Dorset do not cease railing against the cruel Fates that have suddenly taken away Wyatt.') The Durotriges' resistance to the Roman invasion under Vespasian in 43 CE is recorded in Suetonius, but by 70 CE the tribe had been Romanized as part of the Roman province of 'Britannia'.

calidis … thermis: not found in Martial, for example, where the classical usage tends to distinguish grander *thermae* from humbler and often private *balnea*. The adjective *calidis* seems a redundant line filler (pleonasm), especially as Leland stresses in his *Commentarii in Cygneam Cantionem* and *De viris illustribus* that *thermae* were by definition naturally hot.

2 *Quo … loco*: an ablative of place.

9–11 *Tres numero fontes … regius*: Note how the word *balneum* is avoided by referring to the baths as *fontes* (see Introduction) and then by the use of the ellipsis *regius [fons]*. The adverb *rectius* is the comparative of *recte*, 'rightly', 'correctly', with *rectius* used more for the sake of metre than for the refinement of meaning.

11–12 *sedes … sedulitate pia*: 'seats' carved 'with pious care'; probably a reference to the 32 sheltering niches built during the twelfth-century refurbishment of the springs by monks.

14 *Fracta … membra*: The words are fittingly dislocated from one another, while the chiastic phrasing connects healing with the broken and warming with the limbs.

15–16 *Hic urinantum puerorum … cohors*: See Pliny for sponge-harvesting divers dangerously beset by dogfish (*Canicularum maxime multitudo circa eas [sponges] urinantes gravi periculo infestat, Naturalis historia* 9.70). *MS Tanner* has the prosaic *Urinatores pueri stant margine fontis.*

16 *denarios*: At line 23 the boys balance the call for a few pieces against the value of each.

17–26 *Visne . . . opes*: In the 1589 edition, only the opening of the boys' speech is typographically distinct (roman against italic), although the poem makes clear that their engaging of the poet is closed by *Hactenus et pueri* (27). The embedding of the boys' addresses to the poet in the heart of the poem enlivens it, holding apart the primarily descriptive opening and the antiquarian reflections that follow. The boys' words attest the poet's presence at the scene, while their rhetoric – they associate their soliciting with the invitation of the springs themselves – suggests an almost naiadic scene of ritual and votive offering originating in a distant past.

23 *De meliore nota*: 'from the top drawer': see Catullus 68.28. Note the rhythmic lapping of sound in the line ahead of *undas* (24): *De meliore nota paucos nunc proiice nummos.*

24 *graves*: The adjective takes on adverbial significance, 'heavily', also picks up on the more serious value of the preferred coins, and is placed last in an end-stopped line.

25 *insultu facto*: 'with a leap having been made', an ablative absolute defining circumstances connected with the action, here, of searching the floor of the baths for the solicited coins.

27 *doctorum turba virorum*: *turba* likens the learned to the gang (18) of diving boys. Congregations are elsewhere termed *caterva* (13) and *cohors* (16).

29 *Bladudum*: The earliest surviving account of Bladud, father of King Lear, is in the *Historia regum Britanniae* of Geoffrey of Monmouth (*c.* 1095–*c.* 1155). Leland, here and elsewhere, does not draw on the legend of Bladud's exile for leprosy and the subsequent cure he discovered through the health of those of his pigs that rolled in the spring's mud.

31 *Maildulphus*: William of Malmesbury (*c.* 1095–*c.* 1143), author of *Gesta pontificum Anglorum*. In *De viris illustribus* (Leland 2010: 16–17) Leland notes the Saxons' naming of Maildulphesbury after the hermit Maildulph and its subsequent corruption to Malmesbury.

34 *Caesar*: emphatically placed at the end of the sentence and start of the line; similarly, *ille*, which sets up the dismissive *logi* that follows.

et officium praestitit ille: 'and/indeed that man fulfilled his duty' ironically scorns Caesar's flight.

logi: from the Greek *logoi* ('words'), in Latin signifying less neutrally either a jest or *bon mot*, or a nugatory statement.

35 *Induperatores*: an archaism for *imperatores*, found in Ennius and Lucretius.

37 *inque*: The enclitic conjunction *-que* ('and') is attached to the preposition rather than the noun *moenibus* for the sake of the metre.

Quiritum: The Quirites were originally the inhabitants of the Sabine town Cures, and the name was taken by Romulus for the combined Roman-Sabine community. *Quiris* came to signify a Roman citizen. In the *contio*, a public meeting convened by magistrates to address the *populus Romanus*, Cicero used *Quirites* as the term of address to their faces, in contrast with the addressing of a jury in the law-courts or the members of the senate.

39–40 *sic luceat … Tantum sint*: *sic* + optative subjunctive ('thus may') co-ordinated with *tantum*, an adverb of limitation, 'only', 'as long as'.

40 *hospitis usque mei*: *hospitis* and *mei* in apposition, with hyperbaton emphasizing the final *mei*; *usque* picks up *semper* from the previous line; *memor* + genitive = 'mindful of', 'remembering'. The glory of the *thermae* depends on its memorialization by the poet, who transfers the duties of the guest (*hospes candide*, 17) from the offering of coins (21), once votive, to the offering of a poem.

3

The Nature of the Universe

George Buchanan (1506–1582), *De sphaera* 1.1–51

David McOmish

Introduction

De sphaera ('*On the sphere*') was written by George Buchanan (1506–1582), the prolific and well-respected writer and educationalist. After attending local schools in Killearn, the Gaelic-speaking community in the western highlands of Scotland, where he was born, Buchanan studied at the University of St Andrews, leaving in 1525. He then attended the University of Paris, where, after gaining a BA in 1527, he held various teaching and administrative posts (Procurator of the German Nation) and where he also tutored various members of the French and Scottish nobility over a ten-year period. From 1539 until 1550 he worked with other educationalists, especially Elie Vinet, reforming colleges in Bordeaux (Collège de Guyenne), where he taught the French philosopher Michel de Montaigne, and in Coimbra, Portugal, where he was latterly detained (1550–1552) by the Inquisition for confessional transgressions. During this period Buchanan continued his work on the paraphrases of the Psalms of David, publishing many of them in 1556. It was also during this period that Buchanan became tutor to Timoléon de Cossé, son of Charles de Cossé, first Count of Brissac. Buchanan returned to educational reform in 1566, when he was appointed Principal at St Leonard's College, St Andrews. In 1570, he was appointed tutor (along with Peter Young) to the young King James VI of Scotland (future James I of England). During his time as tutor to Timoléon and James, Buchanan wrote and published many of his most famous works – many of which present a stabilizing philosophical message heavily influenced by Stoic moral and natural philosophy – including *De Iure Regni apud Scotos Dialogus* ('*A Dialogue on the Law of Kingship among the Scots*') and *Rerum Scoticarum Historia* ('*A History of Scottish Affairs*').

Despite his many interests and activities, Buchanan dedicated a large part of his life to composing the poem *De sphaera* (McFarlane 1981:

355–62). He began writing it in the mid-sixteenth century, just as the commentary tradition on the *Sphaera Mundi* ('*The Sphere of the World*') of Johannes de Sacrobosco was being reinvigorated as a teaching aid in universities, specifically by Buchanan's friend and colleague Elie Vinet (McOmish 2018: 164). The philosophical stimulus for both Buchanan's poem and Vinet's commentary came from the publication in 1543 of Nicolaus Copernicus' *De Revolutionibus Orbium* ('*On the Revolutions of the Spheres*'), whose heliocentric arguments undermined the natural philosophy on which traditional religious and moral order (essentially Stoic and Aristotelian) depended. The opening section of *De sphaera*, with its literary and philosophical allusions to the classical writers Ovid, Manilius and Lucretius, shows that the promotion of a geocentric universe was Buchanan's ultimate philosophical goal. Also during this time, the mnemonic tradition of technical poetry that had been a mainstay of medical instruction in the medieval Arabic and European schools (especially the *Cantica Avicennae* and *Regimen Sanitatis Salernitanum*, Latin verses used in the universities of Salerno, Montpellier and Paris to memorize the medical precepts of Ibn Sina and others) had taken root in astronomical teaching, thanks largely to Johannes Honter's versification of his own prose work, *Rudimenta Cosmographica* ('*Beginnings of the Universe*') (Kronstadt 1542). That poem's success is attested by the subsequent twenty-plus editions printed over the next forty years.

Buchanan's *De sphaera*, however, did not share in Honter's success. Buchanan did not complete his five-book poem by the time of his death in 1582 (Books 1 to 3 were completed, but 4 and 5 were unfinished), and it has remained something of a historical curiosity, baffling scholars of literature, history and science alike (McFarlane 1976: 206; Russell 1972: 228). It is reasonable to assume, however, from the evidence of the production context outlined above, the albeit formulaic pedagogical dedications to a specific pupil (Timoléon de Cossé) in the poem itself and the subsidiary title of *Rudimenta Caelestia* ('*Heavenly Beginnings*') given to an instructional edition of the text in 1616 (see below), that rudimentary instruction in cosmology was a core concern (see McOmish 2018: 164–6, *pace* McFarlane 1976: 199).

This edition of the opening of Buchanan's poem will focus upon the poem's significance as an educational tool. The text of *De sphaera* below is a faithful reproduction from the only surviving contemporary manuscript of the poem, Adam King's 1616 edition housed in the University of Edinburgh (University of Edinburgh Centre for Research Collections: shelfmark Dk.7.29). In his preface, King states that the text in the manuscript is a faithful transcription of Buchanan's own copy. King's edition was used for instruction in astronomy and mathematics at the University of Edinburgh for large parts of the seventeenth century (McOmish 2018: 159). It introduced generations of students at Edinburgh to the contrasting ideas of Nicolaus Copernicus, Tycho Brahe, Johannes Kepler and Galileo Galilei among many others, and the anti-authority scepticism of Petrus Ramus and the proto-empiricism of the Parisian Pyrrhonists (see Introduction to Text 8). The notes below are based on Adam King's commentary to the poem. They will only draw attention to Buchanan's literary sources when these directly impact his core philosophical message. Buchanan's tendency to mask his philosophical inspiration (be it prose or verse) behind a pleasing appropriation of a favourite poet (Ovid especially) sheds light upon his compositional approach, and as such, instances of this will be noted. Adam King's *Genethliacon*, also included in this volume, plays a literary game with Buchanan's sources. It provides a useful overview of the elemental aesthetics ('tags') of Buchanan's poetry to the interested reader.

Metre: dactylic hexameter

Bibliography

Farrington, B. (1963), 'Polemical Allusions to the *De Rerum Natura* of Lucretius in the Works of Vergil', in L. Varcl and R. F. Willets (eds), *Geras: Studies Presented to George Thomson on the Occasion of his 60th Birthday*, 87–94, Prague.

Gee, E. (2009), 'Borrowed Plumage: Literary Metamorphoses in George Buchanan's *De Sphaera*', in P. Ford and R. P. H. Green (eds), *George Buchanan: Poet and Dramatist*, 35–57, Swansea.

Green, R. P. H. (ed. and trans.) (2011), *George Buchanan: Poetic Paraphrase of the Psalms of David*, Geneva.

King, A. (1616), *De Sphaera Georgii Buchanani*, Unpublished: Edinburgh.

McFarlane, I. D. (1976), 'The history of George Buchanan's *Sphaera*', in P. Sharratt (ed.), *French Renaissance Studies 1540–70*, 194–212, Edinburgh.

McFarlane, I. D. (1981), *Buchanan*, London [355–78].

McOmish, D. (2018), 'The Scientific Revolution in Scotland Revisited: The New Sciences in Edinburgh', *History of Universities*, 31.2: 153–72.

McOmish, D. (2019), '*Scientia* Demands the Latin Muse: The Authority of Didactic Poetry in Early Modern Scotland', in L. G. Canevaro and D. O'Rourke (eds), *Didactic Poetry: Knowledge, Power, Tradition*, 249–73, London.

Naiden, J. R. (1952), *The Sphera of George Buchanan (1506–1582): A Literary Opponent of Copernicus and Tycho Brahe*, Washington.

Ruddiman, T. (ed.) (1725), *Georgii Buchanani opera omnia*, Vol. 2, Lyon [427–535].

Russell, J. L. (1972), 'The Copernican System in Great Britain', in J. Dobrzycki (ed.), *The Reception of Copernicus' Heliocentric Theory*, 189–240, Dordrecht.

Source of the Latin text

The text given here is a reproduction from the only surviving contemporary manuscript of the poem, Adam King's 1616 edition housed in the University of Edinburgh (University of Edinburgh Centre for Research Collections: shelfmark Dk.7.29).

Latin text

Georgii Buchanani Sphaerae Liber I

Quam variae mundi partes, quo semina rerum
foedere conveniant discordia; lucis et umbrae
tempora quis motus regat; aestum frigore mutet,
obscuret Solis vultum, Lunaeque tenebris,
5 pandere fert animus. Tu qui fulgentia puro
lumine templa habitas, oculis impervia nostris,
rerum sancte parens, audacibus annue coeptis:
dum late in populos ferimus tua facta, polique
immensum reseramus opus: gens nescia veri,
10 ut residem longaque animum caligine mersum
attollat caelo, et flammantia moenia mundi
dum stupet, et vicibus remeantia tempora certis,
auctorem agnoscat: tantam qui robore molem
fulciat; aeternis legum moderetur habenis,
15 consilio nostrosque bonus conformet ad usus.
     Tu mihi, Timoleon magni spes maxima patris;
nec patriae minor; aonii novus incola montis,
adde gradum comes, et teneris assuesce sub annis
Castalidum nemora, et sacros accedere fontes;
20 nympharumque choros; populoque ignota profano
otia, nec damnis nec amarae obnoxia curae.
Tempus erit cum tu (veniat modo robur ab annis)
spumantes versabis equos in pulvere belli
torvus; et in patriam assurgens non degener hastam:
25 interea genitor Ligurum sine fulminet arces,
Germanosque feros, et amantes martis Iberos,
consiliis armisque premat; francisque trophaeis
littora Phaebaeos decoret testantia luctus.
     Hoc quodcunque vides, circumque infraque supraque,
30 volvere perpetuo labentia secula motu;
omnia complexum gremio; longaeva vetustas
admirata decus varium, purique nitorem
aetheris, et puros radiati luminis orbes;
uno appellari consensit nomine mundum.

English translation

How changeable are the universe's regions, by what law are different atoms of matter brought together, what force regulates the periods of light and dark, alternates heat with cold, and covers the face of the Sun and Moon in darkness, all of this my mind moves me to disclose. You who inhabit the 5 regions shining with pure light that are impervious to our view, sacred parent of the universe, approve my daring endeavour, while I relate your deeds to people everywhere and reveal the immense structure of the heavens, so that those unfamiliar with the truth may lift up to heaven their sluggish minds, 10 long-mired in darkness, and as they gaze dumb-struck at the flaming walls of the universe, and its times recurring in fixed mutations, they may know its author, who supports so great a mass with his strength, steers it with the unwavering reins of his laws, and in his goodness shapes it providentially for our uses. 15

You, Timoleon, greatest hope of a great father, and no less a hope of your country too, new dweller on the Aonian mount, add your step to mine as my companion, and become accustomed in your early years to approach the groves of the Castalian Muses and sacred fountains; and attend the choruses 20 of the Nymphs, and peaceful contemplation free from bitter worry and loss, unknown to the uninitiated populace. A time will come (let strength but come from your years) when you will sternly wheel seething steeds in the dust of battle, reaching the heights of your father's spear, and no disappointment to your ancestors. For the moment, let your parent bombard the citadels of the 25 Ligurians, and the fierce Germans, and the war-loving Spaniards, and let him overwhelm them with his strategies and arms; and may he decorate with French trophies the shores that bore witness to Apollo's laments for Phaethon.

All around, above, and below, you see that the universe turns the flow of time in never-ending motion. It envelops all in its bosom. Aged antiquity, 30

35 Et quanquam moles omni sibi parte cohaerens
una sit; et nexis per mutua vincula membris
conspiret; positasque semel rectore sub uno
observet leges: Non est tamen omnibus unum
partibus ingenium, non vis nativa: sed orbes
40 astriferi, et nitidi sublimis regia caeli
immunis senii; et vultu immutabilis uno,
perpetuum servat solida et sincera tenorem.
At quicquid gremio lunae complectitur orbis
permutat variatque vices; trepidoque tumultu
45 aestuat; et nunquam sentit pars ulla quietem:
sed ruit in sese, civili vulnere semper
aut cadit aut perimit; alioque renascitur ore;
rursus ut intereat: nam pars haec infima mundi,
quatuor includit genitalia corpora; terram
50 et tenues undas; quique undis altior aer
incubat; et volucrem campos super aeris ignem.

admiring its variegated beauty, the splendour of the pure ether, and the pure globes of radiant light, agreed that it be called by a single name: universe. Yet, 35 although it is a single structure bound together as one whole, and is united by limbs joined in mutual chains, and observes the laws that were set down once and for all by a single ruler, nevertheless all parts do not have a uniform character, or single innate essence. For the star-bearing spheres, and the 40 sublime palace of bright heaven, immune to decay, and unchangeable in appearance, preserves an eternal course, untainted and solid. Yet, whatever is embraced within the orbit of the moon changes utterly and alters its condition, and convulses in restless commotion. No part ever experiences 45 rest, but rather it smashes down upon itself, either destroying or being destroyed by fratricidal blow, and is born again in a different guise in turn to pass away anew. For this lowest part of the universe contains four generative bodies: the earth; its overlapping waters; the air, which, farther up, lies upon 50 the waters; and winged fire above the levels of the air.

Commentary

1–5 *semina rerum* ... *pandere fert animus*: Buchanan recasts Lucretius'
semina rerum (the atoms of Epicurean philosophy) as the four Empedoclean
elements (fire, air, water, earth), following in the polemical anti-Lucretian
footsteps of Virgil (see Farrington 1963), Ovid (see Gee 2009) and Manilius
(see McOmish 2019). For discussion of the literary impact of this Stoic/
Epicurean dialectic upon writers like Girolamo Fracastoro, Buchanan and
other contemporary Scots like David Kinloch, see McOmish 2019: 251–5.
The opening five lines of the poem are indebted to Ovid, *Metamorphoses*
1.1–9, for specific diction (see Gee 2009: 41–5), and Virgil, *Georgics* 1.1–5, for
structure and intent (McOmish 2019: 253). See also the opening to Adam
King, *Genethliacon* (Text 8), for a well-developed contemporary example of
the continued influence upon early modern intellectual discourse.

1 Buchanan's parts of the universe (*mundi partes*) are: the domain of the
heavens and the domain of the terrestrial elements. His poem will relate the
composition of these parts of the universe and explain the nature of variance
and change within them.

1–2 Buchanan's atoms/seeds (*semina*) are discordant in that they are differing
elements, which come together in different admixtures to make divergent
bodies, as he will explain later in the poem (formally introduced at lines
43–50). The process of elemental admixture and mutation operates within the
limitations of God's law (*foedere*).

5 This appeal to the divinity to sanction this work directly appropriates the
language of Latin epic (didactic and heroic): Virgil, *Georgics* 1.40; *Aeneid* 9.625.
However, Buchanan's overt attempt to procure divine favour for his simulation
of divine things (cosmos) has deeper implications for the view of him as poet
and of his poetry: compare Plato's rejection of Homer as mere artist/poet in
favour of a divinely inspired devotee aiming at imitation (mimesis) of the
divine (*Ion*, esp. 534). As Buchanan implies in lines 7–14, the sanction of the
divinity will enable him to reveal the truth in all its glory to his audience.

6 Following in the tradition of Aristotle (*De Caelo* 1.3), Buchanan locates the
home and abode of divinity in the heavens. Cf. also Homer's description of the
pure light permeating the eternal abode of the gods in the sky: *Odyssey* 6.41–6.

9 *nescius*: here takes the genitive case.

11 Cf. Lucretius, *De rerum natura* 1.73. See also n. on King, *Genethliacon*
10–11 (Text 8) for broader discussion of Buchanan's use of this passage from
Lucretius.

13–15 *qui ... fulciat ... moderetur ... conformet*: relative clause of characteristic or generic subjunctive, presenting the type of behaviour and character required (and expected by the viewer) to be the *author* of the universe.

15 An explicit censure of Epicurus' rejection of divine providence or divine intervention in human affairs, delivered allusively by textual rejection (*consilio*) of Lucretius, *De rerum natura* 1.1021; 5.419.

16 Timoléon de Cossé, future Count of Brissac (Anjou), son of Charles de Cossé, first Count of Brissac. In 1555 Charles invited Buchanan to be tutor to Timoléon, while Charles waged a military campaign on behalf of Henri II of France against towns along the banks of the Po river in the Piedmont region of Italy, who were sympathetic to Charles V, Holy Roman Emperor. Buchanan educated the young boy (who was 11 in early 1555) in both France and Italy until 1560. Buchanan mentions Timoléon at *De sphaera* 1.16, 2.1, 3.1 and 5.80.

20–21 Accusatives still conditioned by *accedere* in line 19.

25 The Ligurian cities and region Buchanan refers to encompass the modern regions of Piedmont, Liguria and Western Lombardy, historically known as Ligurian Cisalpine Gaul. It is defined as such by Pliny, *Natural History* 3.5. Pliny's *Natural History* is Buchanan's source for much content throughout *De sphaera* (esp. Book 5). *sine fulminet*: *sino* (here in the imperative form *sine*) takes the subjunctive *fulminet*.

26 A reference to the German soldiers in the service of Emperor Charles V; and an allusion to those from the Iberian peninsula who made up the bulk of the army of Charles V, and their love of Mars (war), a commonplace in Latin poetry: see e.g. Silius Italicus, *Punica* 1.225–8; 3.329–31.

28 This relates to the myth of Phaethon, son of Apollo (Phoebus), who died after crashing the chariot of his father Apollo into the river Eridanus (popularly assumed to be either the Po or near it: e.g. Strabo, *Geography* 5.1.9), plunging his father into grief. For an extended verse version of the myth, accompanied with local Ligurian eye-witnesses to the crash (King of the Ligurians, Cycnus), see Ovid, *Metamorphoses* 2.31–400. Buchanan's reference to the Phaethon myth, while providing geographical specificity to his and his pupil's location, ultimately serves as a warning to Timoléon not to rush into his father's footsteps unprepared (i.e. without Buchanan's instruction). The motif of Timoléon/Phaethon recurs throughout *De sphaera*: for an introductory overview of literary correspondences between Buchanan and Ovid in this regard, see Gee 2009: 50–3. *littora* is here used for *litora*, and *Phaebaeos* for *Phoebaeos*.

29 Buchanan presents the universe in every part and all directions as a single entity, governed by a single ruler. See Plato, *Timaeus* 30–1 (esp. 30D); Pseudo-Aristotle, *De Mundo* 391b2. *quodcunque* is here used for *quodcumque*.

34 Buchanan's idea and specific diction come from Pliny, *Natural History* 2.8 (2.3 old numbering): *consensu gentium moveor; namque et Graeci nomine ornamenti appellavere eum et nos a perfecta absolutaque elegantia mundum* ('I am swayed by the agreement of the nations. For the Greeks also called it after the name for ornament [cosmos], and we have called it *mundus* from its perfection and complete refinement').

35–7 For the universe as a living, breathing entity, see Plato, *Timaeus* 30C.

35 *quanquam* (*quamquam*) here takes the subjunctive instead of the usual indicative. Livy and Tacitus, both of whose work Buchanan knew well (for his reliance upon Livy especially, see his *Genethliacon* on the birth of James VI), use *quamquam* with the subjunctive to state perceived fact with no potential or conditional meaning. Although it is possible that Buchanan may be highlighting the conjectural nature of his narrative, it would be out of keeping with the general tone of certainty of the poem's exordium.

40–2 A literary allusion to and pointed rejection of the process of elemental infestation of the heavens articulated by Lucretius, *De rerum natura* 5.490 and 5.508. See also n. on 15 for the importance of this passage from Lucretius to Buchanan's philosophical position in this introduction. See Naiden 1952: 52–4 and 56–60 for the possibility that Buchanan was also alluding to contemporary astronomers and their work on superlunary change. Adam King, who would later use Buchanan's poem as a point of reference for his academic commentary, conspicuously altered his reference to these lines at *Genethliacon* 10–14, to reflect contemporary evidence for transience in the heavens. *immunis* takes the genitive; *solida et sincera* agrees with *regia*.

43 This line marks Buchanan's formal division of the universe into two: the celestial and the elemental (terrestrial). He will deal with the elemental in Book 1 and with the celestial in Book 2.

49 Buchanan's presentation of the universe ordered according to the four elements follows the ancient authority of Plato, Aristotle and Galen, and those who followed them in the medieval schools. It was a hotly contested subject in Buchanan's time. Girolamo Cardano (*De Sublimitate* 2) and Johannes Pena (*In praefationem ad Euclidis Optica*), along with Tycho Brahe, Christoph Rothmann and other contemporary writers, questioned key aspects of it. Adam King, who often reworks Buchanan's poetry to reflect the

new sciences, studiously avoids stating that there are four elements when referencing Buchanan's poetry from this section: King, *Genethliacon* 16–17.

49–51 Buchanan frames this section of his provisional description of the elemental composition of the universe with lines from Ovid, *Metamorphoses* 15.239–40: *quattuor aeternus genitalia corpora mundus | continet* ('the eternal universe contains four generative bodies'), where Ovid begins his description of the universe; Buchanan then closes the frame with Manilius, *Astronomica* 1.149: *ignis in aetherias volucer se sustulit oras* ('fire in flight bore itself aloft into the etherial regions'), from Manilius' section describing the elemental composition (*opus generabile . . . omnis partus elementa capacia*: 'generative work . . . elements capable of all production', *Astronomica* 1.143–4) of the universe. The content, and often the same specific diction, of this section can be found in both Ovid, *Metamorphoses* 1.26–35 and 15.239–51, and Manilius, *Astronomica* 1.149–70. Adam King, in his *Genethliacon*, when reworking this section of *De sphaera* for his own philosophical ends, often playfully interchanged passages from Ovid with text from corresponding sections in Manilius: see text and notes to *Genethliacon*, esp. 17–25 (Text 8).

4

A Celebration of Queen Elizabeth I's Coronation in Verse

Walter Haddon (1515–1572),
In . . . Elisabethae regimen

Lucy R. Nicholas

Introduction

Walter Haddon (1515–1572) is not a familiar name these days, but if we go back 500 years or so, he was a very well-known figure indeed. He was a luminary of Cambridge University and a leading player in state affairs. The paradox is that Haddon has fallen into obscurity in modern times for precisely the reason he was so renowned in the early modern period: his Latin skills. During his lifetime he enjoyed an unassailable reputation for the quality of his Latin composition: according to the most prominent rhetorician of the day, Thomas Wilson, there was 'No better Latin man within England except Walter Haddon'. Another contemporary compared Haddon to Ovid, Prudentius and Cicero, declaring that Haddon was superior to them all. Haddon was one of the leading Latinists of his day, in both prose and verse. Consequently, he was often required to apply his linguistic expertise in prestigious projects of national importance. The extract set out here relates to one such occasion, the accession of Queen Elizabeth I to the throne of England.

Haddon acquired and developed his Latin talents first at Eton and then at King's College, Cambridge, where he also became a fellow. He specialized in legal studies and was soon appointed Regius Professor of Civil Law. He also held other senior posts at Cambridge, including Master of Trinity Hall and Vice-Chancellor of the University. His life is especially interesting in that it straddled the reigns of four Tudor monarchs, Henry VIII, Edward VI, Mary I and Elizabeth I. Despite being a man of outspoken views and a committed Protestant, Haddon flourished during each of these reigns, for example serving as a Member of Parliament under Mary, and during Elizabeth's reign being appointed as Master of Requests, a very senior legal role.

Haddon wrote many speeches, letters and polemical tracts, but he was also a poet, and a very fine one. He did not write verse for private enjoyment but for public consumption. The broader collection of his poems – about 100 in total – evinces a dazzling versatility. He wrote in a range of classical metres and covered a huge span of topics, from morality, religious life and Scripture to high-profile events and notable individuals. It has been said that in Haddon's verse a history of sixteenth-century England can be found.

In the poem below Haddon writes in celebration of Elizabeth I's coronation, which took place on 15 January 1559. The poem presents the reader with a remarkable fusion of metaphor and fact, the ideal and the actual, the divine and the human. It is a powerful piece, full of classical language (Ovidian, in particular), myth and topoi, but also with a strong religious underpinning and very much a product of its time. It keys in primarily to the principle of the Royal Supremacy. This was a notion first established under Elizabeth's father, Henry VIII, when he broke with the Roman Church and the Pope, and resolved as monarch to lead the Church of England and arrogate to himself all ecclesiastical authority. Immediately upon Elizabeth's accession to the throne in 1558 Henry's Act of Supremacy of 1534 was renewed and replaced (the Act was finally passed in 1559). When Haddon penned this poem, Elizabeth was, by virtue of the new act, about to be declared 'the only supreme governor of this realm, . . . as well in all spiritual or ecclesiastical things or causes, as temporal . . .'. His poem in its emphatic assertion of an essential bond between God and Queen powerfully reinforces this. It also condemns rebellion, a very real problem that had threatened Tudor monarchs during the previous few decades. Haddon, probably out of tact, does not mention Mary I, the Catholic sister of Elizabeth, who had reigned as queen for the five years before Elizabeth. However, the many references in his poem to recent storms and adverse weather could easily be understood as negative comments on her reign, during which the evangelical reforms of Henry and Edward had been reversed and many Protestants were publicly executed.

The motor of this poem is panegyric, a form of public praise with origins in the ancient tradition of rhetoric. Just as in classical panegyric, and now here in its Neo-Latin manifestation, historical events are shaped into an ideal pattern of restored order, a new age of concord and peace. One of the best and most influential classical examples of this theme of restoration is found in Pliny's *Panegyricus* to the emperor Trajan. The theme would continue to be applied through the centuries, and it was also present in Erasmus' early modern verse panegyric to the Archduke Philip, King of Castile (*Illustrissimo principi Philippo*) and, in England, in Thomas More's poem *Gratulatorium Carmen*, which honoured the coronation of Henry VIII. Embedded in such pieces was a hybrid form of oratory that combined the demonstrative (ceremonial/laudatory) with the deliberative (advisory), a form of exhorting to virtue under the pretext of praise. Haddon is not just extolling Elizabeth in this poem but advising her, pointing his queen in the direction of the perfect prince. His poem also offers a good illustration of the patriotic theme that dominated much of Haddon's poetry. He viewed England as a mighty, chosen nation, whose national interest he aligned with true religion and the will of the Creator. This poetical celebration of Elizabeth's accession not only reflects the ideological orthodoxy that would come to characterize the Elizabethan reign, but quite possibly also helped to shape it.

When Haddon entrusted the publication of his Latin works to Thomas Hatcher of King's College in 1567, he was a poet of considerable acclaim. It is likely that his poems had circulated in manuscript before then, and an index of their popularity was the second publication of his verse shortly after his death in 1576. His poetry is graceful and dignified, and has a pronounced moral tone. It is evident that his poems also exerted a strong influence on later contemporaries as well as much more recognized poets like John Dryden.

Metre: elegiac couplet

Bibliography

Binns, J. W. (1990), *Intellectual Culture in Elizabethan and Jacobean England: The Latin Writings of the Age*, Leeds.

Bradner, L. (1940), *Musae Anglicanae: A History of Anglo-Latin Poetry, 1500–1925*, New York and London.

Garrison, J. D. and H. Garrison (1975), *Dryden and the Tradition of Panegyric*, Berkeley and London.

Lees, C. J. (1967), *The Poetry of Walter Haddon*, The Hague and Paris.

Reedijk, C. (ed.) (1956), *The Poems of Desiderius Erasmus*, Leiden.

Ryan, L. V. (1977), 'The Shorter Latin Poem in Tudor England', *Humanistica Lovaniensia*, 26: 101–31.

Source of the Latin text

The full poem is given here and taken from Lees 1967: 169–71, checked against *D. Gualteri Haddoni Poemata*, set out in *Lucubrationes* (London 1567): sigs O3^r–O4^v.

Latin text

In auspicatissimum serenissimae Reginae Elisabethae regimen

Anglia, tolle caput, saevis iactata procellis,
    exagitata malis Anglia tolle caput.
Aurea virgo venit, roseo venerabilis ore,
    plena deo, princeps Elisabetha venit.
5 Quaque venit, festos circumfert undique ludos,
    undique, qua graditur, gaudia laeta ciet,
stella salutaris salve, praesentia serva,
    splendeat ex radiis terra Britanna tuis.
Formosum sydus, patriam caligine mersam,
10   admota propius luce levato nova.
Frigidus horribili Boreas terrore strepebat,
    atque diu terras aspera laesit hyems.
Nunc Zephyrus mollis iucundas commovet auras,
    Anglia vere novo nunc recreata viret.
15 Tu deus ista facis, tu summi rector Olympi,
    prospiciens coelo vulnera nostra vides.
Tu deus es solus, nostri medicina doloris,
    atque tuis servis tempore semper ades.
Tu deus in solio gemmam componis avito,
20   quae patriae lucem sola referre potest.
Rettulit, atque refert, poteritque deinde referre,
    lumine si posthac luceat illa tuo.
Anglia tende deo palmas, et supplice voce
    spiritus ad dominum saepe precando meet:
25 Elisabetha tuis servis praefecta magistra,
    ut domino maneat fida ministra deo.
Sit pia, sit clemens, et sit virtutis amatrix,
    semina doctrinae non peritura serat.
Iustitiam colat, et disponat in ordine certo
30   res, homines, terras, Anglia quicquid habet.
Consiliis rectis attentam praebeat aurem,
    et ferat oppressis, quando rogatur, opem.
Fulminet in vitiis, et corda rebellia frangat,
    supplicibus parcat, quos meliora movent.
35 In domini iusto maneat cultuque, metuque,
    sit similis princeps Elisabetha sui.

English translation

For the most auspicious reign of the most radiant
Queen Elizabeth

England, raise your head, though buffeted by savage storms; though harassed
by evils, England, raise your head. A golden maiden is coming, august with
rosy countenance, suffused with God; our leader Elizabeth is coming. 5
Wherever she comes, she spreads merry sport around in all directions, and
wherever she goes, she excites happy joy in all directions. Salutations, o star of
salvation! Preserve the present state of affairs, and may the land of Britain
shine forth from your rays of light. Beautiful star, with your new light moved 10
closer, relieve your fatherland plunged in darkness. The chill north wind
howled with hellish terror, and for a long time harsh winter tormented the
land. Now the gentle west wind awakens the pleasant breezes, and now
England grows green, restored to life with a new springtime.

   You, God, effect these things, governor of high Olympus, looking out from 15
heaven, you see our wounds. You are God alone, medicine for our suffering,
and you are always present for your servants in season. You, God, place on
our ancestral throne a jewel, the only one who can restore the light to the 20
fatherland. She has restored it and (still) restores it, and will be able to restore
it hereafter, if, henceforth, she can shine with your light. England, stretch your
hands to God and, with suppliant voice, let the spirit through frequent prayer
reach the Lord, that Elizabeth, as a teacher in charge of your servants, may 25
remain a faithful minister to the Lord God. May she be pious, may she be
clement, and may she be a lover of virtue. May she sow seeds of learning not
destined to perish. May she cultivate justice, and arrange in sure order affairs, 30
men, lands, whatever England possesses. May she offer an attentive ear to
upright counsel and, when asked, bring help to the oppressed. May she blast
vice with lightning and crush rebellious spirits, and may she spare suppliants
whom better things motivate. May she abide in the just worship and fear of 35
the Lord; may Elizabeth, our leader, be true to herself. And, when about to die,

Et similem matri prolem moritura relinquat,
    vivere sic patriae post sua fata potest.
Nos miseri, ferro, flamma, morboque, fameque,
40   quos merito tristis puniit ira dei.
Nos miseri, clemens domini quos dextra levavit,
    et quibus ad coelum est rursus aperta via.
Pectore syncero domini mandata tenere
    convenit, et vera relligione frui.
45 Exeat ex regno libertas impia carnis,
    spiritus est liber, res placitura deo.
Mutua nos firmo concordia pectore iungat,
    sic soboles patri grata futura sumus.
Invide livor abi, mendax infamia musset,
50   turpis avaritiae sordida lucra migrent.
Seditio sileat, tollatur iniqua rapina,
    sanguinis et sitiens, dira tyrannis eat.
Mentibus in nostris reverentia principis insit,
    et populo faveas Elisabetha tuo.
55 Sic deus in regno tibi prospera tempora mittet,
    patria sic tecum vivere laeta potest.

may she leave an offspring in the image of its mother; thus she can live on for the fatherland after her own death.

We are miserable whom, in our wretched state, God's wrath has deservedly 40 punished with the sword, flame, plague and famine. We are miserable whom the merciful right hand of the Lord has relieved, and for whom the path to heaven has again been opened. It is fitting to uphold the Lord's commandments and to take enjoyment of true religion with a pure heart. Let wicked licence 45 of the flesh depart from the kingdom; the spirit is free, and this (alone) will be pleasing to God. Let mutual accord join us with a steadfast heart; in this way we are destined to be an offspring pleasing to its father. Be gone, jealous envy; let deceitful disgrace die down, and let the vile pickings of shameful 50 avarice pass away. May insurrection be silent; may unjust pillage be removed; and may awful tyranny, thirsting after blood, go on its way. May deference for our leader be etched in our minds, and may you, Elizabeth, favour your people. In this way God will send prosperous times to you in the kingdom; 55 (and) in this way the fatherland can live joyfully with you.

Commentary

1-2 The repetition and personification of *Anglia* and the repetition of the phrase *tolle caput* ('raise your head') make for an eye-catching opening to this poem. The technique of opening and closing a couplet (at the start of a poem) with the same words is Ovidian: compare *Amores* 1.9.1-2.

3 *Aurea virgo venit*: Haddon does not replicate the wording of Virgil's immensely influential *Eclogue* 4, but its spirit is present. Haddon uses *virgo venit* where Virgil used *iam redit et Virgo* ('Now the Virgin returns', *Eclogues* 4.6), and Haddon applies to this the adjective *aurea* used by Virgil (*Ecl.* 4.9) to denote a golden age. Elizabeth Hoby (see Text 6) would use this form of words to describe her young daughter Anne when she wrote an epitaphic poem in her honour in 1571. *venit* (in the present tense) is subsequently repeated twice in the following two lines as a means to intensify the sense of Elizabeth's arrival, here, of course, her arrival or accession to the throne.

roseo venerabilis ore: Haddon is adapting Ovid's *roseo spectabilis ore* ('visible with rosy blush', *Metamorphoses* 7.705), which describes Aurora, the goddess of dawn. Ovid also used the words *roseo . . . ore* to describe Aurora in *Epistulae ex Ponto* 1.4.58. For Haddon and his readers, an implicit correspondence between Aurora and Elizabeth would be flattering and fitting. Although Haddon, the Christian, would have read Ovid's verse with some circumspection, stylistically Ovid is an important poet for Haddon (see 1-2 n.).

4 Elizabeth is characterized as *plena deo*, metaphorically 'pregnant' with God. On the popularity of the phrase see Seneca, *Suasoriae* 3.5: *aiebat se imitatum esse Vergili(an)um 'plena deo'* ('he [i.e. the declaimer Fuscus Arellius] asserted that he had imitated the Virgilian *plena deo*').

7 *stella salutaris*: Haddon may have had in mind a line from *De rebus coelestibus* by Giovanni Gioviano Pontano, a slightly earlier Italian poet and humanist: *Iovis stella felix esse ac salutaris dicitur* ('The star of Jupiter is said to be lucky and health-bringing': I, sig. Biii^r). The star imagery (taken together with *formosum sydus* in line 9) not only alludes to Christ's nativity, but also brings into focus the classical *virgo* enshrined as a constellation, namely Astraea (see also Virgil, *Ecl.* 4.6). Star imagery would continue to gain prominence in Elizabethan panegyric through her reign. The letter 's' dominates the line, lending a tone of awe and respect.

9 *sydus = sidus. caligo, -inis* (f) can denote actual darkness but also a more metaphorical dullness of perception. It is very common in panegyric of this sort to decry the *status quo* prior to the arrival of the new subject of praise, but this, taken together with references to 'savage storms' (*saevis . . . procellis*) and

'evils' (*malis*) above, might constitute a covert criticism of Elizabeth's Catholic sister, Mary I, who had reigned from 1553 to 1558. The start of the line, *formosum sydus*, is entirely spondaic and is followed by a caesura, investing the phrase with considerable solemnity.

10 *levato*: a formal imperative.

11–14 Haddon describes a shift from winter to spring. Erasmus had also incorporated a pattern of seasonal change into his poem celebrating the return of Archduke Philip (*Illustrissimo principi Philippo feliciter in patriam*), set out in Reedijk 1956: 273, especially in lines 24–31:

> *Sic ubi tristis hyems aquilonibus asperat auras*
> *nuda senescit humus, moerent sine floribus horti,*   25
> *torpescunt amnes, languet sine frondibus arbos,*
> *stat sine fruge seges, marcent sine gramine campi;*
> *rursus ubi zephyris tepidum spirantibus anni*
> *leta [i.e. laeta] iuventa redit, gemmantur floribus horti,*
> *effugiunt amnes, revirescit frondibus arbos,*   30
> *fruge nitent segetes, hilarescunt gramine campi.*

'Thus, when bitter winter makes breezes harsh with north winds, the bare ground lies spent with age, gardens are in mourning without flowers, rivers become sluggish, trees are lifeless, without their leaves, the grain field lies barren of its crop, the plains dry up without grass; again when spring (lit. 'happy youth of the year') returns with west winds blowing warmly, gardens are studded with flowers like jewels, rivers are free to flow, trees become green again with foliage, grain fields flourish in their crop, the plains delight in their grass.'

The use of imagery and language in the poems of Erasmus and Haddon was, in turn, almost certainly influenced by Horace's *Odes* 4.7 (*Diffugere nives . . .*).

12 *hyems* = *hiems*. The phrase *laesit hiems* is a favourite expression of Ovid, often found at the ends of pentameter lines in his exile poetry (for example, *Tristia* 3.8.30 and 5.13.6).

13–14 The repeated *nunc* marks a decisive break with the immediate past.

13 *Zephyrus mollis*: Ovid has *Zephyri molles* in *Ars amatoria* 3.728. A young contemporary of Haddon, Thomas Newton, used the same wording *Zephyrus mollis* in his poem *Qualis Edvardus Phyttonus*: *est Zephyrus mollis, gemmea prata fovens* ('there is the gentle west wind, caressing the bejewelled meadows', line 2).

15–16 ... *tu summi rector Olympi,* | *prospiciens coelo vulnera nostra vides,* though not identical with, is reminiscent of lines from Virgil's *Aeneid*: ... *aequora postquam* | *prospiciens genitor, coeloque invectus aperto* ('... soon as the god, looking forth upon the waters and driving under a clear sky ...', 1.154–5). Virgil is describing how Neptune, god of the oceans, calms the storm, a context which, though it is not drawn explicitly by Haddon, also fits his broader theme. The wording *Tu deus ista facis* is possibly influenced by Psalm 76:15: *Tu es Deus qui facis mirabilia* ('Thou art the God that dost wonders'). Haddon knew the Psalms well and would produce Latin verse paraphrases of several of them. The repeated *Tu Deus* on three consecutive alternate lines imbues Haddon's verse with a prayer-like quality.

17 *Tu deus es solus*: from Psalm 85:10.

nostri medicina doloris: this exact expression was used by the later English poet George Herbert (1593–1633) in his poem *In Obitum Henrici Principis Walliae* ('On the Death of Henry, Prince of Wales'), also at the end of a hexameter line (line 46). Whereas Herbert suggests in his poem that words cannot be a remedy for pain, Haddon declares that God is a remedy for cares (see also S. Knight, '*Juvenes ornatissimi*: the student writing of George Herbert and John Milton', in L. B. T. Houghton and G. Manuwald [eds], *Neo-Latin Poetry in the British Isles*, 51–8, London 2012, at 57).

19 *solio ... avito* is a phrase used in classical works, for example by Ovid in *Met.* 6.650: *ipse sedens solio Tereus sublimis avito* ('[So] Tereus himself, sitting aloft in his high ancestral banquet chair') and Tacitus, *Histories* 1.40: *Pacorum avito Arsacidarum solio depulsuri* ... ('[Then did Roman soldiers rush forward like men who had to drive a Vologeses or] Pacorus from the ancestral throne of the Arsacidae ...').

20–22 Haddon uses repetition of themes and vocabulary to striking effect in these lines. First, in lines 20–21, Haddon applies the verb *refero* ('I restore') four times in order to reinforce the sense of Elizabeth as someone who resurrects and re-builds. Her ability to do this in the past, present and future is underscored through Haddon's use of a range of tenses in line 21: the perfect *rettulit*, present *refert* and infinitive after a future tense *poteritque deinde referre*. This line is also heavily dactylic, injecting it with pace and great immediacy. Haddon's focus on restoration is reminiscent of the constant re-refrain that Horace uses to herald the return of old, Republican standards under Augustus in *Odes* 4.15.5, 6 and 12 (*rettulit, restituit* and *revocavit* respectively). Haddon may also have the famous verses from Revelation in mind which straddle past, present and future: Revelation 1:4, 1:8 and 4:8: *qui est et qui erat et qui venturus est* ('[he] that is, and that was, and that is to come'). Alongside this, Haddon emphasizes the notion of light through *lucem, lumine* and *luceat.*

23 The gesture of outstretched hands has a Virgilian flavour: see, for example, *Aeneid* 1.93 and 10.845. *supplice voce* is a phrase that appears in Ovid, for example in *Met.* 2.396 and 6.33.

27 *Sit pia, sit clemens, et sit virtutis amatrix:* Haddon uses anaphora of *sit* in a rising tricolon as a means to amplify Elizabeth's qualities but also the force of his entreaty. The language used here is reminiscent of the Catholic Marian hymn *Salve Regina* and especially the line *o clemens, o pia, o dulcis Virgo Maria* ('o clement, o loving, o sweet Virgin Mary'). It may be that Haddon knew of this and was deliberately redeploying the fabric of a popular Catholic work in an overtly Protestant context.

29 *Iustitiam colat:* The reference to justice again picks up the common identification of Elizabeth with Astraea, a goddess of justice (see especially F. A. Yates, *Astraea*, London and Boston 1975). *in ordine certo* is a form of words used regularly by the philosopher poet Lucretius (for example, twice in *De rerum natura* 5.731–6).

30 *quicquid habet:* This seems to be in apposition to the previous three terms.

31 *Consiliis rectis:* Such terms indicate that this poem is one of counsel as much as compliment. *praebeo aurem / aures* is a Latin idiom meaning 'to give ear to' or 'to listen'. There may be a yet more subtle way to read this line, namely: 'May she offer an attentive ear when her plans have been overruled / corrected'. Such a reading is suggestive of a quiet confidence on Haddon's part – he has the Queen's ear and is secure in his role of key counsellor.

33–34 Haddon's lines *corda rebellia frangat,* | *supplicibus parcat* ... are different from but reminiscent of the famous words of Anchises in Virgil, *Aen.* 6.853: *parcere subiectis et debellare superbos* ('show mercy to the conquered and fight to the end against the proud').

36 *similis ... sui* (literally, 'similar of herself'): the adjective *similis* can take the genitive (here of the reflexive pronoun).

37 *similis* can also take the dative, as here. The prospect of Elizabeth leaving a child who will perpetuate her image after she (Elizabeth) is gone, may include an allusion to Dido in Virgil's *Aeneid* 4 wanting a child: the use of *moritura* is certainly reminiscent of Dido (*Aeneid* 4.308), and Haddon's line

contains as much hope and expectation for Elizabeth as Dido's speech at 4.327–330 contains wistful regret that she had *not* had a baby with Aeneas.

39 *ferro, flamma, morboque, fameque* is a striking tetracolon. *morboque, fameque* is a phrase that appears in classical works, including Virgil's *Georgics*: *amissis, ut fama, apibus morboque fameque* ('so runs the tale – his bees were lost through sickness and hunger') in 4.318, and applied to bees; and Ovid's *Metamorphoses*: . . . *fractus morboque fameque* ('. . . broken with disease and hunger') in 13.52, with reference to Philoctetes.

39–41 Supply *sumus* with *miseri* in lines 39 and 41. The repetition of *miseri* ('wretched') together with the reference to God's punishment almost certainly captures something of the Protestant Lutheran doctrine of man's inherent sinfulness and need for justification. Line 41 presents men as saved by God alone according to his grace. According to this Protestant view, there was no clerical intermediary such as a priest, just a direct relationship between God and congregant.

40 *tristis* = *tristes*, accusative plural in agreement with *quos. merito* is qualifying *puniit* rather than *tristis*.

43 *syncero* = *sincero*.

44 *relligione* = *religione* (for metrical reasons).

47 *concordia* ('agreement' or 'peace') was an important concept for Haddon as it was in antiquity, championed, in particular, by Cicero.

48 *soboles* = *suboles*.

49–54 Haddon uses the imperative *abi* followed by a series of present subjunctives.

51–2 The modern edition of Haddon's poetry (edited by Lees) has *inique* instead of *iniqua* and *est* instead of *eat*, but these forms cannot be correct. The forms set out above match the version of Haddon's poem printed in 1567.

5

The Latin University Orations of Queen Elizabeth I

Queen Elizabeth I (1533–1603), Speeches of 1566 and 1592

Sarah Knight

Introduction

Elizabeth I (1533–1603; reigned 1558–1603) visited the University of Oxford twice for a week or so in late summer near the start (31 August to 6 September 1566) and the end of her reign (22 to 28 September 1592). On both occasions she delivered a Latin oration to the assembled courtiers and scholars in St Mary's, the University Church on the High Street. Elizabeth prided herself on being *regina literata* ('a well-read, or erudite, or highly educated queen'), a reputation crystallized by the title of a book printed after her 1564 visit to Cambridge, Abraham Hartwell's *Regina Literata: sive de Elizabethae reginae in Academiam Cantabrigiensem aduentu* ('The well-read queen: or on Queen Elizabeth's coming to the University of Cambridge'). Elizabeth had visited Cambridge earlier in her reign, also during the summer, from 5 to 10 August 1564. The two speeches from the two Oxford visits presented here illustrate well how *literata* this particular Tudor *regina* was: Elizabeth's Latin orations demonstrate a thoughtful understanding of how rhetoric functioned and some artful expressions of modesty as well as assertiveness. As she acknowledges in the 1566 speech, she was 'schooled in a variety of many languages' (*in multarum linguarum varietate versata*), and what follows indicates her skill and confidence in Latin oratory. In the second oration of 1592, though, she asserts her own 'loss of familiarity with this language' (*huius linguae desuetudo*), implying, perhaps, that politics has taken her away from academic studies during her long reign.

However fragmented and dysfunctional Elizabeth's family had been, several of its members, both male and female, were keen readers and had scholarly ambitions. In 1566 she attributes her thorough schooling to *patrem meum*, and indeed her father Henry VIII (1491–1547) had been an accomplished Latinist who prized humanist scholarship and had famously defended the Catholic faith against the attack on it by Martin Luther, leading the Pope to confer upon him the epithet *defensor fidei* that is still used by the British monarch. But she was surrounded by other erudite individuals too: her mother Anne Boleyn (*c.* 1501–1536) had spent several years at the court of the French king François I when young, and during her brief reign she supported several humanists, including Nicholas Bourbon. Elizabeth's brother Edward VI (1537–1553) received a thorough reformed humanist education and even while young cultivated a reputation for learning. Her step-mother Katherine Parr (1512–1548) was a thoughtful and studious woman too, as was her cousin Jane Grey (1537–1554): both wrote and translated pious works.

We are fortunate to possess accounts that set the scene for us of Elizabeth's orations in their context of delivery. The first of the two speeches presented below, delivered on 5 September 1566, is based on the manuscript account of Miles Windsor, an undergraduate at Corpus Christi College, who went on to become a prominent university historian. Windsor's lively narrative vividly conjures up the setting: the Queen stands in the University Church, addressing scholars and dignitaries who are hierarchically arranged in ranks around and before her. Many of these men have already delivered their own Latin orations, declaimed and debated with each other, summarized and responded to each other's arguments, but now they are hushed and listening attentively to her words instead:

> After disputacions ended the Quenes Maiestie made an oration in lattyn before her departure owte of the Churche of her owne benignitie to the greate Content of the whole Vniuersitie & delectation of all that were presente./Firste shee desyred the Embassadour, the Earle of Leycester, & mr Secretarye to take yt in hande, wherevpon they refused to doo, she comminge forward & after gyvinge back with a most Gracious, Princelye & reverent regard began to spake as folowethe.

Elizabeth's presumably disingenuous performance of timidity – Windsor tells us she turned to a diplomat, a courtier and a councillor to 'take yt [it] in hande' – followed by her acceptance of the rhetorical challenge, suggests the Queen's skilful knowledge (and deployment) of the modesty topos, designed to win her audience's sympathy. It may be too that within the first decade of her reign, given the confessional turbulence at both universities during the 1550s, Elizabeth was especially cautious, performing deference in this very public speech even when at other moments of the 1566 visit she was more critical or sarcastic in her remarks to various Oxford scholars (Knight 2015).

In 1592 we see a less rhetorically bashful queen: the oration seems more determined, even admonitory, and while Elizabeth might allude to being out of practice as a Latinist, she presents herself as much more rhetorically practised and politically experienced as a queen. Elizabeth delayed her speech since she felt her audience had heard too much Latin oratory from another speaker, Dr Westphaling (1531/2–1602), which, according to Anthony Wood, chronicler of many controversies and much gossip at early modern Oxford, the Queen did her best to stop:

> All that then was disliked in him, was the tediousness in his concluding Oration; for the Queen, being something weary of it, sent twice to him to cut it short, because herself intended to make a publick speech that evening; but he would not, or as some told her, could not put himself out of a set methodical speech for fear he should have marred all, or else confounded his memory.

Westphaling's reluctance to stop a set-piece oration once he had set it in motion tells us something interesting about how careful, almost mechanical, some early modern orators' public speaking clearly must have been. But Elizabeth, Wood makes clear, was not to be thrown off by potential interruption when she gave her speech the next day and demonstrated a shrewd sensitivity to her audience's capacity for concentration. Wood tells us she 'forbeared her speech at that time', presumably because the audience were worn out by Westphaling's Latin, and so gave her speech 'the next morning'. At that point, Elizabeth

> proceeded to her Oration; and when she was in the midst thereof, she cast her eye aside, and saw the old Lord Treasurer Burleigh (Cecil) standing on his lame feet for want of a stool; whereupon she called in all haste for a stool for him; nor would she proceed in her speech till she saw him provided of one. Then fell she to it again, as if there had been no interruption. Upon which one that knew he might be bold with her, told her after she had concluded, that she did it of purpose to shew, that she could interrupt her speech, and not be put out, although the Bishop durst not adventure to do a less matter the day before.
>
> (Wood 1786: 2.253)

Westphaling was an august figure within the university, well established as a former Lady Margaret Professor of Theology and Vice-Chancellor, who had played a prominent part in the 1566 visit, and had been Bishop of Hereford since 1586. We should see Wood's comparison as pointed: the learned humanist theologian could not improvise; the Queen, not herself a career Latinist, could interrupt her speech to show compassion (even if not quite spontaneously) to an old advisor. Elizabeth was just as rhetorically adept as the Oxford scholar, Wood implies, but had learned her rhetorical facility in the worldly sphere of international politics rather than in the academic microcosm.

One of the most famous portraits of Elizabeth, attributed to William Scrots (active 1537–1553) and probably painted around 1546, shows her holding a small book while standing in front of a larger one (see cover image). Elizabeth had been taught by the important mid-Tudor humanist Roger Ascham (1515–1568), who probably began writing his influential pedagogical work *The Scholemaster* (1570) during the early 1560s, when he was still in regular contact with the Queen and they frequently read classical authors together. Ascham took an interest in the university progresses, writing to the Earl of Leicester (then Chancellor of the University of Oxford) that he should learn from the plays he had seen during Elizabeth's visit to Cambridge in 1564: 'I truste you beinge at Cambrige and hearinge Comedies, Tragedies and Disputacions there will moue you [...] to thincke as I doe' (see *REED: Cambridge*, I, 229: Letter from Ascham to Robert Dudley, 5 August 1564). Typically of many Tudor humanists, Ascham thought of drama and staged debate ('Disputacions') as different aspects of academic performance culture: all of these entertainments thrived on the consummate delivery of Latin rhetoric, on both theoretical and applied knowledge of the parts of speech delineated by Greek and Roman authorities beloved of early modern educators, such as Aristotle, Cicero and Quintilian, and on engaging and impressing an erudite and often highly critical audience. Elizabeth entered onto this academic rhetorical stage and performed eloquently and purposefully, as these speeches reported by witnesses convey, although it is worth noting what the recent editors of her *Collected Works* have called the 'irretrievable oral component' of these texts (Marcus, Mueller and Rose 2000: xiii) as well as the complicated textual history of how these ephemeral orations have been handed down to us. Elizabeth's status and the conventions of panegyric to the monarch more or less guaranteed her speeches a warm reception. But these are polished orations, in which the Queen deftly acknowledges the intelligence of her listeners, and even if she seems at times (especially in the earlier speech) to doubt her own capability, we should perhaps see this articulation of humility as a canny deployment of the 'modesty topos' or the *captatio benevolentiae* (literally, the 'taking of goodwill'), intended to get her audience on her side and demonstrating her sound humanist rhetorical training.

Bibliography

Elliott, J. R., Jr. (1988), 'Queen Elizabeth at Oxford: New Light on the Royal Plays of 1566', *English Literary Renaissance*, 18: 218–29.

Elliott, J. R., Jr., A. H. Nelson, A. F. Johnston and D. Wyatt (eds) (2004), *Records of Early English Drama: Oxford*, 2 vols, Toronto.

Keenan, S. (2007), 'Spectator and Spectacle: Royal Entertainments at the Universities in the 1560s', in J. E. Archer, E. Goldring and S. Knight (eds), *The Progresses, Pageants, and Entertainments of Queen Elizabeth I*, 86–108, Oxford.

Knight, S. (2015), 'Texts Presented to Elizabeth I on the University Progresses', in E. Jones (ed.), *A Concise Companion to the Study of Manuscripts, Printed Books, and the Production of Early Modern Texts: A Festschrift for Gordon Campbell*, 21–40, Chichester.

Marcus, L. S., J. Mueller and M. B. Rose (eds) (2000), *Elizabeth I: Collected Works*, Chicago and London.

Nichols, J. (2014), *John Nichols's The Progresses and Public Processions of Queen Elizabeth I: A New Edition of the Early Modern Sources*, 5 vols, ed. E. Goldring, F. Eales, E. Clarke and J. E. Archer, Oxford.

Shenk, L. (2010), *Learned Queen: The Image of Elizabeth I in Politics and Poetry*, New York.

Wood, A. (1786), *The History and Antiquities of the University of Oxford*, ed. J. Gutch, Oxford.

Sources of the Latin text and the English translation

Latin text and English translation are reprinted by permission of Oxford University Press and first appeared in the following publications:

John Nichols's The Progresses and Public Processions of Queen Elizabeth I: A New Edition of the Early Modern Sources. Volume I: 1533-1571 (2014), ed. by Goldring et al. Ass. Gen. eds. Heaton & Knight, pp. 485–87.

John Nichols's The Progresses and Public Processions of Queen Elizabeth I: A New Edition of the Early Modern Sources. Volume III: 1579-1595 (2014), ed. by Goldring et al. Ass. Gen. eds. Heaton & Knight. pp. 628–30.

1566: The text is based on Miles Windsor's account held at Corpus Christi College, Oxford, in MS 259, fols 104–23. The text has been taken from Windsor's 'fair copy' (the tidier version of the manuscript narrative), entitled 'The Receivinge of the Quenes Maiestie into Oxford', fols 104–14; see also Elliott 1988. The speech is also translated in Marcus, Mueller and Rose 2000: 89–91, who use a different manuscript (Bodleian Library, MS Additional A. 63) as their copytext.

1592: The text is based on the British Library manuscript Cotton Titus C.VII, fols 141^r–^{v}. The speech is also translated in Marcus, Mueller and Rose 2000: 327–8, who use a different manuscript (Bodleian Library, MS Bodley 900) as their copytext.

The Latin texts are in their original early modern spelling: in the sixteenth century, for example, *u* and *v*, and *i* and *j* were often used interchangeably –, *ineptiis* appears as *ineptijs* below, to name but one example –, and those original uses have been retained here, as have abbreviations (such as the use of the ampersand *&* instead of *et*), original diacritics (e.g. *malè* for *male*) and diagraphs such as *æ* for *ae*.

Latin text

1566

Qui malè agit, odit lucem. Sic ego, quia nil nisi malè facere possum, odi sane lucem: id est conspectum vestrum.[1] Est autem hoc tempus, & meis ineptijs, peridoneum, & vobis ad audiendum accomodatum. Cum singula repeto quæ hic geruntur, magna me tenet dubitatio, vtrum laudem an[2] vituperem,[3] taceamne an eloquar. Si eloquar patefaciam[4] vobis quam sim literarum plane rudis. Tacere autem nolo ne effectus videar contemptus.[5] Quod vero sum dictura, dividam in duas partes, in laudem, & vituperationem: quarum laus ad vos pertinet, vituperatio ad me ipsam. Vos enim, qui omni literarum genere estis ornati, laudo, proboque. Me verò, quæ ab omnibus bonis studijs & Musis aliena sum, vitupero, damno, & accuso maxime. Etenim, ex quo Oxoniam veni, multa vidi, multa audivi, probavi omnia.[6] Erant, & prudenter facta, & eloquenter dicta. At ea, de quibus in proemijs sese excuserant Theologi,[7] nisi tempore magis, quàm ex animo dixissetis, neque authoritate mea probare vt Regina, neque iudicio vt Christiana potuissem. Cæterum,[8] quia vos semper in exordijs vestris adhibuistis sanctiorem,[9] mihi sane illa non displicuere,[10] imo potius multis a pæne infinitis de causis mirifice mihi placuere.

English translation

1566

Whoever conducts himself badly hates the light. And so I, because I can only do this badly, certainly hate the light: that is, your scrutiny.[1] But this time is both very appropriate for my inadequacies and suited for you to listen. When I recall individual events that have taken place here, great doubt seizes me, whether[2] I should praise or blame,[3] whether I should be silent or speak: if I were to speak, I would expose[4] to you how clearly unskilled I am in learning. But I do not want to remain silent, lest I should seem to convey disdain.[5] So I shall divide what I am about to say into two parts, praise and blame: of these the praise relates to you, and the blame to myself. I praise and think highly of you, who are adorned with all kinds of learning. As for myself, who am a stranger to all noble studies and to the Muses, I blame, condemn, and reproach myself completely. As a matter of fact, from the moment I arrived in Oxford, I have seen many things, I have heard many things, and I have thought highly of everything.[6] There have been both wise deeds and eloquent words. But as for those words for which the Theologians excused themselves in their prologues,[7] which you said rather to suit the circumstances than as a result of your conviction, I neither approve them either under my authority as Queen, nor according to my judgement as a Christian. However,[8] since you always used more pious words in your prologues,[9] that could not displease me,[10] no, on the contrary, for many – almost an infinite number – of reasons, I have been wonderfully pleased.

Nunc venio ad alteram partem, nempe ad vituperationem, atque hæc pars mea propria est. Cum enim hic præsens, intueor vos omnes præsentes, sed ita vt indocta doctos, rudis eruditos, imperita peritissimos alloqui mihi videar,[11] pudore quidem suffundor, pænè subrustico, & in ipso medio pæne cursu deterreor a dicendo.[12] Fateor enim ingenuè, & quod sentio eloquor. Melius vt credo doctrinæ vtilitatem ego nunc carendo intelligo,[13] quam vos fruendo concipere vllo modo potestis. Sane fateor patrem meum curasse,[14] idque diligenter, vt bonis literis instituerer,[15] atque profecto, in multarum linguarum varietate versata (quarum mihi aliquam cognitionem assumo) fui. Quod etsi vere, tamen verecunde dico. Cæterum quas vos eximia quadam amoris abundantia mihi laudes tribuitis, eas ego nec agnosco nec fero libenter. Nam quod attinet ad eruditionem nostram, doleo equidem, sed tamen necessario fateor sum[16] dolore, eam nec authoritate mea, nec expectatione vestra, nec Subditorum meorum opinione dignam esse. Quamobrem cùm vos me abunde laudetis omnes, & ego interim mihi conscia sim quam sim[17] nulla laude digna, finem imponam huic orationi meæ, illiterati illi quidem, & fœminini[18] nimis, si hoc vnum prius optavero,[19] & a Deo optimo maximo demisse postulavero, vt vos me viva sitis florentissimi, me mortua, sitis beatissimi. Dixi.[20]

Now I come to the second part, blame, of course, and this is my own responsibility. For as I stand here, I see you all standing here, but I seem[11] to myself to speak as an unlearned woman to learned men, as an ignoramus to the erudite, as an unskilled woman to highly skilled men, so that I am overcome with shame, almost like a country yokel, and almost at the midpoint of my journey I am discouraged from speaking.[12] For I speak frankly, and articulate what I perceive. I believe that now I understand[13] the usefulness of learning better, though I lack it, than you could grasp by any means, though you possess it. Certainly I admit that my father took care,[14] and did so diligently, to bring me up[15] in noble studies, and indeed I was schooled in a variety of many languages (of which I claim a certain understanding). And I speak truly, but bashfully. However, those merits you attribute to me with an exceptional abundance of love, I neither recognize nor can gladly bear. In relation to my own erudition, I grieve, of course, but I confess[16] with necessary grief that my erudition is worthy neither of my own authority, nor of your expectation, nor of the good opinion of my subjects. Therefore since you all praise me so lavishly, and meanwhile I am myself aware that I am[17] not worthy of any praise, I will put an end to my speech, which is too unlettered and womanly,[18] if first I shall request[19] this one thing, and ask the best and greatest God to grant it, that you may flourish most greatly while I live, and be most blessed when I die. I have finished.[20]

1592

Merita & gratitudo sic meam rationem captiuam duxerunt, vt facere cogant, quæ ratio ipsa negat. Curæ enim Regnorum tam magna pondera habent, vt ingenium obtundere potius quam memoriam acuere solent.[21] Addatur etiam huius linguæ desuetudo, quæ talis & tam frequens fuit vt in triginta et sex annis,[22] trigesies nec tot vsam[23] fuisse meminerim. Sed fracta nunc est glacies: aut inhærere aut euadere oportet. Non sunt laudes eximiæ et insignes sed immeritæ, non doctrinarum in multis generibus iudicationes, narrationes, et explicationes, non orationes multis modis & varijs eruditæ & insigniter expressæ, sed aliud quiddam multo pretiosius atque præstantius, amor scilicet, qui nec vnquam[24] auditus, nec scriptus, nec memoria hominum notus fuit, cuius exemplo parentes carent, nec inter familiares cadit, immo nec inter amantes, in quorum sortem non semper fides incidit experientia ipsa docente.[25] Talis est iste vt, nec persuasiones, nec minæ, nec execrationes delere potuerunt; immo in quem[26] tempus gubernationem non habet, quod ferrum consumit: quod scopulos minuit, id istum separare non potuit. Ista sunt merita: sunt eiusmodi quæ sempiterna futura putarem, si et ego æterna essem. Ob quæ[27] si mille pro vna linguas haberem, gratias debitas exprimere non valerem: Tantum animus concipere potest quæ exprimere nequit. Pro cuius gratitudine accipite tantum votum & concilium. Ab initio Regni mei gubernationis, summa & præcipua mea sollicitudo cura et vigilia fuit, vt tam ab externis inimicis, quam internis tumultibus seruaretur, vt quod diu multis seculis floruerit, sub meis manibus non debilitaretur. Post enim animæ tutelam, in sola mea perpetua solicitudine[28] collocaui: Quod si totius tam semper fuerim vigilans,[29] & quod ista Academia pars non minima putetur, quomodo non & in illam extenditur ista cautio, pro quâ tanta diligentia[30] vsura semper sum, vt nullo stimulo opus erit,[31]

1592

Merits and gratitude have so taken my reason captive, that they force me to do what reason itself forbids. For the concerns of kingdoms possess such great weight, that they usually[21] blunt intelligence rather than sharpen memory. A loss of familiarity with this language should be added too, which has been of such a kind and so frequent during thirty-six years[22] that I do not remember having used[23] it as much as thirty times. But the ice has now been broken: it is necessary either to stand fast or to escape. It is not the excellent and distinguished praises, but the undeserved ones, not the many different sorts of opinions, accounts, and explanations of doctrines, not the speeches which were polished in so many and various ways, and delivered with distinction, but something which is much more precious and outstanding, that is, a love which has never[24] been heard, or written down, or known to men's memory; parents lack an example of this, nor does it occur among friends, no, indeed, not even among lovers, whose destiny is not always shared by loyalty, as experience itself teaches us.[25] This love is of such a kind that neither persuasions, nor threats nor curses can obliterate it. No, time – which devours iron, and wears down rocks – has no control over it,[26] and cannot sever it. Those are your merits: they are of such a kind that I would think they would be eternal, if I were undying too. If[27] I had a thousand tongues instead of one, I would not be able to articulate the thanks that are owed: the mind can imagine what it cannot express. Receive, in gratitude for this, just a prayer and advice. From the beginning of my control of the kingdom, it has always been my greatest and foremost anxiety, concern and object of attention that it should be kept safe from external enemies and internal upheavals, so that something that has flourished for so many centuries should not weaken in my hands. For after the safekeeping of my soul, I have directed my unique and constant concern[28] towards that: if I have always been attentive to the whole,[29] and since this University should not be thought to be the smallest part, how could that guardianship not be extended towards it, for on the University's behalf I shall always employ so much care[30] that there will not be any need for an incentive to prompt me,[31]

ad exercitandam, quæ ex seipsa prompta est ad promouendam,[32] seruandam, et decorandam illam. Nunc quod ad concilium attinet, tale accipite, quod si sequamini non dubito quin erit[33] in Dei gloriam, vestram vtilitatem, & meum singulare gaudium.[34] Vt diuturna sit hæc Academia, habeat inprimis cura vt Deus colatur,[35] non more omnium opinionum, non secundum ingenia nimis inquisita & enquisita, sed vt Lex diuina iubet, & nostra præcipit. Non enim talem Principem habetis, quæ vobis quidquam precipit quod contra conscientiam vere Christianam esse deberet. Scitote[36] me prius morituram,[37] quàm tale aliquid acturam, aut quicquid iubeam, quod in sacris literis vetatur. Si enim corporum vestrorum curam semper suscepi, deberem non animarum?[38] Vetet Deus. Animarum ego curam negligam,[39] pro quarum neglectu, anima mea iudicabitur? Longe absit. Moneo ergo vt non præcatis[40] leges, sed sequamini: non disputetis num meliora possint præscribi, sed obseruetis quæ[41] Lex diuina iubet et nostra cogit. Deinde memineritis vt vnus quisquam in gradu suo superiori obediat[42], non præscribendo[43] quæ esse deberent, sed sequendo quod præscriptum est: hoc cogitando, Quod si superiores agere cæperint[44] quæ non decet, alium superiorem habebunt a quo rogantur, qui illos punire & debeat et velit. Postremo vt sitis vnanimes cum intelligatis[45] vnita[46] robustiora, separata infirmiora & citò in ruinam casura.[47]

for my care itself is ready to promote,[32] maintain and adorn it. Now in relation to my advice, hear this: if you follow it, I do not doubt that it will be[33] to God's glory, in your own interest and to my unique delight.[34] So that this University may last for a long time, its first concern should be to worship God,[35] not after the fashion of everyone's opinion, nor according to overly curious and inquisitive intellects, but as the divine Law orders, and our own teaches. For you do not have the kind of sovereign who teaches you anything that should go against a truly Christian conscience. Understand[36] that I would die[37] before I would do such a thing, or order anything that is forbidden in holy scripture. For should I, who have always looked after your bodies, not look after your souls?[38] God forbid. Shall I overlook[39] the care of souls, for whose neglect my own soul will be judged? Let that not happen. And so I tell you not to address the laws, but to follow them: do not debate whether better laws[40] could be prescribed, but keep to what[41] the divine Law orders and what our own urges. From now on, remember that each person should obey[42] his superior in rank, not by prescribing[43] what ought to be, but by following what has been prescribed, considering this: if superiors start[44] to do what is inappropriate, then they will possess another superior to whom they will have to answer, who both should and would wish to punish them. Finally, you should be unanimous, for you know[45] that unity[46] is stronger, division is weaker, and quickly falls into destruction.[47]

Commentary

1566

1 Elizabeth's grammatical shift in pronoun and verb agreements is striking. She moves from the general and abstract third person (*qui, agit, odit*) to the first-person singular (*ego, possum, odi*) to the second-person plural (*vestrum*), establishing the terms for a rhetorical interaction between orator and audience. The opening words of the oration quote John 3:20, *omnis enim qui mala* [or *malè*, as here] *agit odit lucem* (Vulgate). The verse is spoken by Jesus, who answers a series of questions about faith posed by Nicodemus, 'a man of the Pharises' and 'a ruler of the Iewes' in the 1560 Geneva bible translation; the Geneva translation of John 3:20 is: 'For euery man that euill doeth, hateth the light, neither commeth to light, least his deedes should be reprooued.'

2 *vtrum . . . an*: The indirect question construction Elizabeth uses here is typical of how debate topics were presented and disputed in early modern university rhetoric, as was evident in the speeches by Oxford scholars to which the Queen listened in 1566 and 1592. This speech contains many examples of indirect questions.

3 *laudem an vituperem*: Elizabeth underlines her understanding of two of the main branches of epideictic rhetoric, praise (*laudatio*) and blame (*vituperatio*). Epideictic rhetoric is the kind of public speech typically used on official or ceremonial occasions.

4 *patefaciam*: Elizabeth uses this form as a present subjunctive in a remote conditional clause, not as future indicative.

5 *ne effectus videar contemptus*: The grammar here is unusual, but it looks like a purpose clause in which *ne* ('lest', 'so that . . . not') takes the subjunctive (*videar*): literally, 'so that I should not seem', and in which the masculine noun *contemptus* ('disdain', 'scorn') agrees with the past participle *effectus* ('to have been accomplished'; 'to have been conveyed'). The sense is that the speaker worries that silence might seem aloof and proud. In this oration Elizabeth's rhetorical self-awareness is typical of how early modern university orators often began their speeches to an assembled academic audience, by anticipating critical objections and – as here – introducing (and sometimes then refuting) hypothetical conditions. Obviously, at this stage of a public oration, it is clear that Elizabeth will not remain silent (*tacere*), but she expresses this condition as a courtesy to her audience ('silence' might 'seem' contemptuous).

6 In these two consecutive sentences Elizabeth uses the rhetorical tricolon construction popular among both classical and humanist rhetoricians twice,

to different effects. The first tricolon (*vitupero, damno, & accuso*) is created by a sequence of first-person present verbs and is a form known as asyndeton, like Julius Caesar's famous *veni, vidi, vici* ('I came, I saw, I conquered'). It is also an example of a 'rising tricolon', where the first-person verbs increase in rhetorical and emotional intensity as the clause progresses. The syntactical parallelisms of the second tricolon comprising first-person perfect verbs (*multa vidi, multa audivi, probavi omnia*) are perhaps more conspicuous in the more economical Latin syntax than in the English translation. Again, this second example could also be seen as a 'rising tricolon', in which the plural sensory perceptions expressed twice for 'many things' (*multa*) lead up to the universal admiration for 'everything' (*omnia*).

7 *ea, de quibus in proemijs sese excuserant Theologi*: By suggesting that tactless words have previously been uttered by some scholars present, Elizabeth was probably referring to the Questions in Divinity held earlier that day, in which disputants argued for and against the extremely contentious question: 'A private citizen should not be allowed to take up arms against a particularly unjust prince.' For participants in the debate, see Nichols's *Progresses*, 1.484–5.

8 *Cæterum*: often used in this oration in place of *ceterum*.

9 *sanctiorem*: The implication is that Elizabeth's fellow orators have tended to begin their speeches (an *exordium* is the opening of an oration) in a 'more holy' (*sanctiorem*) manner. The grammar is unusual here: we might perhaps expect the plural *sanctiores* here rather than the singular *sanctiorem*.

10 *displicuere*: At several points in her speech Elizabeth uses a contracted third-person plural perfect verb form (*displicuere* = *displicuerunt*; see also *placuere* for *placuerunt* later in the sentence).

11 *videar*: Elizabeth uses this verb several times in the oration: here, this subjunctive form occurs in the result clause following *ita vt*.

12 *dicendo*: Elizabeth uses a number of ablative gerunds in the speech, some governed by a preposition (as *a dicendo* here) and others without a preposition (*carendo* and *fruendo* in what follows, both ablatives of cause).

13 *intelligo* = *intellego*.

14 *curasse* = *curavisse*.

15 *instituerer*: Elizabeth uses an unusual verb form, the imperfect passive subjunctive dependent on *curasse ut* (see n. 14).

16 *fateor sum*: In the peroration (formal ending) of her speech Elizabeth's unusual syntactical choice might be intended to emphasize – and, rhetorically,

to perform – the personal emotions she describes. The two first-person verbs *fateor* and *sum* foreground both the words she speaks and the way she feels.

17 *conscia sim quam sim*: The two first-person present subjunctive verb forms perform different functions within the sentence, despite their proximity. The first *sim* is used as a subjunctive following *cum* (like *laudetis* earlier in the sentence), and the second is a subjunctive used in an indirect question (*quam sim*).

18 *fœminini = feminini*.

19 *optavero*: Elizabeth uses the first-person future perfect form to indicate a future completed action (as does *postulavero*).

20 Following the text of Elizabeth's speech, Miles Windsor tells us what happened next during the royal progress: 'This daye at nighte was playde before the Quene in the Commonhall at Christe Churche, a Lattyn Tragedy named Progne made by Mr. Dr. Caulfhil.' James Calfhill, a canon of Christ Church, had been one of the opponents in the Divinity disputations (see n. 7). His tragedy *Progne* is not extant, but was perhaps an adaptation of the Venetian dramatist Gregorio Corraro's (or Correr) Latin tragedy *Progne* (Venice 1558), based on Book 6 of Ovid's *Metamorphoses*: see F. S. Boas, *University Drama in the Tudor Age*, Oxford 1914, 104–5 and *REED: Oxford*, II, 832.

1592

21 *solent*: We might perhaps expect to find the subjunctive form *soleant* in a result clause.

22 *in triginta et sex annis*: Elizabeth acceded in 1558, so by 1592 she had been on the throne thirty-four years.

23 *vsam*: *me* needs to be understood with *vsam*.

24 *vnquam = umquam*.

25 *experientia ipsa docente*: an ablative absolute.

26 *in quem*: In this section Elizabeth uses a sequence of connecting relative pronouns in which she expects her audience to retain an understanding and keep up in their inferring of the nouns she has previously articulated. Here, for instance, *quem* refers back to *amor*.

27 *Ob quæ*: *quæ* refers back to *merita* (see n. 26).

28 *in sola mea perpetua solicitudine*: The positioning of the adjectives *sola* and *perpetua* – without, say, a conjunction like *et* ('and') is unusual, but the

point is that Elizabeth's 'concern' (*solicitudine*) is both 'unique' (*sola*) and 'constant' (*perpetua*).

29 *totius tam semper fuerim vigilans*: The genitive *totius* is dependent on *vigilans*.

30 *tanta diligentia*: the ablative object of *vsura* . . . *sum*, since *utor* takes the ablative case.

31 *nullo stimulo opus erit*: The impersonal clause *opus est* (here in the future form) takes the ablative case, hence *nullo stimulo*.

32 *ad exercitandam*, . . . *ad promouendam*: gerundives expressing purpose, dependent on the preposition *ad*.

33 *non dubito quin erit*: Expressions of doubt using *quin* more usually take the subjunctive rather than the indicative as here.

34 *in Dei gloriam, vestram vtilitatem, & meum singulare gaudium*: Elizabeth again uses the tricolon structure (see n. 6).

35 *habeat inprimis cura vt Deus colatur*: Compared with her 1566 speech, Elizabeth focuses much more concertedly on the status of the assembled scholars as her subjects and argues strongly for their obedience and conformity in religious matters.

36 *Scitote*: an example of the emphatic imperative form. These forms are particularly associated with legal discourse.

37 *me . . . morituram*: The verb *esse* needs to be understood, i.e. *morituram esse*.

38 *animarum*: Again, Elizabeth's Latin might seem elliptical and relies on her listeners supplying words already mentioned to complete the sentence. The genitive *animarum* is dependent on the noun *curam* introduced in the previous clause.

39 *negligam* = *neglegam*.

40 *præcatis*: More typically spelled *precatis*, this is the second-person plural form of *preco*, an attested late-antique and patristic variant form of what is a deponent verb in classical Latin (*precor*). Usually, we would expect the subjunctive rather than indicative in the *vt*-clause.

41 *quæ*: In addition to this relative pronoun, *ea* should be understood (lit. *ea quæ* = 'those things which'). Elizabeth uses a similar implied construction twice in the following sentence (*quæ esse* and *quæ non decet*).

42 *obediat = oboediat.*

43 *præscribendo*: an ablative gerund, like *sequendo* and *cogitando* later in the sentence.

44 *cæperint = coeperint.*

45 *intelligatis = intellegatis.*

46 *vnita*: As with *separata* in the next clause, and as in other points of this oration, Elizabeth expects her audience to supply the verb *esse* to accompany these neuter plural forms.

47 See Wood, *History and Antiquities*, 2.253, for what Elizabeth did next: Wood records that her final valediction to the assembled scholars and local dignitaries was also 'in the Latin Tongue': 'Her speech being done, she talked with the Vicechancellor and Doctors a little while, and then retired. In the afternoon she left Oxford, and going through Fishstreet to Quatervois, and thence to the East Gate, received the hearty wishes (mixt with tears) of the people; and casting her eyes on the walls of St Mary's Church, All Souls, University and Magdalen Colleges, which were mostly hung with Verses and emblematical expressions of Poetry, was often seen to give gracious nods to the Scholars. When she came to Shotover Hill (the utmost confines of the University) accompanied with those Doctors and Masters that brought her in, she graciously received a farewell Oration from one of them, in the name of the whole University. Which being done, she gave them many thanks, and her hand to kiss; and then looking wistfully towards Oxford, said to this effect in the Latin Tongue: "Farewell, farewell, dear Oxford, GOD bless thee, and increase thy sons in number, holiness, and virtue, &c."'

6

Female Funerary Verse

Elizabeth Cooke Hoby Russell (1540–1609), Epitaphic Poems

Lucy R. Nicholas

Introduction

Elizabeth Cooke Hoby Russell (1528–1609) (henceforth 'Russell') was an English noblewoman, one of the five daughters of the influential courtier Anthony Cooke and his wife, Anne Fitzwilliam, and personally known to Elizabeth I. Rather like the Mitford sisters or the Brontës, the Cooke daughters, all highly learned and accomplished, enjoyed a reputation as formidable women in their own right. This five-fold *fama* notwithstanding, their reputations were also secured to a large degree through their marriages. Russell had two husbands, and both were important national figures. Her first husband was Thomas Hoby (English ambassador in France and the translator into English of Castiglione's *Courtier* and Martin Bucer's *Gratulation to the Church of England*). Following Hoby's death in 1566, she married Lord John Russell, second Earl of Bedford, who predeceased her in 1585. Russell had three children by her first husband Thomas Hoby, including two daughters, Anne and Elizabeth, and was pregnant with a fourth when Thomas died in France. She would go on to have two (possibly three) more children with her second husband, Lord Russell.

Russell's family life is not unrelated to her poetry. She became known during her lifetime as a talented author of epitaphs, and the poems featured in this section were written upon the deaths of: (a) her first husband, Thomas Hoby; (b) her daughters (both of whom predeceased her); and (c) her father, Anthony Cooke. Her verse was largely inspired by her immediate domestic circle, but it should not be thought that Russell's epitaphic poetry was a wholly private affair. Historians are increasingly conscious of the profound overlap between private and public in this period. Almost no realm of activity – family, death or religion – was private in the modern sense:

virtually all life was public, or at least had a public, social or communal dimension. This quickly becomes apparent in Russell's commemorative works. Alongside the pathos and heart-wrenching grief that the deaths of loved ones elicit, readers will note numerous references in her poems to public service, to the country (*patria*) and to the monarch, as well as allusions to Ovid. Although Russell was not a professional poetess (she published very little in her lifetime), she became well known through the circulation of her manuscripts.

We should also be alive to the fact that Russell's funerary verse belongs to a broader religious context. The monuments and epitaphs she created seem almost to convey a conversation between mourner and departed that traverses the border between life and death. However, Russell's poems are also implicated in the then widespread ferment of the English Reformation, and there is evidence that she was a keen promoter of Reformed religion. The growing schism between Catholics and Protestants encouraged a wholesale re-evaluation of all aspects of life. This included re-evaluation of death, and scholars argue that thanatology, in particular, was a crucial barometer of religious change. New approaches to death helped to define Protestantism, to establish it as a separate confession and to decouple it from a Catholic past and papal opponents. Two of the most seminal Catholic doctrines concerning death were purgatory and intercession, which gave rise to a complex relationship between the living and the dead, including prayers for the dead, the communion of saints and the practice of indulgences (see Text 9, Epigram 6(2).18 with commentary). It is possible to discern in Russell's epitaphic poems a strong rejection of these doctrines. There is no mention at all of any interim state between the dead and the living. The poems are also silent about any clerical intermediary role in the management of death. Fulsome praise of the moral qualities of the deceased is another index of Protestant allegiance, for positive moral qualities were understood as essential signs of inward faith that operated within a framework of the doctrine of justification, the seminal Protestant doctrine originally developed by Martin Luther. Another possible index of her Protestantism is Russell's emphasis on the family. Recent scholarship has argued that Protestants placed a far greater emphasis on family life, viewing the family unit as a church in microcosm, as opposed to the weight placed by Catholics on monasticism and the Virgin Mary.

The fact that the other authors showcased in this Neo-Latin Anthology are men, with the exceptions of the present author and Queen Elizabeth I (see Text 5), might not come as a particularly great surprise. Women of the time did not generally receive a formal education; yet the fact that some women did use Latin and Greek should perhaps alert us to the fact that male monopoly over Latin and Greek was less absolute than is sometimes thought. Cooke followed the unusual path of educating both his sons and his daughters, and it in fact transpired that his intellectual legacy would be continued far more effectively by his daughters than his sons. Russell herself is a shining example of a woman of the early modern period who composed verse in both Latin and Greek; indeed, she employs Greek in one of the poems set out below. Russell is often dubbed 'the English Sappho'; her poems are sophisticated, metrically adept and replete with classical vocabulary and allusions. It is also worth noting how she celebrated the learning of the figures she writes about, presenting them as exemplars of humanist values. There is nothing faint-hearted or equivocal about these poems: Russell is central in them and resolutely examines death from a woman's perspective.

Metre: elegiac couplets

Bibliography

Allen, G. (2013), *The Cooke Sisters: Education, Piety and Politics in Early Modern England*, Manchester.

Heal, F. (1996), 'Reputation and Honour in Court and Country: Lady Elizabeth Russell and Sir Thomas Hoby', *Transactions of the Royal Historical Society*, 6: 161–78.

Hosington, B. M. (2012), '"The Well-Wrought Verses of an Unknown Bard": Renaissance Englishwomen's Latin Poetry of Praise and Lament', in A. Steiner-Weber (ed.), *Acta Conventus Neo-Latini Upsaliensis*, 1.81–104, Leiden and Boston.

McDiarmid, J. F. (1996), 'Classical Epitaphs for Heroes of Faith: Mid-Tudor Neo-Latin Memorial Volumes and their Protestant Humanist Context', *International Journal of the Classical Tradition*, 3: 23–47.

Phillippy, P. (with translations by J. Goodrich) (2011), *The Writings of an English Sappho / Elizabeth Cooke Hoby Russell*, Toronto.

Schleiner, L. (with verse translation by C. McQuillen and L. E. Roller) (1994), *Tudor and Stuart Women Writers*, Indiana.

Stevenson, J. (2005), *Women Latin Poets: Language, Gender, and Authority from Antiquity to the Eighteenth Century*, Oxford [267–8, quoting Passage 1].

Stevenson, J. and P. Davidson (eds) (2000), *Early Modern Women Poets: An Anthology*, Oxford.

Source of the Latin text

The text has been taken from Phillippy's *The Writings of an English Sappho* (Phillippy 2011), though some amendments (for example, 'j' changed to 'i') and certain corrections (where indicated below) have been made. The first two poems have been checked against the transcriptions from the actual tombs, as offered in E. Ashmole, *Antiquities of Berkshire*, 3 vols, London 1719: vol. 2. The third poem has been checked against F. Chancellor, *The Ancient Sepulchral Monuments of Essex*, London and Chelmsford 1890: vol. 1.2.

Latin Text

Poem 1

Elizabetha Hobaea coniunx ad Thomam Hobaeum, Equitem Maritum

O dulcis coniunx, animae pars maxima nostrae,
    cuius erat vitae vita medulla meae.
Cur ita coniunctos divellunt livida fata?
    Cur ego sum viduo sola relicta toro?
5 Anglia foelices, foelices Gallia vidit,
    per mare, per terras noster abivit amor,
par fortunatum fuimus dum viximus una,
    corpus erat duplex, spiritus unus erat.
Sed nihil in terris durat, charissime coniunx,
10   tu mihi, tu testis flebilis esse potes.
Dum patriae servis, dum publica commoda tractas,
    occidis, ignota triste cadaver humo.
Et miseri nati flammis febrilibus ardent.
    Quid facerem tantis, heu, mihi mersa malis.
15 Infoelix coniunx, infoelix mater oberro,
    Te vir adempte fleo, vos mea membra fleo.
Exeo funestis terris, hinc rapta cadaver
    Coniugis, hinc prolis languida membra traho.
Sic uterum gestans, redeo terraque marique
20   In patriam luctu perdita, mortis amans.
Chare mihi coniunx, et praestantissime Thoma,
    Cuius erat rectum, et nobile quicquid erat;
Elizabetha, tibi quondam gratissima sponsa
    Haec lacrimis refert verba referta piis.
25 Non potui prohibere mori, sed mortua membra,
    Quo potero, faciam semper honore coli.
Tu Deus, aut similem Thomae mihi redde maritum,
    Aut reddant Thomae me mea fata viro.

English translation

Poem 1

Elizabeth Hoby, wife, to Thomas Hoby, Knight and her Husband

O dear partner, the greatest part of my soul,
Whose life was the very quintessence of my life.
Why do the envious fates tear apart those thus united in love?
Why am I alone, abandoned on a widow's bed?
England saw us happy, France saw us happy,   5
Our love travelled over the sea, over lands,
We were a charmed pair while we lived together:
the body was twofold; the spirit was one.
But on the earth nothing abides, dearest husband,
and you, you can be my mournful witness to that.   10
While you were serving the fatherland, while you were attending to the
    public good,
You perished, an unhappy corpse on foreign soil.
And our wretched children are ablaze with feverish flushes.
What was I to do, alas, sunk in misfortunes of such magnitude?
Joyless partner, I, a joyless mother, drift around,   15
I weep for you, husband, carried off, I weep for you, my children.
I depart from these grief-bringing lands; from here I, robbed, drag the corpse
of my partner, from here I drag the weak limbs of our offspring.
In this way, carrying our unborn child, I return, by land and by sea
to the fatherland, lost in mourning, a lover of death.   20
Partner so dear to me, and my most distinguished Thomas,
who was endowed with whatever was right and whatever was noble:
Elizabeth, once your most beloved bride,
returns these words brimming with tender tears.
I wasn't able to keep you from dying, but your dead limbs   25
I will always, to the best of my ability, cause to be cherished with honour.
You God, either restore to me a spouse resembling Thomas,
or may my death restore me to my husband Thomas.

Poem 2

Elizabethae Hobeae, Matris, in obitum duarum filiarum Elizabethae, et Annae, Epicedium

Elizabetha iacet, (eheu mea viscera) fato
  Vix dum maturo virgo tenella iaces,
Chara mihi quondam vixisti filia matri,
  Chara Deo posthac filia vive patri,
5 Mors tua crudelis, multo crudelius illud,
    Quod cecidit tecum iunior Anna soror.
Anna, patris matrisque decus, post fata sororis,
  Post matris luctus, aurea virgo iaces!
Una parens, pater unus erat, mors una duabus,
10   Et lapis hic unus corpora bina tegit.
Sic volui mater tumulo sociarier uno,
  Una quas utero laeta gemensque tuli.

Istae duae generosae, optimaeque spei
Sorores, eodem Anno, viz. 1570,
15 Eodem mense, viz. Februario,
Paucorum dierum spatio
Interiecto, in Domino
Obdormiverunt.

Poem 2

An Epitaphic Lament of Elizabeth Hoby, a Mother, on the death of her Two Daughters Elizabeth and Anne

Elizabeth (ah, my very core) lies felled by a death
scarcely timely; you lie dead, delicate girl.
You once lived, dear to me, a daughter to a mother;
live hereafter, dear to God, a daughter to a father.
Yours was a cruel death; it was much crueller   5
Because your younger sister Anne fell with you.
Anne, pride of your father and mother, following your sister's death
and a mother's grief, you lie dead, beautiful girl!
There was one mother, one father, one death for two girls,
and this one stone covers their two bodies.   10
Thus, as their mother, I wanted them to be united in a single tomb
together, those whom I bore in the womb, then joyous, now grieving.

These two noble sisters, with the most hopeful future,
fell asleep in the Lord in the same year, namely 1570,
and in the same month, namely February,   15
in the space of a few days
of each other.

Poem 3

In obitum clarissimi, literatissimi Domini Antoni Coci equitis aurati carmen Ἐπιτάφιον

Clare vir (Antoni), cum nil tua funera fletus
   Adiuvet, has laudes concelebrabo tuas
Foelix illa fuit, qua nascebaris in hora:
   Quippe decus generi, lausque, futurus eras,
5 Te Pallas docuit generosa stirpe creatum
   Et Musae mores instituere tuos.
Ut tempus crevit sic crevit tempore virtus
   Et pietas vera cognitione dei.
Tunc Deus uxorem nulli probitate secundam
10   Donat honore tibi, et nobilitate parem.
Anna tibi fuerat quamvis pulcherrima coniunx,
   Diminuit studium non tamen Anna tuum.
Bibliotecha fuit, gaza praestantior omni:
   Librorum facerent nomina nuda librum.
15 Hinc pulchros flores, fructus hinc promis amaenos:
   Hinc mentis pastus, deliciaeque tuae.
Τὰ γνωσθέντα λέγων, καὶ μὲν τὰ δέοντα γιγνώσκων,
   Τοῦ πλούτου κρείττων, καὶ φιλόπατρις ἔης.
Cur te (Roma) facit Cornelia docta superbam?
20   Quam multas tales, et mage, Cocus habet?
Quinque sciunt natae coniungere Graeca Latinis,
   Insignes claris moribus atque piis.
Has tu nobilibus (res est bene nota) locasti:
   Qui Christum vera religione colunt.
25 Et quorum prodest prudentia summa Britannis:
   Qui virtute valent, consiliisque graves.
Quinque peregrinis vixti regionibus annos,
   Dum revocat princeps te Elisabetha domum.
Utque solet Phoebus radiis nitidissimus almis
30   Nubibus excussis, exhilarare diem,
Sic regina potens regali sede locata
   Et Coco et natis omnia fausta tulit.
Haec inter vitam, foelicia (Coce) beatam
   Traduxit, cupiens coelica regna senex.
35 Et veluti recidunt maturo tempore poma

Poem 3

A Funeral Song on the Death of the most Distinguished and Most
Learned Sir Anthony Cooke, Decorated Knight

Illustrious man (Anthony), since weeping profits
your last rites in no way, I will instead celebrate these praises of yours.
That hour when you were born was a propitious one:
Since you were destined to be the pride and glory of your kith and kin,
goddess Minerva gave you instruction, you born of noble stock,   5
and the Muses set in place your way of life.
As time advanced, so with time your virtue advanced,
so too your religious mission through true knowledge of God.
Then God granted a wife inferior to no one in goodness,
and a perfect match for you in honour and birth.   10
Anne, although you had in her a most beautiful wife,
nonetheless she did not detract from your life of learning.
The library was more extraordinary than every treasure.
The names of the books alone would make a book.
It was from here that you brought forth beautiful flowers, from here
    gratifying fruits;   15
here it was where the mind was nourished, and your pleasure.
Gathering the things that are known, and knowing the things that are needful,
You transcended the influence of money, and were a lover of your country.
Why, o Rome, does learned Cornelia make you haughty?
How many of such a kind, and more, does Cooke have?   20
Five daughters, outstanding for their upstanding and dutiful
way of life, know how to yoke Greek to Latin.
You married them to noblemen (the fact is well known):
who worship Christ in the true religion,
and whose supreme statesmanship profits Britons.   25
They are strong in virtue, and grave in counsel.
You lived for five years in foreign lands,
Until our leader Elizabeth recalled you home.
And just as the most radiant god Apollo is accustomed,
once the clouds have been routed, to gladden day with life-giving rays, 30
thus our vigorous queen, set on a royal throne,
bestowed all these favourable gifts upon Cooke and his children.
He (Cooke) among these happy things led a blessed life,
and as an old man, longing for heavenly kingdoms.
And just as apples fall ripe in season,   35

Sic facili coelum morte solutus adis.
Hocque simul tumulo, duro cum marmore structo
   Doctus eques, coniunx intemerata cubant.
Quos socialis amor, pietas, quos iunxit, et alma
40   Virtus in terris vos Deus unus habet.

so, set free by a painless death, you go to heaven.
And together in this tomb, fashioned from enduring marble,
The learned knight and his chaste wife lie asleep.
Those whom conjugal love, devotion, and whom bountiful
virtue united on earth, one God now keeps you. 40

Commentary

Poem 1

This poem was composed by Russell upon the death of her first husband, Thomas Hoby, in 1566. While it should be evident from the notes that follow that this is a work of multiple literary tributaries, an important general source of inspiration for Russell's composition is Ovid's *Heroides*, a collection of poems in elegiac couplets and presented as though written by a selection of aggrieved heroines in address to their heroic lovers who have in some way abandoned them.

1 For *o dulcis coniunx* see Creusa's address to Aeneas at Virgil, *Aeneid* 2.777. The poet is perhaps also adapting (and improving upon) Horace's words to Virgil, *animae dimidium meae* ('half my soul'), at *Odes* 1.3.8.

2 The juxtaposition of *vitae vita* underscores how close this couple were.

3 Ashmole (1719: 467) has *invida* (also meaning 'envious') for *livida*.

4 This is an adaptation of Giovanni Pico della Mirandola's *moxque ego sum viduo sola futura thoro* ('and soon I will be alone on a widow's bed'), which appears in an unpublished poem entitled *Martia conqueritur Pici discessum, qui ad exteras gentes ire parabat et studiis incumbere*, line 18.

5 *foelices = felices*: this applies *mutatis mutandis* throughout the poems. Both England and France are referred to since Hoby was sent to France from England after his appointment as an ambassador.

6 *abivit*: Russell does not mean that their love went away, just that it travelled where they went.

7 *par*: Hoby deftly incorporates a nice switch to *par* after *per . . . per* in the line above.

7–8 *una . . . duplex . . . unus*: The focus on numbers underscores the bond of the married couple. *par fortunatum* may recall Virgil's address *fortunati ambo* to the inseparable lovers Nisus and Euryalus at *Aeneid* 9.446.

9 *charissime = carissime*: this applies *mutatis mutandis* throughout the poems.

10 There is an ambiguity in the adjective *flebilis*, which could mean 'tearful' but also 'one who is to be wept for'.

11–12 *dum . . . servis, dum . . . tractas, occidis*: The construction, together with the present tense in all clauses, helps to highlight with great immediacy the point that Hoby died while in post; normally one would expect to find a present tense with *dum* in an 'interrupted *dum* clause', but where the verb in the main clause is in the perfect tense.

13 *febrilibus*: *febrilis, -e* is a medieval rather than classical Latin word. Russell must mean here that the children fall dangerously ill at the same time as their father passes away. There is also a possible play on *flebilis* in line 10.

15-18 The lines convey well the cohesion of the family unit even after the death of one of its most vital members.

16 *adempte* is reminiscent of Catullus' epitaphic poem on his brother (Cat. 101.6: *heu miser indigne frater adempte mihi* – 'oh, poor brother, taken away from me unworthily'). *mea membra*: lit. 'my limbs', but this must mean her children in the context. Russell had four children by her husband Hoby (including one born after his death). The focus on weeping is reminiscent of Orpheus lamenting Eurydice in Virgil, *Georgics* 4.

18 *languida*: This could point to the fact the children are ill.

19 *uterum gestans*: Russell was pregnant with their fourth child when Thomas Hoby died; he was Thomas Posthumus (1566–1640).

redeo terraque marique: This phrase seems to pick up *per mare, per terras* of line 6, effecting a poignant contrast between then and now. There might also be another generically appropriate suggestion of the opening of Catullus' poem on his brother (Cat. 101.1: *Multas per gentes et multa per aequora vectus*: 'Carried through many nations and over many seas'). There may even be a play on *mari* as *male* ('badly').

21/23 The ends of these hexameter lines are strikingly similar – *praestantissime Thoma* and *gratissima sponsa*: both have a superlative followed by a two-syllable word ending in 'a' – again perhaps as a way to highlight the emotional proximity between the poet and her addressee. The vocative *Thoma* may be playing on the Greek word θῶμα (or θαῦμα) meaning 'marvel'.

24 *refert . . . referta*: The two verbs are unrelated, the former from *refero* and the latter from *refercio*, but in these forms they sound very similar, with the second almost forming a mournful echo after the first.

25 *prohibere mori*: *prohibeo* tends to be used with the infinitive, i.e. to 'prevent' or 'stop' someone from doing something.

26 *facio* + passive infinitive has the force of causing something to be done. Hoby was buried in the village of Bisham, in the Royal Borough of Windsor in Berkshire, where a monument was erected and can be visited today.

27-8 The repetition of her husband's name injects the final two lines with considerable feeling and intensity.

Poem 2

Elizabeth had four children by Thomas Hoby. The two girls, Elizabeth and
Anne, both died in childhood in 1570, within days of each other. They were
also buried in Parish Church of All Saints, Bisham in Berkshire.

1 *iaceo* can denote lying in death, for example, *Aeacidae telo iacet Hector*
('Hector lies prostrate under the spear of Aeacides': Virgil, *Aeneid* 1.99). For
the second-person singular of the verb used in epitaphic addresses to the
deceased, see e.g. Propertius 1.7.24; Ovid, *Amores* 2.6.20. *viscera* conveys real
physicality: in the New Testament it stands as the seat of the emotions, for
example in Colossians 3:12.

2 *Vix dum* = *vixdum*. *maturo* seems to offer a sad play on *matri* at the end of
line 3.

3–4 It is noteworthy how Russell unites the family through the use of familial
terminology and careful word order.

4 *patri*: This constitutes a reference to God the Father (in apposition to *Deo*)
with the suggestion that her daughters, who have lived dear to their mother,
will now live in God and be dear to him. There is a possible secondary meaning
too, though, that they are dear to their father Thomas Hoby, who died in 1566.

5 *crudelis ... crudelius*: The use of adjective plus its comparative helps
amplify the sense of grief.

8 *aurea virgo*: picks up the earlier *virgo tenella*, but may also allude to Virgil's
Eclogue 4. For *iaces* in literary epitaphs, see note on line 1.

9–12 Note the emphasis on and repeated use of numbers to unite the family
and to accentuate the sense of double loss. In line 12 Ashmole prints *Una*
(translated here as 'together'), but modern editors alter this to *uno*, agreeing with
utero ('in a single womb') and balancing *tumulo ... uno* in the preceding line.

11 *sociarier* = *sociari* (passive infinitive).

13 *optimae ... spei*: lit. 'of the most excellent hope'.

17–18 *in Domino obdormiverunt*: This sounds Scriptural – see, for example,
Acts 7:60: *obdormivit*.

Poem 3

Anthony Cooke (1504–1576) was Russell's father. He was a celebrated scholar
and courtier and tutor to Edward VI. He was 72 when he died.

1–2 There is an interesting detachment from grief and instead a focus on the
qualities of the man.

5 Pallas was a name for the Greek goddess Athena (or Minerva in the Roman pantheon), associated with (*inter alia*) wisdom.

7 *crevit . . . crevit*: the repeated verb underscores the degree to which Cooke continually flourished.

8 Phillippy's text has *vita* rather than *vera*, but *vera* is used in the transcription in Chancellor (1890: 238) and this seems preferable in the context: it would be difficult to argue that *vita* on its own can mean 'in life'; furthermore, taking *vita* as the first of two elements in asyndeton ('through life, [and] through knowledge of God') is problematic because that meaning could easily have been made explicit simply by adding *et* after *vita* with no damage to the metre.

9–11 Cooke married Anne Fitzwilliam, the daughter of Sir William Fitzwilliam, by whom he had four sons and five daughters.

15 *amaenos = amoenos*. Russell here seems to pun on the idea of rhetorical conceits. But this imagery, which is bound up with fertility, may additionally reflect the fact that Cooke was a great landowner (he owned estates in Essex and lands in Warwickshire). There may also be a stress on his multiple children.

16 In Phillippy *deliciae* stands without *-que*, but it needs this in order for the line to scan.

17–18 Russell demonstrates her Greek learning in these lines.

17 δέοντα in Greek can mean things that are lacking or necessary.

18 ἦης is an epic form of the second-person singular imperfect of the verb 'to be'.

19 Cornelia, presumably a reference to the daughter of Scipio Africanus and mother of the Gracchi, was universally admired at Rome as a woman of the most enlightened understanding and learning, especially in philosophy. It might also possibly be alluding to Pompey's last wife, Cornelia, who was trained in geometry and philosophy.

20 The direct contrast with the ancient world is interesting as it situates this poem in a broader Renaissance drive to build on but also outdo the antiquity that was so admired.

21 Presumably the reference to 'yoking Greek and Latin' refers to the ability to switch from one ancient tongue to another and, more specifically, to be able to render Greek into Latin, an exercise that was central to the Renaissance and the Reformation. The truth of the claim is demonstrated by the poet's own switch from Latin into Greek in the preceding lines (17–18).

22 By describing the daughters as *claris*, Hoby indicates their inheritance from their father, Cooke, the epithet having been used of him in the first line.

23 *locasti = locavisti.*

24 It is probable that by 'true religion' Russell means Protestantism.

26 In Phillippy *consiliis* stands without *-que*, but it needs this in order for the line to scan.

27 *vixti = vixisti.* The reference to five years is a clear allusion to the fact that Cooke went into self-imposed exile during the Catholic Mary I's reign (1553–1558). He was, in fact, committed to the Tower of London under Mary on suspicion of complicity in the movement to put Lady Jane Grey on the throne instead of Mary. He travelled widely and returned to England upon the accession of Elizabeth I.

29 Phoebus, viz. Apollo, god of sun and light.

33 Note the mimetic placing of *vitam* in the middle of *haec inter . . . foelicia* (his life is literally 'among those happy things').

34 *coelica = caelica.*

36 *coelum = caelum.*

37 Cooke was buried in Romford, and there is still an elaborate memorial to him in St Edward the Confessor Church. It incorporates this epitaph.

7

On Writing about Britain

William Camden (1551–1623), Prefatory Letter to *Britannia*

Gesine Manuwald

Introduction

William Camden's *Britannia*, which earned him the name of the 'British Strabo', is the first detailed description of the history and geography of the whole of Britain; therefore it is an important historical source for the shape of Britain at the time and for contemporary views on the country's history, as well as a significant element in developing a national identity and a scholarly discourse about the country.

The author William Camden (1551–1623) was educated at Christ's Hospital and St Paul's School and from 1566 at Oxford University. He left Oxford for London in 1571 without a degree. In 1575 he became Second Master (or Usher) and in 1593 Headmaster of Westminster School. In 1597 he was appointed Clarenceux King of Arms. After his death Camden received a monument in Poets' Corner in Westminster Abbey in London.

Camden wrote a number of works on the political history, geography and traditions of Britain and also a Greek grammar for use in schools and Latin poems. Nowadays he is best known for *Britannia*, a comprehensive description of the topography and history of the British Isles as well as features of their inhabitants. As the title indicates, the book covers all parts of Britain: this interest in the whole of Britain might have been inspired by recent political developments, especially the Union of the Crowns, when James VI, King of Scots, became King James I of England and Ireland in 1603 (a full formal union eventually followed in 1707).

The contemporary concern for historical geography and ways of documenting it had been initiated by the Dutch, led by Abraham Ortelius. Camden had met Ortelius when the latter visited Britain in the 1570s, and the two men had extensive correspondence afterwards. A forerunner of such a description (for a different country) was Flavio Biondo's (1392–1463) *Italia illustrata* (publ. 1474); there were also German predecessors and some attempts in Britain, but not on the scale of Camden's work. Camden's *Britannia* contributed to the project of a full historical and geographical description of Europe and to improving knowledge about Britain on the Continent. It also took a stand in contemporary discussions on the relative merits of legends concerning the origin of Britain.

   Britannia was originally written in Latin and first published in 1586. Because of the volume's popularity, five further editions soon followed (1587, 1590, 1594, 1600, 1607), each with additional material. The 1607 edition (reproduced here) was fully illustrated and consisted of almost 500 leaves; it was the first to include a complete set of maps of the English counties. The first translation into English (provided as an appendix below) appeared in 1610; it included additions by Camden himself. The translator was Philemon Holland (1552–1637), a schoolmaster, physician and translator (who also translated works by Greek and Roman writers). The fact that *Britannia* (like other contemporary works first written in Latin) was translated into English soon after its appearance demonstrates its perceived importance at the time and the aim to make it available to a large domestic readership (however, as an early seventeenth-century English translation might not be an immediate help in understanding the Latin for today's readers, a modern English translation is also given here). Further editions and reprints of *Britannia* were produced at the end of the seventeenth century and again in the eighteenth and into the nineteenth centuries. Beyond Britain, the work made an impact on the Continent, with several editions of the Latin version printed there.

   Britannia gives an account of the history of the country and describes all parts of the British Isles county by county (inspired by ancient territorial divisions); it provides information on historical periods, early inhabitants, the locations of settlements, the history of place names and their equivalents in earlier periods, topographical and geographical features as well as antiquarian details. The work aims at comprehensiveness, copiousness and variety. In order to compile the information (as he indicates in the extract below), Camden travelled widely through the country to view sites and documents, read a large number of documents and descriptions, for which he even learned Welsh and Old English, and requested details from his network of correspondents. This attempt at proper research and an evidence-based approach was remarkable at the time.

   Like many early modern publications, the 1607 edition of *Britannia* came with a significant amount of paratextual material, i.e. texts about or in relation to the work: in this case the book opens with a frontispiece, a dedication to King James, a title page, a letter to the reader and various Latin poems by others before the start of the main text (similar material was included in the earlier editions). Such material offers crucial information for putting early modern books into their social, historical and intellectual contexts and for obtaining details about the publication process. In the letter to the reader (of which the beginning and end are reproduced below) Camden sets out the aim of his work and the anticipated reaction of the audience. In the early modern period letters were an important and widespread means of communication among learned men within the same country and within the so-called international 'republic of letters'. Camden wrote many letters, some of which were later collected and published. In addition, the literary genre of the letter was used separately in place of introductions, dedications or prefaces, as is the case in *Britannia*.

In this letter, adopting classical conventions, William Camden introduces his work and his achievements with mock modesty: he claims that he only embarked on this enterprise since he was prompted by Abraham Ortelius; this endeavour, he says, is a work of extreme difficulty, he only undertook it in fear, and it might be subject to envy. When he says that he trusts in his own industriousness and the support of God, he brings a contemporary Christian twist to a scholarly exercise. Camden's approach to scholarship is progressive, when he asserts that he is cautious in uncertain matters, has tried to investigate and establish by autopsy as much as he could, and provides verbatim quotations of the main sources for the sake of truth even if they have 'barbarian' elements. In a *captatio benevolentiae* directed towards potential readers Camden expresses his hope for understanding and approval from upright and discerning readers, which will inspire all readers to assign themselves to this category. The combination of moral worth and the appropriate approach to such a piece is in line with ancient notions of the role of character.

William Camden's *Britannia*, then, is both steeped in classical traditions and an important milestone in scholarly research about one's own country, aiming at a better understanding of its history through a return to its beginnings.

Bibliography

Guillén, C. (1986), 'Notes toward the Study of the Renaissance Letter', in
    B. Kiefer Lewalski (ed.), *Renaissance Genres. Essays on Theory, History, and Interpretation*, 70–101, Cambridge (MA) and London (Harvard English Studies 14).
Herendeen, W. H. (1996), 'William Camden (2 May 1551 – 9 November 1623)',
    in D. A. Richardson (ed.), *Dictionary of Literary Biography 172: Sixteenth-*

Century British Nondramatic Writers, 25–37, Detroit, Washington (DC) and London.

Herendeen, W. H. (2007), *William Camden. A Life in Context,* Woodbridge.

Levy, F. J. (1964), 'The Making of Camden's *Britannia', Bibliothèque d'Humanisme et Renaissance,* 26: 70–97.

Rockett, W. (1990), 'Historical Topography and British History in Camden's *Britannia', Renaissance and Reformation / Renaissance et Réforme,* 14: 71–80.

Rockett, W. (1995), 'The Structural Plan of Camden's *Britannia', Sixteenth Century Journal,* 26: 829–41.

Vine, A. (2014), 'Copiousness, Conjecture and Collaboration in William Camden's *Britannia', Renaissance Studies,* 28: 225–41.

Source of the Latin text

BRITANNIA, | SIVE | FLORENTISSIMORUM | REGNORUM ANGLIÆ, | SCOTIÆ, HIBERNIÆ, ET | *Inſularum adiacentium ex intima antiquitate* | Chorographica deſcriptio: | *Nunc postremò recognita, plurimis locis magna acceßione* | adaucta, & Chartis Chorographicis | *illuſtrata.* | GUILIELMO CAMDENO Authore. | LONDINI, | *Impensis* GEORGII BISHOP & | IOANNIS NORTON. M. DC. VII. (copy from Folger Shakespeare Library, available on Early English Books Online) [with some spelling conventions standardized].

Latin text

LECTORI.

Quae prima huius libri editione ante annos viginti[1] praefatus eram, eadem et iisdem verbis, pauculis adiunctis, in hac postrema editione benevolo Lectori nunc denuo praefari haudquaquam dispudet. Eximius veteris Geographiae restaurator Abrahamus Ortelius[2] ante annum tricesimum mecum pluribus egit ut BRITANNIAM nostram, antiquam illam illustrarem: hoc est, ut Britanniae antiquitatem, et suae antiquitati Britanniam restituerem,[3] ut vetustis novitatem, obscuris lucem, dubiis fidem adderem;[4] et ut veritatem in rebus nostris, quam vel scriptorum securitas, vel vulgi credulitas proscripserant, quoad fieri posset, postliminio[5] revocarem. Opus sane arduum, et plusquam difficile, in quo quantopere sit sudandum ut nemo fere sentit; sic nemo plane credit, nisi qui ipse aliquando periculum fecit.[6] A proposito tamen, quantum rei difficultas me deterruit, tantum ad id ipsum aggrediendum charissima patriae gloria excitavit. Itadum simul onus subire metui, et patriae gloria, quantum in me sit, deesse nolui, res diversissimas, timiditatem et audaciam, quae nunquam in eundem hominum cadere posse putavi, nescio quo pacto, in me coniuncta animadverti. Verumenimvero DEO auspice, comite INDVSTRIA rem aggressus omni animo, cogitatione, opera, et assidua meditatione in eandem succisivis horis totus incubui.[7] In Britanniae ETYMON[8] et primos incolas timide inquisivi, nec in re dubia quicquam asseveranter affirmavi. Gentium enim origines vetustate nimia, velut quae magno loci intervallo vix cernuntur, esse obscuras,[9] immo incertas certo novi; perinde ac magnorum fluminum noti sunt decursus, nota diverticula, noti confluentes, nota ostia,[10] fontes[11] autem ipsi plerumque latent ignoti. Britanniae divisiones antiquas pervestigavi, florentissimorum Regnorum Angliae, Scotiae, et Hiberniae[12] Ordines et Tribunalia compendio memoravi. In singulis horum regionibus qui sunt limites, (non tamen exiliter ad decempedam[13]) quae terrae dotes, quae antiquioris memoriae loca, qui Duces, qui Comites, qui Barones,[14] et quae familiae vetustiores et splendidiores (nec sane singulas, quis enim poterit?) paucis[15] percensui. Quid praestiterim dicant qui recte iudicare norunt,[16] nec illi quidem facile diiudicent. Tempus autem testis incorruptus edocebit, cum invidia quae vivos sectatur, conticescat. Hoc tamen dicam, quae ad latentem antiquitatis veritatem eruendam inprimis

Modern English translation

To the reader.

What I had said by way of preface in the first edition of this book twenty years ago,[1] to say the same and with the same words, with just a few added, now again, by way of preface, to the benevolent reader in this latest edition does not at all displease [me]. The distinguished restorer of ancient geography, Abraham Ortelius,[2] encouraged me eloquently more than thirty years ago that I should illustrate our old Britain: that is, that I should restore antiquity to Britain and Britain to its antiquity,[3] that I should give novelty to old things, light to obscure ones, trust to doubtful ones,[4] and that I should recall anew,[5] as far as possible, the truth in our matters, which the carelessness of writers or the credulity of the masses had outlawed. A hard task certainly and more than difficult because of the fact that, just as hardly anyone knows how much one will have to sweat in this, so, nobody completely believes it, unless he himself has had made trial of it on some occasion.[6] Yet, as much as the difficulty of the matter deterred me from this plan, so much the most esteemed glory of our country stirred me up to approach this very thing. Thus, while, simultaneously, I was afraid to undertake the burden and did not want to fail our country, as far as I could, I noticed very different things, fear and boldness, which I did not believe could ever fall to the same person, somehow joined in me. But in fact, with God as patron, with industry as my companion, I embraced the matter with my entire mind, thinking and effort, and with constant reflection I devoted myself entirely to that in leisure hours.[7] I enquired cautiously into the etymology[8] of Britain and the first inhabitants, and in such an uncertain matter I have not asserted anything emphatically. For I know that the origins of nations, owing to excessive antiquity, just like things that can hardly be perceived owing to a great distance in space, are obscure,[9] in fact I know for sure that they are uncertain; just as of great rivers the courses are known, the branches are known, the meeting places are known, the mouths are known,[10] but the sources[11] themselves are mostly hidden and unknown. I have explored the ancient divisions of Britain, I have recorded briefly the orders and courts of the most flourishing kingdoms of England, Scotland and Ireland.[12] In each of these regions, I have enumerated briefly[15] what the borders are (not, though, narrowly according to the measuring-rod[13]), the dowries of the soil, the places of rather ancient memory, the dukes, the earls, the barons[14] and the older and more eminent families (not, however, indeed, each individually; for who will be able to?). How I have excelled they should say who know[16] how to judge correctly, and not even they should judge readily. But time, the incorruptible witness, will inform, when envy, which pursues the living, falls quiet. This only I will say: what is

faciant,[17] a me neutiquam fuisse neglecta; subsidio mihi antiquissimae linguae Britannicae, et Anglo-Saxonicae[18] notitiam qualemcumque comparavi; Angliam fere omnem peragravi;[19] versatissimum et peritissimum quemque[20] in sua regione consului. Scriptores patrios, Graecos, Latinos qui vel semel Britanniae meminerunt, studiose evolui.[21] Publica regni Commentaria, sacra scrinia, et archiva, Bibliothecas plures, urbium et Ecclesiarum Tabularia, monumenta, et veteres schedas excussi; eaque quasi testimonia de coelo omni exceptione maiora advocavi; et certe ipsissimis quibus loquuntur verbis licet barbarie infuscatis,[22] ut Veritati suus integer constet honos, in medium, cum res postulare videretur, produxi.

...

Haec tamen interea a te, humanissime Lector, tua humanitas, mea industria, patriae communis charitas, et Britannici nominis dignitas mihi exorent, ut quid mei sit iudicii, sine aliorum praeiudicio libere proferam, ut eadem via qua alii in his studiis solent, insistam, et ut erratis,[23] si ego agnoscam, tu ignoscas. Quae ut ab aequis, et bonis magis speranda, quam petenda sentio:[24] ita iniquos, et malos, qui omnes in conviviis rodunt, in circulis vellicant,[25] invident, calumniantur, obtrectant, nihil moror. Obtrectationem enim stultorum esse thesaurum, quem in linguis gerunt, e Comico[26] didici; et Invidiam (dicam Invidia[27] adstante) non in alio, quam degeneri, minuto, et ieiuno animo domicilium sibi collocare explorate cognovi. Candida et proba ingenia ut invidiam facile contemnunt, ita ne norunt quidem invidere. Me autem et mea scripta omnia piorum et doctorum iudicio in singulis, ea qua par est reverentia, demississime submitto et subicio: quibus professione pietatis in patriam hic labor, si non approbetur, certe, ut spero, excusetur. Vale, fave, et fruere.

particularly useful for finding out the hidden truth of antiquity[17] has not been in any way neglected by me; in assistance I have obtained whatever record there is in the most ancient British and Anglo-Saxon tongue;[18] I have travelled through almost the whole of England;[19] I have consulted all the most learned and most experienced people[20] in their own region. I have eagerly read the writers in the language of our country, the Greek and the Latin ones who even just once mention Britain.[21] The public records of the realm, sacred documents and archives, several libraries, the depositories of cities and churches, documents and old charters I have examined; and I have adduced them as if testimony from heaven beyond all exception; and I have certainly put them forward, whenever the matter seemed to require it, in the very same words that they speak, even if stained with barbarity,[22] so that for Truth her due honour may stand intact.

. . .

Meanwhile, however, may your humanity, my industry, the love for our common country and the dignity of the British name ask this of you, most humane reader, for me, that I may put forward freely whatever my judgement is without a preceding judgment of others, so that in the same way in which others are accustomed to in these studies, I may press on, and that you pardon errors,[23] if I acknowledge them. Just as I feel that this is more to be hoped from just and good people than to be asked,[24] so I waste no time on unjust and bad people, who all slander at dinner parties, taunt in company, are envious, depreciate and denigrate.[25] For that disparagement is the treasure of stupid people, which they bear in their mouths, I have learned from a comic poet;[26] and that envy (I will say this with Envy[27] standing by) does not settle down anywhere else than in a degenerate, small and feeble mind I have surely experienced. As honest and upright minds easily look down upon envy, so they do not even know how to envy. But myself and all my writings I most humbly submit and subject to the judgement of pious and learned people in each instance, with the respect that is deserved: as regards these, because of [my] declaration of piety towards our country, this toil, if it is not approved, will certainly, as I hope, be excused. Farewell, be well disposed and enjoy.

Commentary

1 The first edition of *Britannia* appeared in 1586, just over twenty years before this edition, published in 1607. Among its paratextual material, the first edition also had an introductory letter addressed *Benevolo Lectori*: it indeed features some of the same phrases and motifs as this text, but the entire letter is not exactly the same.

2 Abraham Ortelius (1527–1598) was a Brabantian cartographer and geographer. He is regarded as the creator of the first modern atlas (*Theatrum Orbis Terrarum*) in 1570, which sparked great interest in cartography and geography, and he compiled a kind of dictionary of classical place names and their modern equivalents (*Synonymia geographica*) in 1578, which stimulated research into the history and etymology of countries and settlements.

3 This sophisticated rhetorical phrase (employing parallelism in structure and chiasmus in the arrangement of vocabulary) implies that this work will make Britain again aware of its history.

4 This sentence recalls the opening letter to the *Natural History* of Pliny the Elder (Plin. *HN, praef.* 15: *res ardua vetustis novitatem dare, novis auctoritatem, obsoletis nitorem, obscuris lucem, fastiditis gratiam, dubiis fidem, omnibus vero naturam et naturae suae omnia.* – 'It is a difficult matter to give novelty to old things, authority to new things, brilliance to ordinary things, light to obscure things, attraction to things despised, credibility to doubtful things, indeed nature to all things and all things to their nature.').

5 *postliminio* in post-classical Latin simply denotes 'anew'; it literally means 'return behind one's threshold'.

6 *in quo* is a connecting relative. *quantopere sit sudandum* is an indirect question (with an impersonal gerundive construction) placed before the verbs governing it, linked by *ut . . . sic* (*sentit . . . credit*).

7 When Camden claims that he has worked on *Britannia* in 'leisure hours', this is mock modesty; the work is thus presented as something less serious that can be looked at more leniently. This presentation slightly contradicts the emphasis on the amount of effort spent in compiling the evidence. Belittling one's own work as a rhetorical topos is a widespread feature in classical literature (cf. e.g. Cicero, *Orator* 1–2; Catullus 1).

8 *ETYMON* is a transliterated Greek word, meaning 'the true sense of a word according to its origin, its etymology'.

9 What Camden notes here about the obscurity of ancient material is similar to what Livy says about information on the early period described in his historical work (Liv. 6.1: *res cum vetustate nimia obscuras, velut quae magno ex intervallo loci vix cernuntur* – 'matters obscure owing to excessive antiquity, just as things that can hardly be perceived because of a great distance').

10 A tetracolon (sequence of four elements) with emphatic repetition of the first word (anaphora).

11 While *fontes* ('sources') here is an element in the illustrative simile, it may recall the phrase *ad fontes*, which is well known as a concise expression of the aim of humanism to go back to the sources and study Greek and Roman antiquity.

12 As in the title of the entire work, only England, Scotland and Ireland, but not Wales, are listed here, since Wales is covered along with England.

13 *decempeda* is a 'measuring-rod': it is thus indicated that the borders defined have not been measured out accurately.

14 *Barones* is not a classical word, and the other terms in this sequence have been adapted to express different types of British noblemen.

15 Supply *verbis* with *paucis*.

16 *norunt* is a contracted form of *noverunt*.

17 *faciant* is construed with *ad* + noun and gerundive, to express purpose.

18 The 'most ancient British and Anglo-Saxon tongue' is probably to be seen as a double expression (hendiadys) and refers to Old English.

19 The Latin verb (*peragro*) literally means 'travel through'; in a transferred sense it implies 'search through' and also a certain amount of labour.

20 Superlative + *quisque* expresses universality ('all the most . . . people').

21 Camden claims that he consulted writers from Britain as well as Greek and Roman authors, even if they only mentioned Britain once, thus indicating his thoroughness. Comments on Britain are included, for instance, in the account of the Gallic Wars by C. Iulius Caesar and in the imperial writer Tacitus' biography of his father-in-law Cn. Iulius Agricola, who was governor of Britain in the late first century CE. References can also be found in works of the Greek scholars Strabo and Ptolemy. A kind of ancient road map appears in the so-called *Antonine Itinerary* in the section *Iter Britanniarum*.

22 The phrasing here might be inspired by a passage in Cicero's *Brutus* about the use of language (Cic. *Brut.* 258: *sed omnes tum fere, qui nec extra urbem hanc vixerant neque eos aliqua barbaries domestica infuscaverat, recte loquebantur* – 'but at that time almost all who had not lived outside the city of Rome or whom some domestic barbarity had not stained spoke correctly').

23 *ignoscere* takes the dative: this is supplied by *erratis*, used as a noun.

24 *sentio* governs a gerundive construction in the infinitive (with *esse* not expressed); the neuter plural gerundives agree with *quae*.

25 The phrase is taken from Cicero's speech *Pro Balbo* (Cic. *Balb.* 57: *more hominum invident, in conviviis rodunt, in circulis vellicant ...* – 'As people usually do, they display envy, they slander at dinner parties, they taunt in company ..').

26 The quotation (equally without precise attribution) also appears in John Owen (see Text 9).

27 A description of personified Invidia can be found in Ovid's *Metamorphoses* (Ov. *Met.* 2.760–82). In the early modern period Envy was among the seven deadly sins, particularly important in Catholic doctrine, but referred to frequently in contemporary art and literature.

Appendix: contemporary English translation

BRITAIN, | Or | A CHOROGRAPHICALL | DESCRIPTION OF THE MOST | flouriſhing Kingdomes, ENGLAND, | SCOTLAND, and IRELAND, and the | *Ilands adioyning, out of the depth of* | ANTIQUITIE: | BEAVTIFIED WITH MAPPES OF THE | *ſeverall Shires of* ENGLAND: | Written firſt in Latine by *William Camden* | CLARENCEUX K. of A. | Translated newly into Engliſh by *Philémon Holland* | Doctour in Physick: | Finally, reviſed, amended, and enlarged with ſundry | Additions by the ſaid Author. | LONDINI, | *Impensis* GEORGII BISHOP | & IOANNIS NORTON. | M. DC. X. [copy from Yale University Library, available on Early English Books Online]

The Author to the Reader.

I Hope it shall be to no discredite, if I now use againe by way of Praeface, the same words with a few more, that I used twenty foure yeares since in the first edition of this worke.[1] Abraham Ortelius the worthy restorer of Ancient Geographie[2] arriving heere in England, above thirty foure years past, dealt earnestly with me that I would illustrate this I'e of BRITAINE, or (as he said) that I would restore antiquity to Britaine, and Britain to his antiquity; which was as I understood, that I would renew ancientrie, enlighten obscuritie, cleare doubts, and recall home Veritie by way of recovery, which the negligence of writers and credulitie of the common sort had in a manner proscribed and utterly banished from amongst us. A painfull matter I assure you, and more than difficult; wherein what toyle is to be taken, as no man thinketh, so no man beleeveth but hee that hath made the triall. Neverthelesse how much the difficultie discouraged me from it, so much the glory of my country encouraged me to undertake it. So while at one and the same time I was fearefull to undergoe the burden, and yet desirous to doe some service to my Country, I found two different affections Feare, and Boldness; I knowe not how, conioined in me. Notwithstanding by the most gratious direction of the ALMIGHTY, taking INDVSTRIE for my consort, I adventured upon it, and with all my studie, care, cogitation, continuall meditation, paine, & travaile I emploied my selfe thereunto when I had any spare time.[7] I made search after the Etymologie of Britaine and the first inhabitants timerously, neither in so doubtfull a matter have I affirmed ought confidently. For I am not ignorant that the first originalls of nations are obscure by reason of their profound antiquitie, as things which are seene very deepe and farre remote:[9] like as the courses, the reaches, the confluents, and the out-lets of great rivers are well knowne, yet their first fountaines and heads lie commonly unknowne. I have succinctly runne over the Romans government in Britaine, and the inundation of forraine people thereinto, what they were, and from whence they came: I have traced out the ancient divisions of these Kingdomes,[12] I have summarily specified the states, and iudiciall Courts of the same.

In the severall Counties I have compendiously set downe the limites (and yet not exactly by pearch and pole to breed questions) what is the nature of the soile, which were the places of greatest antiquitie, who have beene the Dukes, Marquesses, Earles, Vicounts, Barons,[14] and some of the most signall, and ancient families therein (for who can particulate all?) What I have performed, I have to men of judgment. But time the most sound & sincere witnesse will give the truest information, when envie which persecuseth the living, shall have her mouth stopped. Thus much give mee leave to say, that I have in no wise neglected such things as are most materiall to search, and sift out the Truth. I have attained to some skill of the most ancient, British and English-Saxon tongues:[18] I have travailed over all England for the most part, I have conferred with most skillfull observers in each country, I haue studiously read over our owne countrie writers, old and new; all Greeke and Latine authors which have once made mention of Britaine.[21] I have had conference with learned men in other parts of Christendome: I have beene diligent in the Records of this Realme. I have looked into most Libraries,

Registers, and memorials of Churches, Cities, and Corporations, I have poored upon many an old Rowle, and Evidence: and produced their testimonie (as beyond all exception) when the cause required, in their very owne words (although barbarous they be) that the honor of veritie might in no wise be impeached.

...

Meanwhile let your kinde courtesie, my industry, the common love of our common mother our native Country, the ancient honour of the British name obtaine so much upon their entreaty, that I may utter my judgment without prejudice to others, that I may proceed in that course that others have formerly done in the like argument, and that you would pardon my errours upon my acknowledgement, which may be aswell hoped as requested, from good indiffrent and reasonable men; so I passe not for the unresonable, and worser sort which gnaw upon all at tables, carpe in conventicles, envy, backbite, sclaunder, and detract. For I have learned of the Comicall Poet,[26] that sclaunder is the treasure of fooles which they carry in their tongues, & I know for certainty that Envy is seated (I will say it although Envy[27] stood at my elbow) in none but in degenerous, unnoble, and base mindes. The honest good and noble natures as they detest envy, so they cannot envy. As for my selfe, and this worke, I doe most humbly submit it to the censure of the godly honest and learned with all respective reverence of whom if it be not approved, I hope in regard of my professed loue to our native Country, that it may be excused. Farwell.

8

A Birthday Poem for Christ

Adam King (*c.* 1560–1620), *Genethliacon Iesu Christi* (*c.* 1586)

David McOmish

Introduction

The *Genethliacon Iesu Christi* (or '*Poem on the Day of Christ's Birth*'; henceforth abbreviated to *GIC*) is the first part of a three-poem cycle on the life of Christ that deals with his life, passion and resurrection. It was written by Adam King (born *c.* 1560; died 10 August 1620), the son of an Edinburgh lawyer. From 1580 until 1595 King had a distinguished academic career at the University of Paris, where he was professor of mathematics and philosophy at the Collège de Lisieux, Procurator of the German Nation (twice) and leading candidate for Rector of the whole university (1589).

Two variants of *GIC* are extant, neither of which provides a date for its composition. A printed version was produced in 1637 as part of the Neo-Latin anthology *Delitiae Poetarum Scotorum*. The other copy is in a manuscript that contains Adam King's entire poetic corpus (University of Edinburgh Centre for Research Collections: shelfmark Dk.7.29). It was owned by William King, Adam's nephew, a regent/lecturer at the University of Edinburgh. Bound in with King's poetic corpus is a large cosmological commentary on George Buchanan's poem *De sphaera* (see Text 3), written by King after his return to Scotland from France in 1595. It sets out in detail the content and outline of his intellectual and pedagogical approach to the science and philosophies of Nicolaus Copernicus, Tycho Brahe, Christoph Clavius, Johannes Kepler and Galileo Galilei, among many others.

This commentary was taught to and memorized by generations of students at the University of Edinburgh. King's commentary is thus significant for our understanding of the development of modern science and philosophy in Scotland. As a commentary on poetry, it also provides evidence of the important role poetry played in approaches to the new sciences within formal education in Edinburgh in the period immediately before the city and its university became one of the centres of the Enlightenment in Europe.

The evidence from the dateable poems contained in the manuscript suggests chronological arrangement and a date for the *GIC* of the mid-1580s. Internal evidence from the poem also strongly suggests this timeframe. The opening of the *GIC* contained in this edition addresses two topics that were particularly pressing at this time in Scotland and Europe: the Reformation and the new sciences. The religious context is apparent in King's manipulation of one of his primary literary inspirations: the *De sphaera* of the Scottish educationalist and writer George Buchanan (see Text 3). Throughout the opening section King recalibrates Buchanan's text to emphasize the specifically Christian and Catholic nature of the god who created the universe (lines 7–10), and to encourage the reader to venerate this god in the time-honoured fashion, on formalized and sanctified feast days (lines 5–6). From 1583 onwards, Calvinists in Scotland were actively trying to ban the observance of Christmas (especially) and other 'papist' festivals. In the period between 1584 and 1588 King produced some vernacular work (catechismal and calendrical) dealing with the observance of the sacraments and holy days; *GIC* should be viewed as part of his Counter-Reformation activities.

The second topic addressed in *GIC* is that of the new sciences of the late sixteenth and early seventeenth centuries. We have few details of what King taught while in Paris for over a decade. The circumstantial evidence suggests that the scepticism and anti-authority approaches of sixteenth-century Parisian intellectual culture would have been part of it. Petrus Ramus, the educational reformer, was one of the most active anti-Aristotelians in Paris, and he advocated the use of Copernicus in schools to undermine the authority of Aristotle, even while retaining a sceptical view of Copernicus. Despite Ramus' fame as a Protestant martyr, King, a professed Catholic, described himself as a 'Ramist' professor of mathematics, aligning his scientific and philosophical approach to that of Ramus. The Collège de Lisieux, King's place of work, was the first college in Paris to teach Ptolemy and Copernicus side by side. However, rejection of authority was not confined to the Ramists at this time in Paris, as a more pointed and comprehensive sceptical approach was practised by the so-called Pyrrhonists (named after a work by Sextus Empiricus, whose texts were keenly read by Parisian sceptics, including King). *GIC* shows that King had begun to accept at an early stage some of the new ideas and approaches, such as the rejection of Aristotelian cosmology and celestial spheres (lines 11–13) and scepticism towards the doctrine of terrestrial immovability (lines 45–50), which he would later set down in more detail in his commentary, especially in relation to the observations of Tycho Brahe, Christoph Clavius and William Gilbert.

Metre: dactylic hexameter

Bibliography

Durkan, J. (2001), 'Adam King: A Church Papist', *The Innes Review*, 52: 195–9.

Green, R. P. H. (ed. and trans.) (2011), *George Buchanan: Poetic Paraphrase of the Psalms of David*, Geneva.

Lattis, J. M. (1994), *Between Copernicus and Galileo: Christoph Clavius and the Collapse of Ptolemaic Cosmology*, Chicago.

McOmish, D. (2018), 'The Scientific Revolution in Scotland Revisited: The New Sciences in Edinburgh', *History of Universities*, 31.2: 153–72.

McOmish, D. (forthcoming), 'Windows on the World: The Literary Revolutions of Adam King's *Genethliacon*', in E. Tarantino, C. Burrow, S. Harrison and M. McLaughlin (eds), *Literary Windows: Imitative Series and Clusters from Classical to Early Modern Literature*, Oxford.

Naiden, J. (1952), *The Sphera of George Buchanan (1506–1582): A Literary Opponent of Copernicus and Tycho Brahe*, Washington.

Ruddiman, T. (ed.) (1725), *Georgii Buchanani opera omnia*, Vol. 2, Lyon [427–535].

Scot of Scotstarvit, J. (ed.) (1637), *Delitiae Poetarum Scotorum*, Vol. 2, Amsterdam [236–54].

Source of the Latin text

The text of *GIC* given here is a reproduction of the text in the Edinburgh manuscript (University of Edinburgh Centre for Research Collections: shelfmark Dk.7.29).

Latin text

Adami Regii Genethliacon Iesu Christi

Eia age qui puros caeli revolubilis ignes
aspicis immenso diffundere lumina mundo,
partirique vices rerum: iam lucida certus
sidera moliri nutu, terrasque iacentes
5 munificum curare deum: lux ista quotannis
dum recolit pura natum de virgine numen;
agnoscas quibus officiis, quantoque favore,
humano indulsit generi Deus ille salutem:
quaque tuos largus dextra providit in usus
10 omnia quae fecit: nitidi tibi flammea caeli
moenia, et immensi radiatos aetheris orbes
immunes senii, cursusque tenore sub uno
aeternos, certis accendere legibus ignes
iussit, perque vices caeca ferrugine vultus
15 induere, obductaque tegi telluris ab umbra.
Ille tibi propriis genitalia semina rerum
disposuit foecunda locis: sine pondere flammis
ire sub astra dedit: niveo quas aurea phoebe
ambiret complexa sinu, celerique per orbem
20 raptaret gyro: tenues his aeris auras
supposuit; mediique leves per inania mundi
explicuit: vasto demum stagnata profundo
aequora, quae solidam sinuato gurgite terram
alluerent; iam prona sua gravitate deorsum
25 impulerat: terraeque parem glomerasset in orbem;
humanae nisi gentis amor, iussisset in altum
tollere se clivos; summorumque ardua montum
praerupto late latera exhorrescere dorso:
submissasque premi valles, stagnare lacunis
30 Nerea, praescriptis et plangere littora metis.
    Tunc et iussa suo tellus proferre colono
munera: ut humanus quaecunque exposceret usus,
divite proventu, et magno cum foenore rerum
sufficeret: sobolemque aeterna lege propaget.

English translation

Come now, you who see that the uncorrupted fires of the turning heavens spread out their light through the vast universe, and that they apportion changes across the world: now you see clearly that a generous god controls the bright stars by his will, and that he manages the lands below. And when   5
that annual day brings again to our mind the divinity born of a pure virgin, may you acknowledge with what duty and how much good-will *that* God granted salvation to the human race, and with what a hand he generously gave for your employment all that he made. He ordered that fires light up in   10
fixed laws the fiery walls of glittering heaven for you, and the radiant globes of the vast firmament, which are immune to decay, and their eternal courses under his control alone; and by turns that they cover their faces in the   15
sightless dark and lie hidden from the enveloping shadow of the earth. For you he has distributed the fertile life-giving seeds of the universe in their most fitting places: he made the flames without weight travel beneath the stars, for golden Phoebe to envelop them after clasping them to her snowy bosom, and to seize them in a swift orbit around her globe. And he set thin   20
breezes of air under these, and he spread out the light air through the empty space of the middle zone of the world; then the seas flowed out from the vast depths, to lap upon the solid earth in billowing torrent, after he had struck them downwards with their own sinking force: and he would have gathered   25
them into a sphere covering the earth, if his love for the human race had not demanded that the hills rise up towards the heights, and the steep sides of the highest mountains menace far and wide with their overhanging ridge, that the low-lying valleys sink down, that the sea be checked by chasms, and that   30
it strike the shores in predetermined boundaries.

Then the earth too was ordered to furnish gifts for its own inhabitants, so that human employment might seek out everything, and to supply them with its rich produce and the great profit of its materials, and by eternal law

35 Nec minus ambitas circum amplectentia terras
    aequora squammigeras per regna liquentia gentes
    didere iussa; suas nunc se cumulante profundo
    paulatim viduis undas subducere arenis:
    nunc laxo diffusa sinu, lateque refractis
40 obiicibus vasto sua littora plangere fluctu:
    dum nova pallentes sine lumine Delia vultus
    induit; aut tenui fingit sibi cornua flamma,
    atque iterum in plenum consumptis cornibus orbem,
    candenti tacitas despectat imagine terras:
45 iussaque phoebaeis facibus glomerata sub auras
    nubila, nunc sylvis lapidosa grandine frondes
    decutere; atque altos niveo sub vellere montes
    sternere; nunc pluviis sitientes imbribus agros,
    squalentesque situ tristi, siccumque fluentes
50 in cinerem vincire; levique aspergere rore.
    Unde Ceres nostros sese genialis ad usus
    induat in florem; et gravibus flavescat aristis:
    unde tepescentes assurgat odora sub auras
    herba; nemus viridi pubescat fronde; racemis
55 luxuriet tumidis vitis foecunda: pecusque
    tondeat herbosi pratis nova gramina foeni.

produce offspring. Moreover, the seas, which embrace all around the 35
surrounded land, were ordered to distribute the scaly race throughout their
watery kingdoms, and now, with their deep piled up upon itself, to withdraw
their waves little by little from the empty sands, and now, spread out along the
wide bay, and with sea walls smashed far and wide, to strike their own shores 40
with mighty wave, as the new Moon dons a waning front without light, or
fashions crescent horns for herself with a slender flame; and with her crescent
again having given way to a full globe, she looks down upon the silent earth
with a shining appearance. And the clouds, gathered together in the 45
atmosphere by Phoebus' flames, were now ordered to strike down upon the
foliage of the forests with hailstones, and to cover the high mountains beneath
a snowy fleece, then also to shower with their light moisture the fields
thirsting for a rainy downpour, and to surround and care for those fields that
lie untilled in sad neglect, and flow away into dry ashes. Through this process, 50
may fertile Ceres cover herself in flower for our enjoyment, and may she turn
yellow with plump ears of corn; and through this process, may fragrant grass
rise up under the warming atmosphere, may the forest be covered with green
leaves, may the fruitful vine abound in swollen grapes, and may the cattle 55
pluck fresh grass from the meadows of a grassy hayfield.

Commentary

1–2 These two opening lines are closely related to lines 9–10 and provide a frame to a 10-line poetic exordium, setting out the poem's philosophical intention: a vision of the universe as evidence of God's design. King's chief literary and intellectual inspiration for this 'frame' is Manilius, *Astronomica* 2.23–4: *omniaque immenso volitantia lumina mundo,* | *pacis opus, magnos naturae condit in usus* ('and all the lights flying across the immense universe, a structure of harmony, he created for nature's great uses'). For King, the changes described in line 2 are cosmic and terrestrial variation, from the seasonal on earth (cycles of weather and life and birth) to material degradation and mutation more generally. See also the notes to the opening lines of Buchanan, *De sphaera* (Text 3).

3 *certus*: subject continued from previous clause.

5–10 *dum recolit . . . agnoscas . . . in usus*: King appropriates the structure and terminology from the introduction to Buchanan, *De sphaera* 1.8–15 (*dum . . . reseramus . . . agnoscat . . . ad usus*), which itself is indebted to Manilius, *Astronomica* 2.23–4 (especially *De sphaera* 1.9 and 1.15). For a detailed discussion of the textual and philosophical interplay between King, Manilius and Buchanan, see McOmish: forthcoming.

6 *pura natum de virgine numen*: This line and the following description of the sacrifice of the divinity in lines 7–8 represent a recognizable departure from the literary and intellectual influence of Buchanan and Manilius. The language here is liturgical, closely following the Eucharistic hymn 'Ave Verum Corpus' (*Ave verum corpus, natum de Maria virgine*). During the same period in which King composed this poem, he also made a Scots translation of Peter Canusius' Catholic Catechism in 1588. Fifteen pages of King's edition were used to assert the specific theological and ceremonial importance of the Eucharist and the observance of the feast day of the birth of Christ (Christmas), which Calvinists in Scotland were actively seeking to ban at this time: McOmish: forthcoming.

8 *humano indulsit generi Deus ille salutem*: It is no oversight or mistake that the King manuscript (and not the 1637 edition) moves from the lower case of god (*deum*) at line 5 to the upper-case God (*Deus*) here. Line 5 is directing the reader to the conclusion that, upon looking at the universe, one must conclude (*pace* Lucretius, *De rerum natura* 1.1021; 5.419) that *some* god is responsible for it. Here, King is fine-tuning Ovid's conclusion that some god is responsible for it: *quisquis fuit ille deorum* ('whichever of the gods it was': Ovid, *Metamorphoses* 1.33). However, he is also engaging with Buchanan, *De* *sphaera* 1.70–1: *Scilicet humano generi pater optimus olim | prospiciens ...* ('Clearly the greatest parent, in his care for the human race ...'). King is subsuming Ovid's and Buchanan's generic god and his activities into a specific definition and promotion of *the* Christian God.

10–11 *nitidi tibi flammea caeli | moenia*: cf. Lucretius 1.73 (and by extension 5.450). However, as in his use of Manilius above (1–2; 9–10), King is moving between Buchanan's text and what King sees to be Buchanan's own sources: firstly, Buchanan's full appropriation of Lucretius at *De sphaera* 1.11 and 1.74 (*flammantia moenia mundi*, 'the flaming walls of the universe'), and secondly line 1.40 (*nitidi sublimis regia caeli*, 'the sublime palace of bright heaven').

11–13 These lines, which are otherwise a fairly close paraphrase of Buchanan, *De sphaera* 1.40–2, highlight again (see 6 n.) how King uses Buchanan's text to articulate a markedly divergent philosophical position. King has changed the incorruptibility (*immunis senii*) of the heavens (*regia*) found in Buchanan, which is Buchanan's rejection of the confluence of terrestrial and celestial elements (*pace* Lucretius 5.490–4). Instead, King presents the incorruptibility (*immunes senii*) as an aspect of the matter of individual celestial bodies, in this case the Sun and Moon in the firmament (*radiatos ... orbes* – language Buchanan uses for planetary bodies at *De sphaera* 1.33). A very important change, which highlights how early Adam King had begun to accept one of the central ideas of the new sciences: the corruptibility of the heavens above the moon – no change could happen in the traditional cosmological models of Aristotle and Ptolemy. The findings of Christoph Clavius and Tycho Brahe, published independently of each other, on the comets that appeared in the sky in 1572 and 1577 led to King's rejection of Aristotle and Ptolemy (see Lattis 1994: 147–50). King explicitly cites the data of Brahe and Clavius in his prose commentary of the early seventeenth century, when explaining his decision to reject the unchanging and solid celestial spheres (King MS, fols 39^v–40^r). See McOmish 2018 and forthcoming.

14–15 ... *ferrugine vultus | induere, obductaque tegi telluris ab umbra*: see Buchanan, *De sphaera* 1.112–13: *ferrugine vultus | induit, oppositae in medio telluris ab umbra* ('[the moon] bears a face of red-hue from the shadow of the earth that sits between sun and moon'). King's version emphasizes the subjection of eclipses to divine law, while in Buchanan the emphasis is on the curvature of the shadow of the earth as proof of its sphericity. See Naiden 1952: 96.

16–17 *genitalia semina rerum | disposuit foecunda locis*: King uses the terminology of Buchanan, *Psalms* 104.30–1: *foecundaque rerum | semina* ('the fertile seeds of the universe'; King reuses this passage from *Psalm* 104 again at lines 50–1). Both *Psalms* 104.30–1 and *De sphaera* 1.49 are Buchanan's own refashioning of Ovid, *Metamorphoses* 1.419, and knowing rejection of Lucretius 1.58–9 via Ovid, *Metamorphoses* 15.239, respectively. The *semina rerum* of both Buchanan and Ovid reflect the Stoic reworking of Lucretius' Epicurean atoms (*semina rerum*) into the four elements of fire, air, water and earth. Interestingly, King here (and indeed throughout his poetry) never explicitly states that there are four elements, as Buchanan does (*quattuor ... genitalia corpora*, 'the four generative bodies': *De sphaera* 1.49), even though, as here, he speaks of fire, air, water and earth as key generative bodies. King's reticence may be due to his intimate familiarity with the work of the many early modern intellectuals who were sceptical about the doctrine of the four elements as traditionally conceived, especially Tycho Brahe, Girolamo Cardano, Johannes Pena, Christoph Rothmann and Johannes Kepler (King MS, fol. 4ʳ).

propriis ... | disposuit ... locis: Compare Buchanan, *De sphaera* 1.53: *disposuere locis* ('[lightness and heaviness] put [the four elements] in their proper places'). The emphasis in King's text is upon the loving Christian God providentially placing the generative seeds in their places; in Buchanan, the physical mechanics play a more prominent role.

17–25 These lines present a particularly concentrated example of Adam King's awareness of Buchanan's literary and philosophical inspiration. King's primary point of reference is Buchanan, *De sphaera* 1.49–69. However, the content, form and structure of Buchanan's text is found in Ovid, *Metamorphoses* 1.26–35 and 15.239–51, and Manilius, *Astronomica* 1.149–70 (cf. Buchanan, *De sphaera* 1.51, and Manilius, *Astronomica* 1.149). King includes two knowing references to the Ovid and Manilius passages, at lines 20–1 and 24–5. Firstly, 20–1, *tenues his aeris auras | supposuit; mediique leves per inania mundi*, references Manilius, *Astronomica* 1.152–3: *in tenuis descendit spiritus auras | aeraque extendit medium per inania mundi* ('air became thin breezes and spread out through the empty space of the middle zone of the world'); and 24–5 reimagines *De sphaera* 1.54–5 with specific diction from Ovid, *Metamorphoses* 1.30–1.

17 King's treatment of comets, his *sine pondere flammis* at the end of this line, represents another subtle deviation from Buchanan's natural philosophy. Buchanan, *De sphaera* 1.48–51 is King's point of reference, where Buchanan explicitly places the light flames (comets) in the sublunary universe (see 11–13 n.). Although King subjects the comets to the moon's general sphere of influence (necessary for a pre-Newtonian physical explanation of impetus to

motion), they are not explicitly sublunar; their only stated area of activity is beneath the stars (*sub astra*).

26–9 *humanae nisi gentis amor, iussisset in altum | tollere se clivos; summorumque ardua montum | praerupto late latera exhorrescere dorso: | submissasque premi valles*: King's text closely follows Buchanan, *De sphaera* 1.66–9: *nisi cura Dei se attollere montes | iussisset, vallesque premi* ... ('had not the love of God ordered that the mountains rise, and the valleys sink down ...'). Buchanan's own text is a condensed, streamlined presentation of providential intervention found in Ovid, *Metamorphoses* 1.33–48.

30 *Nerea*: third declension Greek accusative form of Nereus, sea god, here used as metonymy for the sea.

praescriptis et plangere littora metis: King shows his awareness that Buchanan, *De sphaera* 1.66–9, is not the first time Buchanan has reworked Ovid, *Metamorphoses* 1.33–48. King takes this line from Buchanan, *Psalms* 104.20– 1: *limitibus compressa suis resonantia plangit | litora, praescriptas metuens transcendere metas* ('contained within their boundaries, [the waters] struck the resounding shores, fearing to go beyond their prescribed limits').

31–9 Following on from the switch from cosmological to religious poetry in line 30, King's poetic point of reference now firmly moves to Buchanan's *Psalms*. These lines are a close paraphrase (and, at times, literal appropriation) of Buchanan, *Psalms* 104.56–61: *Nec tantum tellus, genitor, tua munera sentit, | tam variis fecunda bonis, sed et aequora ponti | fluctibus immensas circumplectentia terras, | tam laxo spatiosa sinu. Tot milia gentis | squamigerae tremula per stagna liquentia cauda | exsultant* ... ('And not only does the earth, father, so fertile with a diversity of good things, receive your gifts, but also the waters of the sea, extending vast with broad embrace, that encircle immense swathes of earth with their waves. So many thousand members of the scaly tribe with quivering tails rejoice in the clear seas ...', trans. R. P. H. Green 2011).

41–4 Paraphrase of Buchanan, *Psalms* 104.43–7, in which Buchanan articulates the phases of the moon. Although King re-employs some of Buchanan's diction (e.g. *tacitas ... terras*), his description of the phases is more detailed (new moon) and defined (waxing to full) than Buchanan's.

41 *Delia* is Diana, the virgin huntress and moon-goddess, who was said to have been born with her brother Apollo on the island of Delos (hence 'Delian'). She is here presented metonymically as the Moon.

45–50 King takes his core poetic inspiration from Buchanan, *De sphaera* 1.297–9: *Nube polus densa latet obrutus, humida molles | vis abit in pluvias, aut grandine ruris honorem* | *decutit, aut operit, niveo ceu vellere montes* ('The heavens lie hidden, obscured by thick cloud, whose watery force falls down in gentle rain, or strikes down in hail upon the beauty of the countryside, or conceals the mountains, as if under a snowy fleece'). King refashions these lines to present the reader with a picture of the phases of the water cycle, which eshews the core intellectual point of Buchanan's text – terrestrial immovability (*pace* Copernicus and others).

52 Another interesting example of King moving between Buchanan and his sources. Here King takes the language and image directly from Buchanan, *De sphaera* 3.518. However, King was aware of Buchanan's own source for the phrase and faithfully reproduces Virgil, *Eclogues* 4.28, in his supplement to Buchanan, *De sphaera*: *Supplementum Sphaerae Buchanani* 4.566.

55–6 Proleptical use of *foeni* ('hay'), denoting the intended use of the field for hay production, but rendered with the seemingly paradoxical adjective *herbosi* ('grassy', 'still-green') to emphasize the freshness of the still-living pasture. The apparent incongruity of *herbosi . . . foeni* perhaps contributed to the decision of the editor of the *Delitiae Poetarum Scotorum* to replace *herbosi* with *auricomi* ('golden-haired') in that edition (vol. 2, p. 202); *herbosis* would have been an easier change.

9

On Poetry, Politics and Religion

John Owen (1560?–1622), Selection of Epigrams

Gesine Manuwald

Introduction

John Owen is known for his large collection of witty and poignant Latin epigrams, which he started to write from an early age. Because of their similarity to the output of the Roman imperial poet Martial, European contemporaries called him the 'British Martial'.

Owen was born at Plas Du, Llanarmon (near Snowdon in Wales); he studied first at Winchester College and then at New College, Oxford. He was a fellow of New College from 1584/5 to 1591, graduating as a bachelor of law in 1590; afterwards he became a schoolmaster at Trellech (near Monmouth) and then at King Henry VIII School at Warwick, though he seems later to have lived in London, supported by wealthy patrons. He was a supporter of Protestantism (with his works even put on the Catholic *Index librorum prohibitorum*) and the Tudor monarchy (which had Welsh roots). Owen was buried in the old St Paul's Cathedral in London.

Owen's Latin epigrams now consist of twelve books; they were published in several instalments of small groups of books from 1606 onwards, so that originally there were several books bearing the number one until they were numbered consecutively in later editions (reprinted frequently in Britain and on the Continent). Nowadays there are twelve books numbered continuously (containing about 1,500 poems), though Book 11 is probably spurious and Book 12 consists of fragments. For the excerpts given below early editions have been used; therefore, book numbers have been given in both the consecutive and the individual numbering (the latter in brackets). The first three books reproduce the poems that Owen wrote as a student. The various books, as well as some of the poems, are dedicated to a range of members of the nobility, political figures, friends and acquaintances. Owen's epigrams were soon translated into a number of European languages, besides English; the most complete near-contemporary translation into English is Thomas Harvey's *The*

Latine Epigrams of John Owen (1677). In turn, Owen was influenced by continental writers such as Desiderius Erasmus of Rotterdam (1466–1536), Joseph Justus Scaliger (1540–1609) and Justus Lipsius (1547–1606).

The literary genre of epigrams (understood as a short poem in elegiac distichs, often making a pun) was becoming popular in the early modern period; contemporaries in Britain also turned to epigrams in English and Latin, including Thomas Campion (1567–1620) and Charles Fitzgeoffrey (*c.* 1576–1638).

Most of John Owen's epigrams consist of one or two couplets, with a few slightly longer ones (950 consist of a single couplet only), and are marked by thematic variety; they frequently make use of puns, rhymes, anagrams and name-play; the poet sometimes adds footnotes to explain allusions. The selection of Owen's epigrams presented here, put together from the different collections, illustrates a number of characteristic themes and stylistic features of his poems. Between them, these epigrams cover the following topics: comments on politics with a focus on the kings and the union of Britain (3.4; 3.202; 3.204; 5[1].58; 9[2].16); notes on famous contemporaries (2.38; 3.4; 5[1].58; 9[2].50); critical notes on religious matters (6[2].18); literary statements (2.179); witty play with different languages and the use of puns (1.48; 9[2].16; 9[2].67); play with famous lines from ancient poetry and concepts from the ancient world (1.48; 2.38).

Bibliography

Doelman, J. (2016), *The Epigram in England, 1590–1640*, Oxford.

Durand, S. (ed.) (2016), *John Owen, Épigrammes / Epigrammata. 1606–1612. Édition, introduction, traduction et notes*, Paris (Les classiques de l'Humanisme 46).

Harries, B. (2004), 'John Owen the Epigrammatist: A Literary and Historical Context', *Renaissance Studies*, 18: 19–32.

Jansen, J. (2009), 'The Microcosmos of the Baroque Epigram: John Owen and Julien Waudré', in S. de Beer, K. A. E. Enenkel and D. Rijser (eds), *The Neo-Latin Epigram. A Learned and Witty Genre*, 275–99, Leuven (Suppl. Humanistica Lovaniensia XXV).

Martyn, J. R. C. (ed.) (1976 /1978), *Ioannis Audoeni Epigrammatum. Vol. I: libri I–III / Vol. II: libri IV–X*, Leiden (Textus minores in usum academicum XLIX / LII).

Martyn, J. R. C. (1979), 'John Owen and Tudor Patronage. A Prosopographical Analysis of Owen's Epigrams', *Humanistica Lovaniensia*, 28: 250–7.

Sources of the Latin text

Books 1–3: EPIGRAMMA- | *TVM LIBRI* | TRES. | Autore Ioanne Owen Bri- | tanno. Noui Collegii | Oxonienſis nuper | Socio. | Londini. | Apud *Ioannem*

Windet, Sumptibus | *Simonis Watersonii.* | 1606. [copy from Harvard University Library, available on Early English Books Online] Books 5(1) and 6(2): *Epigrammatum* | IOANNIS | OWEN OXONI- | ENSIS, CAMBRO- | *BRITANNI, LIBRI* | *TRES.* | *AD HENRICUM PRINCI-* | *PEM CAMBRIÆ DVO.* | *AD CAROLVM EBORA-* | *CENSEM UNVS.* | *Editio prima.* | LONDINI. | Ex officina Nicolai de Quercubus; Sumti- | bus Simonis Waterſon. 1612. [copy from Bodleian Library, available on Early English Books Online] Book 9(2): *Epigrammatum* | IOANNIS | OWEN | CAMBRO-BRITANNI, | *OXONIENSIS,* | Collegij B. MARIÆ, (quod vulgò | NOVUM *vocant) nuper Socij,* | Quæ hactenus prodierunt. | *Libri Decem.* | Editio quarta LONDINENSIS. | Ex officina Nicolai de Quercubus, | ſumtibus S. Waterſon. | 1612. [copy from Folger Shakespeare Library, available on Early English Books Online]

Latin text

1.48: *Ad Philopatrum*
Pro patria sit dulce mori licet, atque decorum,
  Vivere pro patria dulcius esse puto.

2.38: *Franciscus Drakus*
Drake pererrati novit quem terminus orbis,
  Quemque semel mundi vidit utrumque latus.
Si taceant homines, facient te sidera notum,
  Atque Polus de te discet uterque loqui,
5 Plus ultra Herculeis inscribas, Drake, columnis,
  Et magno, dicas, Hercule maior ego.

2.179: *Epigramma. Satyra*
Nil aliud Satyrae quam sunt Epigrammata longa,
  Est praeter Satyram nil Epigramma brevem,
Nil Satyrae, si non sapiant Epigrammata, pungunt;
  Ni Satyram sapiat nil Epigramma iuvat.

3.4: *Elizabethae nuper Anglorum Reginae-virginis Partus*
Scotia nobiscum gentem concrescit in unam.
  Iste tuae Partus Virginitatis erat.
Est unire magis, quam multiplicare, beatum;
  Tuque magis foelix non pariendo Parens.

3.202: *In eosdem*
Ergo novam in cineres voluistis vertere Troiam,
  Periuri fato quo periere Phryges?
Non fuit infando lux Martis idonea fato,
  Mercurii cinerum nam solet esse Dies.

3.204: *Ad Angliam de Unione Britannica*
Interna aeterna Britones iam pace fruemur,
  Ternus enim populus qui fuit, unus erit.
Wallia cui vallum contingit, Scotia scutum,
  Anglia, securam iam licet esse tibi.

English translation

To a lover of their country
To die for one's country may be sweet and glorious,
    But living for one's country, I believe, is sweeter.

Francis Drake
Drake, whom the end of the traversed world knows
    and whom both sides of the world have seen once.
If people are silent, the stars will make you well known,
    and both poles will learn to talk about you,
You, Drake, may inscribe 'further beyond' on the Pillars of Hercules,   5
    and you may say 'I am greater than great Hercules'.

Epigram, Satire
Satires are nothing other than long epigrams,
    an epigram is nothing other than a short satire;
satires, if they do not have smack of epigrams, do not prick;
    if an epigram does not smack of a satire, it has no point.

The giving-birth of Elizabeth, lately virgin-queen of the English
Scotland is growing together with us into a single nation.
    This was the offspring of your virginity.
To unite is a more blessed action than to multiply;
    And you are a happier parent by not giving birth.

On the same
Did you then want to turn the new Troy into ashes,
    you perjurers, by the calamity by which the Phrygians perished?
The light [i.e. day] of Mars was not suitable for the abominable calamity,
    for the day of Mercury is usually that of ashes.

To England on the British union
We, the British people, will now enjoy eternal internal peace,
    for what was a threefold nation, will be one.
You, whom Wales, the rampart, touches, and Scotland, the shield,
    you, England, it is now possible for you to be free from danger.

5(1).58: *Ad Iacobum regem doctiss.*
Esse *bonum*, res est, me iudice, rara poetam;
    Esse *virum* res, me iudice, rara *bonum*.
Esse *bonum*, res iudice me rarissima, *regem*;
    Tu tamen es *vates*, *vir* quoque, *Rexque* Bonus.

6(2).18: *De Papa & Luthero*
Papa pater multas *indulgentissimus* unus
    Ex purgativo liberat igne animas.
Martinus Papis pater *indulgentior* unus
    Omnibus est; omnes eximit inde Luther.

9(2).16: *L'argent faict tout.*
Unde fit ut *Francus* post tot, post bella tot *Anglus*
    Integer in solito regnet uterque solo?
Protexit generosa tuum te, Francia (a) *Scutum*,
    (b) *Angelus*, est *custos*, Anglia tuta, tuus.

[a] *L'escu.* [b] *L'angelot.*

9(2).50: *Ad G. Camdenum, Magnae Britanniae illustratorem maximum*
Insula paene suis obliviscenda Britannis
    Mox in lethaeos praecipitanda lacus,
Hoc tibi, quod superest, *Camdene*, *Britannia* debet.
    Tu quoque, *dum superest* illa, *superstes* eris.

9(2).67: *De Pane & Butyro*
Invenio nostrae veneranda vocabula linguae,
    In Genesi (a) Bara, *Menin* in Iliade.

[a] Bara *prima vox Genesis.* [b] Menin *prima Iliadis.* Bara *autem Cambro-Brittanico panem,* Menin *butyrum significat.*

To the very learned king James
To be a good poet is a rare thing, in my judgement;
  to be a good man is a rare thing, in my judgement.
To be a good king is a very rare thing, in my judgement;
  you, however, are a good poet, man, and king.

On the Pope and Luther
The Pope, the single most indulgent father,
  frees many souls from the fire of purgatory.
Martin Luther is the single father more indulgent than all the Popes:
  he removes all [souls] from there.

Money does everything.
How does it happen that the Frenchman after so many wars, the
    Englishman after so many,
  Each of them reigns in their accustomed land unharmed?
Your shield (a) has protected you, noble France,
  The angel (b) is your guardian, safe England.

(a) Old gold coin. (b) Old gold coin.

To W. Camden, Great Britain's greatest illustrator
The island, almost to be forgotten by her Britons,
  soon to be thrown down headlong into the waters of Lethe,
the fact that she survives, Britannia owes to you, Camden.
  You too, while she survives, will be surviving.

On bread and butter
I find words of our language to be held in awe:
  in *Genesis bara* (a), *menin* (b) in the *Iliad*.

(a) *Bara* is the first word of *Genesis*. (b) *Menin* is the first word of the *Iliad*. *Bara* also means 'bread' in Welsh, *Menin* 'butter'.

Commentary

1.48 This epigram takes the well-known line from one of Horace's *Odes* on dying for one's country (Hor. *Carm.* 3.2.13: *dulce et decorum est pro patria mori* – 'it is sweet and proper to die for one's country'), changes the word order (to integrate the phrase into a different grammatical structure and accommodate the change of metre) and juxtaposes it in the second line with the contrasting idea, based on the general notion that people typically prefer living to dying even if it is for one's country; tellingly, the notion of *decorum* ('glorious, proper') is not repeated in that line.

Philopater or Philopator is originally a Greek word and means 'father-loving'; when used in Latin, with the close connection of *pater* ('father') and *patria* ('fatherland, country'), it can be extended to mean 'lover of one's country', though this sense does not seem to be attested in the classical period.

2.38 (39 in some editions) Francis Drake (*c.* 1540–96) is well known for having circumnavigated the world and having been Vice Admiral in the battle against the Spanish Armada in 1588.

The 'Pillars of Hercules' is the ancient name for the promontories at the entrance to the Strait of Gibraltar, thought to represent the furthest point that Hercules had reached; there was a tradition that they were inscribed with *ne plus ultra* ('no further beyond') since they marked the transition into the unknown.

The poem celebrates the achievements of Drake since he has been to the end of the world by sailing round the globe and thus got even further than the ancient hero Hercules. *plus ultra* was also the motto of the Holy Roman Emperor Charles V, the father of Philip II of Spain, who sent the Armada against England.

William Camden (see Text 7) records that this poem was among those that were 'set up the same day upon the main Mast [of Drake's ship], written by the Scholars of Winchester School' in praise of Francis Drake upon his return to England in 1580 (William Camden, *The History of the Most Renowned and Victorious Princess Elizabeth, Late Queen of England; Containing All the most Important and Remarkable Passages of State, both at Home and Abroad (so far as they were linked with English Affairs) during her Long and Prosperous Reign. The Fourth Edition*, London 1688, p. 254 [available on Google Books]); thus, it must have been written when Owen was still a teenager.

2.179 (181 in some editions) This epigram talks about the relationship of the literary genre Owen uses, epigram, to a related literary genre, satire. The piece starts by acknowledging their close relationship and distinguishing them merely by a difference in length. Then it goes on to state that neither of them can be successful if it does not have elements of the other, which implies a difference in substance. This is probably based on the idea that satires have a critical tendency and epigrams are witty, as discussed in contemporary poetics: a bit of both is needed for the poems to provide enjoyment and have a pedagogical effect. The discussion of the characteristics as well as similarities and differences of literary genres reflects the early modern awareness of generic features (see Introduction).

A phrase similar to the one used here in lines 3 and 4 appears in a poem by Martial that describes his literary genre in contrast to others (Mart. 10.4.10: *hominem pagina nostra sapit* – 'our page smacks of the ordinary human being'), which might have been an inspiration for Owen.

3.4 Queen Elizabeth I (1533–1603) had recently died when this epigram was first published; upon her death, since Elizabeth I did not have any offspring, King James VI of Scotland also became James I of England and Ireland. The epigram claims that this 'offspring', the Union of the Crowns in 1603, is a much better deed than physically bearing children and thus increasing one's own family, which would have prolonged the separation of England and Scotland under different rulers. The first-person plural (*nobiscum*) refers to England, or possibly England and Wales, which were already united. The poem must have been topical at the time since the issue of marriage and the production of royal heirs had been a national theme during the reign of Elizabeth I.

3.202 This epigram, like the preceding one in the collection (3.201: *In Coniuratores qui 5. Novembris 1605*), is about the men who conspired to blow up Parliament at Westminster on 5 November 1605 (see John Milton's *In Quintum Novembris*: Text 13).

Legend had it that Britain was founded by Brutus, a refugee from Troy; therefore, London could be called 'new Troy' and its potential fate compared to the fall of Troy (inhabited by Phrygians), which was eventually conquered and destroyed by the besieging Greek army by means of the treacherous ruse of the Trojan Horse.

5 November 1605 was a Tuesday (*lux Martis*; compare French *mardi*); thus, the poet comments that the plot was unsuccessful as it was scheduled for the wrong day: ashes (as a result of fire) are associated with Wednesday (*Mercurii Dies*; compare French *mercredi*), alluding to Ash Wednesday.

3.204 This epigram comments on the contemporary issue of a united Britain. This alludes primarily to the Union of the Crowns in 1603, when James VI of Scotland also became James I of England and Ireland. The three parts of

Britain mentioned, however, are Wales, Scotland and England. The political and administrative union of England and Wales had been achieved by the Laws in Wales Acts 1535 and 1542. As a Welshman, the poet presumably wanted to include Wales, and / or he was thinking of the three parts of the country on the same island. The speaker is included in the general term 'Britons'.

This selection of countries enables a pun based on the similarity of the sound of the names for parts of Britain and the Latin words *vallum* ('wall, rampart, palisaded earthwork') and *scutum* ('shield') and on the different meanings of *contigit* ('fallen to [England's] lot' and 'become close'): thus, the poem can conclude with the security achieved for England, the addressee of the poem, now protected by the other, bordering countries.

5(1).58 This epigram is addressed to King James VI and I (of Scotland from 1567 and also of England and Ireland from 1603 to 1625). King James had been educated by George Buchanan (see Text 3) and was the patron of a group of poets called the Castalian Band; he himself wrote poetry and also a treatise entitled *Some Reulis and Cautelis to be observit and eschewit in Scottis poesie* (1584), describing poetic traditions in Scotland.

The effect of the poem is achieved by the repetition of *bonus* in every line (at the beginning in lines 1 and 3 and at the end in lines 2 and 4) and the build-up that being 'good' in each of the three areas is claimed to be rare (with a superlative for the goodness of a king mentioned in the third line) when James is then said to manage to be 'good' in all three of them.

6(2).18 This epigram provides a comparison between the Pope, the leader of the Roman Catholic Church, and Martin Luther (1483–1546), an important figure in the Protestant Reformation. Among other things, Luther denied the existence of purgatory and criticized the practice of indulgences operated by the Catholic Church at the time (*The Ninety-Five Theses*; *The Smalcald Articles* 2.2.12). The poet here says as much; by using the same words applied to the description of the Pope, he wittily presents Luther as doing what he is criticizing and on an even larger scale (since he is *indulgentior* than someone who is *indulgentissimus*, which is almost impossible, and offers 'indulgence' to all souls). The plural *Papis ... Omnibus* (lines 3–4) suggests a general statement rather than a comparison with a particular Pope.

9(2).16 This epigram is both a comment on the political situation in the context of wars between England and France, most notably the Hundred Years' War (1337–1453), and a play with different meanings of the same word in different languages. That the title is in French gives a clue that interaction of languages will be relevant, and the prominent mention of money (*l'argent*) in the heading indicates the kind of secondary meaning to be expected even before consulting the notes added by the poet. If the Latin words *scutum* ('shield') and *angelus* ('angel') are interpreted in their standard meanings (as in the English translation here), the sentences make perfect sense, especially in a military context, but there is no reference to money. This nuance is only added if these words are seen as standing for similar-sounding and etymologically connected French words denoting coins (as explained in the notes). Then it becomes clear, in an elaboration of the title, that the two nations have maintained their positions not by military prowess, but by the use of money.

The French term *écu* (Old French *escu*) derives from Latin *scutum* because the coin originally showed a shield with a coat of arms. The French word *angelot* (from late Latin *angelotus*, diminutive of *angelus*) denotes an old French gold coin bearing the image of archangel St Michael and then also an English gold coin with the same design, which became a popular and iconic coin (see 8.52.1–2 with Owen's note). Thus, *scutum* and *angelus* both describe protection and a particular coin associated with each of the two countries.

9(2).50 This poem celebrates the achievements of William Camden (see Text 7; also mentioned in 4.244), who by providing a comprehensive description of Britain in his book *Britannia* saved the country from oblivion. 'Britannia' here denotes the country, but equally alludes to the title of the work. The second half of the poem plays with the notion that a work of literature preserves the memory of its subject and also that of the writer.

Lethe is a river in the underworld in Greek mythology: it creates forgetfulness in those who drink from it.

9(2).67 This epigram is a clever play with sequences of letters/sounds that exist in different languages with different meanings and with the use of these words. The first (actually the second) word of the biblical book of Genesis in Hebrew (*bara*, meaning 'created') and the first word of the Homeric epic *Iliad* in Greek (*menin*, meaning 'anger' and referring to the wrath of Achilles) are famous on account of the fact that they are placed at the beginning of these works and are important for their themes. The same words denote the everyday items 'bread' and 'butter' in Welsh; the poem implies that these words command respect because of the role of these sequences of sounds and letters in venerable literary works in other languages. While the poem is in Latin, 'our language' refers to Welsh. The notes added by the poet indicate that readers are not expected to know Welsh (though *bara brith*, literally 'speckled bread', may be familiar to people outside Wales even today). This poem is the only instance of Welsh in the Latin text of the epigrams, while expressions in this language occur occasionally in the notes.

10

A Comic Exorcism

George Ruggle (1575– *c.* 1622), *Ignoramus* IV 11 (Excerpt)

Daniel Hadas

Introduction

George Ruggle was baptized on 3 November 1575 in Lavenham, Suffolk. In 1589 he matriculated at St John's College, Cambridge. In 1593 he became a scholar of Trinity College, Cambridge, graduating BA the same year and MA in 1597. In 1598 he was elected a fellow of Clare College, where he remained until 1620, probably dying shortly after. We possess few other details of his life, and no works other than *Ignoramus* are attributed to him. *Ignoramus* is a Latin comedy in five acts, in the classicizing tradition of university dramas (on this tradition in England, see Boas 1914). It was written for the 1615 royal visitation of James I to Cambridge and performed at Trinity College, before the king, by students and fellows of the university, on 8 March 1615. The performance lasted over five hours. James was greatly taken by the play and returned to Cambridge on 13 May 1615 to have it performed again (for Ruggle and his play, see Ruggle's *DNB* entry; Sutton 2014; and above all Hawkins 1787).

Ignoramus is a loose adaptation of the *Trappolaria* (1596) of the Neapolitan polymath Giambattista della Porta, itself inspired by Plautus' *Pseudolus*. The plot is complex, but its core is the successful attempt by the young hero Antonius to extract his beloved, Rosabella, from the clutches of the English lawyer Ignoramus, to whom she has been betrothed by her guardian, the pimp Torcol. The play is set in contemporary Bordeaux; so, while the bulk of the dialogue is in Latin, the audience is meant to imagine that this Latin is French. Characters repeatedly refer to Latin as if it were French, whereas, when they speak English or Portuguese, dialogue is rendered in those languages, not in Latin.

The lawyer Ignoramus is the source of much of the play's comedy (for other contemporary plays targeting lawyers, see Tucker 1977: xxxiii–xxxvi).

He is a stock figure, the lustful old fool led a merry dance by the young lovers. But comedy comes above all from Ignoramus' use of Latin, a use that in turn forms the basis of a savage parody by Ruggle of the language of English Common Law (see Tucker 1977). On the Continent, lawyers studied the Roman law of antiquity and had joined in the humanist project to write a classicizing Latin. But English lawyers had remained faithful to the island's medieval Common Law tradition (see Maitland 1901). Legal procedure was carried out, and legal documents were written, in highly anglicized forms of French ('Law French') and of Latin (see Baker 1998). Thus Ignoramus mostly speaks a grotesquely non-classical Latin. Within the play's linguistic universe, as Latin stands in for French, he is probably to be imagined as attempting to speak Law French in France – an intrinsically ludicrous enterprise. He is also law-crazed, so that all his dialogue is permeated with legal technicalities.

Ignoramus was well targeted to delight its audience. Cambridge and Oxford students were taught to write and speak humanist Latin, and they could study only Roman Law, not Common Law (this was taught at the Inns of Court).[1] James I was himself an accomplished Latinist and was on poor terms with his Chief Justice, Edward Coke, the greatest common lawyer of his day. However, *Ignoramus'* success was more than occasional: it remained popular for the next 150 years. Its title has entered our language. In Latin, it was repeatedly performed in schools (Hawkins 1787: lxxxvi–lxxxvii; schools abridged the play) and was printed at least twelve times (Tucker 1987a: xlvii), the last edition (Hawkins 1787) including an expansive commentary. Although the humour is largely untranslatable, three English versions were produced for the London stage: two in 1662 (cf. Codrington 1662; Tucker 1987a), and a third – adapted from the first two – in 1678 (Ravenscroft 1678). However, by the nineteenth century the play was largely forgotten. This was doubtless due in part to the declining role of Latin in education, but its satire had also lost its relevance: in 1731 English became the sole language of the Common Law (as lamented by Ignoramus in Bramston 1736) and, in due course, the common lawyer spewing a barbaric French and Latin became an unrecognizable figure. Nevertheless, an abridgement by David Money and Cressida Ryan was performed in Cambridge in 2000 and at King's College London in 2018.

In this extract (from IV 11) Antonius' accomplices, the ne'er-do-well bookseller Cupes, his shrewish wife Polla and the drunken, lecherous friar Cola, pretending to think Ignoramus is possessed, carry out a mock exorcism on him. Their aim is to shut Ignoramus up in Cola's monastery, so as to keep him away from Rosabella. Mock exorcisms are frequent in plays of the period (Tucker 1977: xxxix; Dijkhuizen 2003), and have an anti-Catholic flavour.[2] But *Ignoramus'* exorcism also marks the culmination of the play's linguistic comedy: Ignoramus responds to his tormentors with his usual legal jargon and barbarisms, and they pretend to take such terms as the names of the demons possessing him (for the importance of demons' names in early modern exorcisms, see Chave-Mahir 2011: 329; Levack 2013: 53–5, with examples of ludicrous names).

Notes

1 Ruggle may also be satirizing one Francis Brakyn, a lawyer who had represented the mayor and corporation of Cambridge in a 1611–12 dispute with the university (Hawkins 1787: xii–xiii; contra Sutton 2014: §§ 23–5).

2 Exorcism was effectively banned in the Church of England in 1604: see Young 2018: 48–56 (my thanks to the author for an advance copy).

Bibliography

Baker, J. H. (1998), 'The Three Languages of the Common Law', *McGill Law Journal*, 43: 5–24.

Boas, F. S. (1914), *University Drama in the Tudor Age*, Oxford.

Bramston, J. (1736), *Ignorami Lamentatio super Legis Communis Translationem ex Latino in Anglicum*, London.

Chave-Mahir, F. (2011), *L'exorcisme des possédés dans l'Église d'Occident (X^e–XIVe siècle)*, Turnhout.

Codrington, R. (1662), *Ignoramus: A Comedy*, London.

Crosswhite, A. B. (2002), 'Women and Land: Aristocratic Ownership of Property in Early Modern England', *New York University Law Review*, 77: 1119–56.

van Dijkhuizen, J. F. (2003), *Devil Theatre: Demonic Possession and Exorcism in English Drama, 1558–1642*, Leiden.

Greenberg, D., ed. (2010³), *Jowitt's Dictionary of English Law*, 2 vols, London.

Hawkins, J. S. (ed.) (1787), *Ignoramus, Comoedia, Scriptore Georgio Ruggle*, London.

Holdsworth, W. (1937²), *A History of English Law*, vol. 8, London.

Levack, B. P. (2013), *The Devil Within: Possession & Exorcism in the Christian West*, New Haven.

Maitland, F. W. (1901), *English Law and the Renaissance*, Cambridge.

Ravenscroft, E. (1678), *The English Lawyer: A Comedy*, London.

Sodi, M. and J. J. Flores Arcas (eds) (2004), *Rituale Romanum: Editio Princeps (1614)*, Rome.

Sutton D. F. (2014²), *George Ruggle. Ignoramus (1615). A Hypertext Edition* (http://www.philological.bham.ac.uk/ruggle/).

Tucker, E. F. J. (1977), 'Ruggle's *Ignoramus* and Humanistic Criticism of the Language of the Common Law', *Renaissance Quarterly*, 30: 341–50.

Tucker, E. F. J. (ed.) (1987a), *A Critical Edition of Ferdinando Parkhurst's Ignoramus the Academical Lawyer*, New York.

Tucker, E. F. J. (ed.) (1987b), *George Ruggle: Ignoramus*, Hildesheim.

Young, F. (2018), *A History of Anglican Exorcism*, London.

Source of the Latin text

The Latin text is based on that of D. F. Sutton (2014^2); but readings have been checked in one manuscript (Oxford, Bodleian Library, Douce 43: facsimile in Tucker 1987b) and in editions of 1630, 1707 and 1787 (Hawkins). The choice of readings is my own. A new critical edition is needed.

Latin text

IGNORAMUS,[1] CUPES, COLA, POLLA, EXORCISMI POMPA

COL. Vos qui cum palmis astatis et herbis benedictis,[2] arcte illum ad cathedram alligate.

IGN. Quid me attachiatis[3] cum funis[4] et cordis?

CUP. Tace.

IGN. O Dulman,[5] Dulman! Dixisti quod pugnares tanquam diabolus pro me. Ubi es nunc, Dulman?

COL. Exorcizo te,[6] Dulman. Fuge, maledicte Dulman, fuge.

IGN. Fugit semel hodie.[7] Sed si nunc venit Dulman …

COL. Invocat Dulman. Certe Dulman nomen est.

IGN. Cum peste vobis,[8] nomen est Ignoramus.

CUP. Discede, Ignoramus.

IGN. Discedite vos, nebulones ut estis,[9] cum vestra *riota* et *routa*.[10]

COL. Duplex daemon, cede, Riota et Routa.

CUP. Prodi, nequissime spiritus,[11] Ignoramus. Coniuro[12] te, Ignoramus. Iusticiae declinator, seductor hominum, sator discordiae, veri transgressor, dissipator pacis. Exorcizo te. Quod est nomen magistri tui?

IGN. Ego sum magister.

COL. Est ipse Beelzebub. Fuge, ipse magister. Coniuro te: quam cito vis exire?

IGN. Tam cito quam possum ex vestris nebulonum digitis.

CUP. Coniuro te, quapropter hoc tibi accidit?

IGN. Propter Rosabellam. Ob eam ita torqueor.

CUP. Abscede, Rosabella, abscede.

IGN. *Diable*,[13] abscessit.

CUP. Coniuro, unquamne dedisti illi animam antehac?

IGN. Quid id ad vos? Imo dedi animam et corpus et bona illi.

POL. O sceleratum!

IGN. Et praeter *iuncturam*,[14] si maritasset[15] me, post mortem habuisset *francum bancum*.[16]

COL. Profuge sis, Francum Bancum. Separa te, Francum Bancum.

IGN. Imo iam non habebit, ne timete. Sed si amasset me, habuisset multa bona privilegia, *infangthef*,[17] *outfangthef, sac, soc, tol* et *tem*.

COL. Quam multi sunt! Exite omnes, Ninantef, Nonantef, Tac, Toc, Tol et Tem. Exorcizo omnes vos malignos spiritus, sive sitis in pileolo diurno[18] aut nocturno, in duplici lingua, aut sub lingua, in barba, vel in capite.

English translation

IGNORAMUS,[1] CUPES, COLA, POLLA, An EXORCIST PROCESSION

COL. You who stand by with palms and blessed herbs,[2] bind him tightly to the seat.

IGN. Why do you attach[3] me with ropes[4] and cords?

CUP. Silence.

IGN. O Dulman,[5] Dulman! You said that you would fight like the devil for me. Where are you now, Dulman?

COL. I exorcize you,[6] Dulman. Flee, accursed Dulman, flee.

IGN. He fled once today.[7] But if Dulman comes now ...

COL. He invokes Dulman. Surely the name is Dulman.

IGN. With a plague on you,[8] the name is Ignoramus.

CUP. Begone, Ignoramus.

IGN. You begone, scoundrels that you are,[9] with your *riot* and *rout*.[10]

COL. Yield, double demon, Riot and Rout.

CUP. Go forth, most wicked spirit,[11] Ignoramus. I conjure[12] you, Ignoramus. Avoider of justice, seducer of mankind, sower of strife, transgressor of truth, destroyer of peace. I exorcize you. What is your master's name?

IGN. I am the master.

COL. It's Beelzebub himself. Flee, o master himself. I conjure you: how quickly will you agree to get out?

IGN. As quick as I can, from you rascals' fingers.

CUP. I conjure you: why did this happen to you?

IGN. Because of Rosabella. It's for her that I'm tormented in this way.

CUP. Go away, Rosabella, go away.

IGN. The devil![13] She's gone away.

CUP. I conjure you: have you ever before given your soul to her?

IGN. What's it to you? Worse still, I have given my soul and body and possessions to her.

POL. O, the wretch!

IGN. And besides the *jointure*,[14] if she had married[15] me, she would have had *frankbank*[16] after my death.

COL. Flee, if you please, Frankbank. Detach yourself, Frankbank.

IGN. But now she won't have it, fear not. But if she'd loved me, she would have had many fine privileges: *infangthef,*[17] *outfangthef, sac, soc, tol* and *tem.*

COL. There are so many of them! Get out, all of you, Ninantef, Nonantef, Tac, Toc, Tol and Tem. I exorcize all you evil spirits, whether you be in the day-cap[18] or the night-cap, in the double tongue, or under the tongue, in the beard, or in the head.

IGN. O asini! Putatis quod diabolus tenet *in capite*?[19] Tenet in froccis et soccis[20] et calvis coronis[21] vestris, fratres diaboli.

POL. Invocat fratres suos diabolos.

COL. Tace. Eradicemini,[22] sive sitis in diploide manicata vel tunica, sive in manicis, vel in capsulis, vel in calamo, vel in cera, aut sigillo, vel in cornugraphia.[23]

IGN. Erat in cornu[24] hodie.

CUP. Coniuro te, pessime daemon, exi e cornu.

IGN. Pestilentia de vobis et omnibus cornubus, nisi de cornu quod cornuat ad prandium.[25]

COL. Explantemini, sive sitis in syngraphis, membranis, chartis scriptis vel non scriptis, verbis cum sensu vel sine sensu.

IGN. Vel in Greyfryers vel in Blackfryers vel in Crotchedfryers.[26]

COL. Exorcizo vos. Fugite, pessimi daemones, Grayfryers, Blackfryers, Crotchedfryers. Fugite, sive sitis in braccis oblongis vel rotundis, vel in intestinis maioribus vel minoribus, vel in coleotheca.[27]

POL. Ibi est: video.

IGN. Ibi est in te, video[28] – nisi facio te tenere manum sursum.[29] O felones,[30] quis habet manum in pocketto[31] ibi? Estis *backbarend* et *handabend*.[32]

CUP. Fugite, Backbarend et Handabend.

IGN. Si fugiunt, est directe felonia.[33]

CUP. Sive estis in loculis aut in crumena, vel in auro vel in argento, sive bene parto sive male parto.

IGN. Illud est daemonium quod desideratis, scio, robbatores[34] ut estis.

COL. Adiuro vos, nequissimi spiritus, Robbatores, si estis in femoribus vel inter femora, exite simul ab omnibus membris huius creaturae.

IGN. Hoc est bene, si vult ire sic.

COL. Et in pollicem sinistri pedis[35] veniatis.

POL. Ibi est, video. Contundam ne ascendat.

IGN. O, o, meos cornos![36] O Pythonissa, quid vis? Unum *Magnum cape*[37] de magno diabolo capiat vos omnes et singulos.

CUP. Iam saevit, frater. Da salem exorcizatum,[38] ignem benedictum.[39] Exorcizo te, profumigo te.[40]

IGN. Ignis ardeat vos. Si dagarias[41] capio, rumpam calvas coronas vestras.

COL. Coniuro te, prodi, Dagarias.

IGN. Utinam possint se defendendo.[42]

COL. Tentemus si sit obediens. Repete nunc quod dico tibi in aurem. Buz, buz, buz.

CUP. Adiuro te, responde quod quaero. Mum, mum, mum.

IGN. O you asses! Do you think that the devil holds *by the head*?[19] He holds by your frocks and sandals[20] and bald crowns,[21] brother devils.

POL. He is invoking his brother devils.

COL. Silence. May you be uprooted,[22] whether you be in the sleeved doublet or in the tunic, whether in the sleeves, or in the boxes, or in the pen, or in the wax, or in the seal, or in the inkhorn.[23]

IGN. He was in the horn[24] today.

CUP. I conjure, you most wicked demon, get out of the horn.

IGN. A plague on you and on all horns, except for the horn that blows for dinner.[25]

COL. May you be ripped out, whether you be in contracts, parchments, papers written or unwritten, words with meaning or without meaning.

IGN. Or in Grey Friars or in Black Friars or in Crossed Friars.[26]

COL. I exorcize you. Flee, most wicked demons, Greyfriars, Blackfriars, Crossedfriars! Flee, whether you be in the long breeches or the round ones, or in the great intestine or the small one, or in the codpiece.[27]

POL. There he is. I see him.

IGN. That's where he is in you: I see him[28] – unless I make you lift up your hand.[29] O felons,[30] who has his hand in my pouch[31] there? You are *backbarend* and *handabend*.[32]

CUP. Flee, Backbarend and Handabend.

IGN. If they flee, that's a felony straightaway.[33]

CUP. Whether you be in the pockets or in the purse, or in the gold or in the silver, whether well-gotten or ill-gotten.

IGN. That's the demon you're after, I know – robbers[34] as you be.

COL. I adjure you, most evil spirits, Robbers, if you be in the thighs or between the thighs, get out all at once from every limb of this creature.

IGN. That's nice, if he wants to go that way.

COL. And come into the toe of the left foot.[35]

POL. There he is – I see him. I'll smash him, so he can't climb up.

IGN. O, o my corns![36] O you witch, what do you want? May one *Great take*[37] from the great devil take each and every one of you!

CUP. Now he's raving, brother. Hand over the exorcized salt,[38] the blessed fire.[39] I exorcize you, I fumigate you.[40]

IGN. May fire consume you. If I get some daggers,[41] I'll break your bald crowns.

COL. I conjure you, go forth, Daggers!

IGN. Would that they could, in self-defence![42]

COL. Let's test if he's obedient. Repeat now what I say to you in your ear. Buz, buz, buz.

CUP. I adjure you: answer what I ask. Mum, mum, mum.

IGN. Nihil intelligo.

CUP. Mum, mum.

IGN. Quid mummatis et moppatis[43] ita ut simiae?

COL. Mum mum. Non iam sentis abisse daemones?

IGN. Sentio ad minimum[44] tres adesse hic.

POL. Tres adhuc?

IGN. Imo tres. Puto hodie sum indiabolatus[45] in bono serio.[46] Si sum, tu es sorciera[47] quae fecisti primum, et vos estis eius condiaboli,[48] qui abettatis[49] illam.

COL. Frater, ut video, opus adhuc opera multa. Ad fratres deferatur, si placet, ad monasterium.

CUP. Fiat. Aliqui vestrum eum intro huc auferte.

IGN. In nomine diaboli, quo portatis me? *Fowle porridge-bellied[50] fryars. Harroul! Harroul! Je scay 'Le grand customier[51] de Normandy'. Harroul. The Divell take you all.*

IGN. I don't understand anything.

CUP. Mum, mum.

IGN. Why are you mumbling and grimacing,[43] just like monkeys?

COL. Mum, mum. Don't you feel that the demons have gone now?

IGN. I feel that at least[44] three are right here.

POL. Three, still?

IGN. Three, indeed. I think today I am bedevilled[45] in good earnest.[46] If I am, you're the sorceress[47] who did this first, and you are her co-devils,[48] who are abetting[49] her.

COL. Brother, as I see it, there is still a lot of work to do. Let him, if you please, be brought to the brothers in the monastery.

CUP. So be it. Some of you, take him inside, over here.

IGN. In the devil's name, where are you carrying me? Foul porridge-bellied[50] friars. *Harroul! Harroul!* I know the 'Great Customary[51] of Normandy'. *Harroul!* The Devil take you all.

Commentary

Unless otherwise stated: medieval Latin and English lexicographical information is from, respectively, the *Oxford Dictionary of Medieval Latin from British Sources* (*DMLBS*) and the *Oxford English Dictionary* (*OED*); legal definitions are quoted or paraphrased from Greenberg 2010.

Exorcism rites are quoted from those collected by Hieronymus Mengus (Girolamo Menghi) in the *Flagellum Daemonum* (Bologna 1577) and *Fustis Daemonum* (Bologna 1584, mentioned at *Ignoramus* II 3; both cited here from the 1608 Lyon reprint) or from the official rite of the 1614 *Rituale Romanum* (Sodi / Flores Arcas 2004). For other early modern exorcism rites, and for their medieval and late antique sources, see Chave-Mahir 2011: 94–7, 324–34.

1 *Ignoramus*: For the name 'Ignoramus', see Tucker 1987a: 229–30. A Grand Jury returns a verdict of *ignoramus* ('we ignore') when they think the evidence presented to them insufficient for further enquiries. Before Ruggle, the name is given in the anonymous Elizabethan history play *Woodstock* to the brother of the bailiff of Dunstable, the latter being an associate of the wicked lawyer Robert Tresilian. The *-mus* ending of *ignoramus* is that of a first-person plural verb, but *Ignoramus* is treated by Ruggle as the nominative of a second declension noun: Ignoramus' very name is bad Latin.

2 *herbis benedictis*: *Flagellum Daemonum* 4: *Exorcista poterit aggredi diabolum obsidentem corpus humanum rebus exterioribus, ut aqua benedicta, incenso sulphure, ruta et medicina, ac aliis potationibus, quae omnia debent esse exorcizata et benedicta* ('An exorcist can attack a devil who is besieging a human body with external materials, like blessed water, burning sulphur, rue and drugs, and other potions, all of which should be exorcized and blessed').

3 *attachiatis*: Like much of Ignoramus' non-classical vocabulary, *attach(i)are* is well attested in British medieval Latin texts. It is found from the twelfth century onwards in its legal sense ('to apprehend by commandment of a writ') and from the thirteenth onwards in the general sense 'attach'.

4 *funis*: The reading of all the manuscripts. Printed editions emend to the correct third declension form *funibus*; but see *DMLBS*, s.v. *funis* for attested second declension forms. Ruggle probably wanted Ignoramus to make a grammatical error.

5 *Dulman* etc.: Dulman is Ignoramus' clerk and fellow-ignoramus. Ignoramus refers to his promise in IV 8.

6 *Exorcizo te*: Cola's and Cupes' use of first-person declarations (*exorcizo, adiuro*) and of imperatives of *ire* ('go'), *cedere* ('withdraw') and *fugere* ('flee')

or derivatives is taken from genuine exorcisms: cf. *Rituale Romanum* 204–8; *Flagellum Daemonum* and *Fustis Daemonum, passim*; Chave-Mahir 2011: 97–9. However, Ruggle omits the voluminous invocations of God, Christ, angels and saints usually present in exorcisms: their use in a burlesque would have been irreverent.

7 *Fugit semel hodie*: In IV 8 Dulman runs from Ignoramus, who wishes to beat him because Dulman has been tricked into believing that Polla is Rosabella.

8 *Cum peste vobis*: Like *pestilentia de vobis*, below, one of Ignoramus' many Anglicisms, where he creates unnatural Latin by translating English word for word.

9 *ut estis*: another Anglicism, repeated below (*robbatores ut estis*).

10 *riota* et *routa*: Both words are well attested in late medieval British Latin. In Common Law, a rout is an assembly of persons who intend to riot, while a riot is a 'violent disturbance of the peace by a crowd'. For the development of law on riot, see Holdsworth 1937: 324–31. In Ruggle's time a crowd of three was sufficient to form a riot, and three persons are here attacking Ignoramus. So 'riot and rout', like many of Ignoramus' legal references, is distorted, but not irrelevant.

11 *nequissime spiritus* etc.: Compare the name-calling of Satan at *Rituale Romanum* 204: *inimice fidei, hostis generis humani, mortis adductor, vitae raptor, iustitiae declinator, malorum radix, fomes vitiorum, seductor hominum, proditor gentium, incitator invidiae, origo avaritiae, causa discordiae, excitator dolorum* ('enemy of the faith, enemy of the human race, bringer of death, thief of life, avoider of justice, root of evils, fomenter of vices, seducer of mankind, betrayer of nations, inciter of envy, source of avarice, cause of discord, instigator of trickery'); still more such imprecations at *Fustis Daemonum* 147–8. Cupes has chosen among the devil's titles those that might apply equally well to Ignoramus: hence he does not use e.g. *mortis adductor*.

12 *Coniuro*: translated by its English derivative 'conjure', which, from the thirteenth century onwards, could signify 'To call upon, constrain (a devil or spirit) to appear or do one's bidding, by the invocation of some sacred name or the use of some spell' (*Oxford English Dictionary* III.5.a).

13 *Diable*: Only one manuscript preserves the French, against Latin *diabole*, but French was more likely to be turned into Latin in the process of copying, than the reverse.

14 *iuncturam*: Found in its legal sense from Bracton (thirteenth century) onwards. A jointure is 'provision made by a husband for the support of his

wife after his death', generally a rent or annuity. Ignoramus reads part of her jointure to Rosabella in I 4.

15 *maritasset*: *maritare* is used, albeit rarely, in classical Latin of providing a husband to a bride, providing a bride to a husband and marrying a wife. All of these senses subsist in medieval Latin, and 'marry a wife' becomes common (see *DMLBS* and other medieval Latin dictionaries). But the sense 'marry a husband' is not attested, so this is another Anglicism.

16 *francum bancum*: 'A custom ... for the wife to have for her dower all the tenements which were her husband's'. A jointure often replaced a dower, and a dower was conventionally set at one third of the husband's property. So Ignoramus' offer is truly generous (but bogus: at I 4 he states that he intends to take Rosabella as a mistress, rather than marry her).

17 *infangthef* etc.: *Infangthef* is a lord's right to hang a thief caught stealing goods on his lands; *outfangthef* is his right to hang certain thieves who had stolen outside his own lands; *sac, soc, tol* and *tem* are not clearly distinguished, but all designate a lord's rights to mete out justice, impose fines and collect revenues on his lands. Ignoramus' new claims are absurd. These rights were normally granted by the king, and a husband could only grant them to his wife if he already held them (unlikely for a jobbing lawyer), and then only in the event of his death: see Crosswhite 2002. Also, *infangthef* and *outfangthef* had been obsolete for circa 300 years, as capital punishment had become reserved to the Crown.

18 *in pileolo diurno* etc.: Ruggle parodies the exhaustive lists of body parts and possibly possessed objects in genuine exorcisms: extensive examples from *Fustis Daemonum* in Hawkins 1787: *ad loc.*

19 *tenet in capite*: A tenant *in capite* ('tenant-in-chief') is generally, in a feudal system, one who holds his land directly from the Crown. Ignoramus perhaps means that the devil's hold over mankind does not stem directly from God, but from the activities of wicked friars.

20 *froccis et soccis*: monastic clothing: *froccus* for 'religious habit' is attested in British sources from the fourteenth century onwards, while *soccus* (a classical word) can designate a form of monastic shoe (Du Cange, *Glossarium Mediae et Infimae Latinitatis*, s.v.).

21 *coronis*: From the sixth century onwards, *corona* ('garland, crown') can designate the tonsure (Blaise, *Dictionnaire Latin-Français des auteurs chrétiens*, s.v.), whence evolves the medieval sense 'crown of the head'.

22 *Eradicemini*: *Rituale Romanum* 204: *immundissime spiritus ... eradicare et effugare* ('most foul spirit ... be uprooted and routed').

23 *cornugraphia*: 'inkhorn' is the translation of Codrington 1662. *atramentarium* is found for 'inkstand/horn' in the Vulgate Bible, and *cornu* ('horn') is so used in medieval sources, but the dictionaries give no instances of *cornugraphia*. Cola is apparently using his Greek and Latin to parody Ignoramus' coinages.

24 *cornu*: perhaps 'erect penis': the devil had stirred Ignoramus' loins via Rosabella. But the dictionaries give no Latin examples, and this sense of 'horn' is not cited in English until 1785.

25 *cornuat ad prandium*: *cornuare* is attested from the thirteenth century onwards (*DMLBS*; Du Cange; Niermeyer, *Mediae Latinitatis Lexicon minus*, s.v.). It is not an Anglicism: 'to horn' is not found in this sense before Thomas Hardy. Hawkins (1787: *ad loc.*) refers to the horn that called students of the Inns of Court to dinner.

26 *Greyfryers* etc.: Grey Friars are Franciscans, Black Friars Dominicans, Crossed Friars (*Fratres cruciferi*) a now defunct medieval Augustinian order.

27 *coloetheca*: 'codpiece' is again taken from Codrington 1662. Formed from Greek *kōlē* ('penis') and *thēkē* ('box'). Apparently a coinage, like *cornugraphia*, above.

28 *Ibi est in te, video*: Ignoramus perhaps means that a devil dwells in Polla's genitals.

29 *tenere manum sursum*: an Anglicism. Hawkins (1787: *ad loc.*) explains this as a reference to the practice of the defendant in a Common Law court holding up his hand when the indictment against him is read out. Codrington 1662 and Parkhurst (= Tucker 1987a) understood likewise, as both translate 'hold up your hand at the bar'.

30 *felones*: found in Latin from the ninth century onwards, meaning both 'rascal' and 'vassal' (Niermeyer).

31 *pocketto*: in British Latin documents from the thirteenth century onwards, as 'pouch' rather than 'pocket'.

32 *backbarend et handabend*: caught carrying stolen goods on one's back or in one's hands, respectively. Obsolete and pedantic English by Ruggle's time.

33 *felonia*: in Latin from the twelfth century onwards in its Common Law sense, 'serious premeditated crime against the King's Peace'.

34 *robbatores*: derived from Germanic *rauba* ('booty, spoils'), attested in Latin from the seventh century onwards. *robbator* appears in French and English texts starting in the twelfth century (Niermeyer; *DMLBS*).

35 *sinistri pedis*: Tucker 1987a: xxxviii–xxxix identifies the source for the devil in the toe as Samuel Harsnet's *A Declaration of Egregious Popish Imposture* (London 1603), an attack on exorcisms.

36 *cornos*: apparently Ignoramus' own coinage.

37 *Magnum cape*: In a dispute over tenements, a writ of *magnum* or *grand cape* summoned the demandant and tenant before the court (*parvum* or *petit cape* summoned only the tenant). So called because the court orders the sheriff to take (*capere*) the land in dispute into the Crown's temporary possession. In effect, Ignoramus is saying no more than 'the devil take you'.

38 *salem exorcizatum*: For the exorcizing of salt, see *Dictionnaire de théologie catholique*, s.v. 'exorcisme', III.3; *Dictionnaire de spiritualité*, s.v. 'sel', 4. For the use of such salt in exorcizing the possessed, see *Flagellum Daemonis* 149–50, 171–80.

39 *ignem benedictum*: For blessings of fire, see *Dictionnaire de spiritualité*, s.v. 'feu', 4.3.

40 *profumigo te*: *Flagellum daemonis* 70: *Si nec audire nec obedire voluerit, accipe ignem et sulphur, et daemoniacum, velit nolit, diu super dictum sulphur et ignem facias fumigari* ('If [the demon] does not wish to hear or to obey, take fire and sulphur, and have the demoniac fumigated for a long time, whether he likes it or not, over said sulphur and fire').

41 *dagarias*: Feminine *dagaria* is unattested, but masculine *dagarius* and neuter *dagarium* are found in British Latin from the fourteenth century onwards. Cola emphasizes the word's barbarism by repeating the accusative form *dagarias* as if it were a vocative.

42 *se defendendo*: the standard Common Law phrase for pleas of self-defence. See Greenberg 2010, s.v. 'private defence', for the development of the law. Ignoramus' (arguable) point is that he is in a good position to use a dagger and invoke the doctrine.

43 *mummatis et moppatis*: probably coined from English 'to mop and mowe': 'to grimace, to make faces'.

44 *ad minimum*: Classical Latin uses *saltem* or *dumtaxat* for 'at least'. *ad minimum* is calqued on the English: compare French 'au moins', Italian 'almeno', Spanish 'al menos'. The usage is poorly covered in medieval Latin dictionaries, although the *Lexicon mediae et infimae latinitatis Poloniae*, s.v. 'minimus' (s.v. 'parvus') records the phrase as frequent in Polish sources from the fifteenth century onwards (*ad minimum* also calques Polish 'przynajmniej', as Agata Zielinska kindly informs me).

45 *indiabolatus*: apparently not medieval. English 'indevil' is first attested in 1604, and, for Neo-Latin, Ramminger (www.neulatein.de/) cites our passage and an instance from John Rainolds (1549–1607).

46 *in bono serio*: another Anglicism.

47 *sorciera*: found in Latin from the ninth century onwards (Niermeyer, s.v. 'sortiarius, sortiaria').

48 *condiaboli*: I cannot find any other instances of *condiabolus*.

49 *abettatis*: *abettare* is found from the thirteenth century onwards in English legal texts, where (as here) it refers to the actions of accomplices to a crime.

50 *porridge-bellied*: OED omits this, but has 'porridge belly' (first usage: 1580), as 'large, fat abdomen', and cites W. Robertson, *Phraseologia Generalis* (1681): 'a huge, great . . . porridge-belly friar'. Was the phrase a stock insult?

51 *Le grand customier* etc.: The *Grand customier* is a thirteenth-century compilation, in both French and Latin, of customary law for the Duchy of Normandy. Edition of French and Latin texts: W. L. de Gruchy (ed.), *L'ancienne Coutume de Normandie* (Jersey 1881). Critical edition of Latin text: E. J. Tardif (ed.), *Coutumiers de Normandie. Textes Critiques. Tome II: La Summa de legibus Normannie in curia laicali* (Paris and Rouen 1896). List of early modern editions and commentaries in de Gruchy, 339–47. English translation of de Gruchy's Latin text: J. A. Everard, *Le Grand Coutumier de Normandie* (St Helier 2009). Customary Norman law was abolished in Normandy at the Revolution, but remains in force in Jersey and Guernsey.

The *harroul* or *haro*, like Common Law 'hue and crie', is a cry for help made by the victim of a crime, which obliges all bystanders to come to their assistance. See chapter 53 (Tardif) = 54 (de Gruchy) of the *Grand customier*: *Non enim debet exclamari nisi in discrimine criminoso, ad ignem videlicet, vel ad latronem, vel homicidium, vel roberiam, vel in aliquo huiusmodi imminente periculo, ut si quis erepto gladio irruat in alium furibunde* ('For it should not be cried out, except in a criminal matter, namely for a fire, or for a thief, or a murder, or a robbery, or in some imminent danger of this sort, as when one man attacks another furiously with drawn sword') – see, however, de Gruchy (*ad loc.*) for its extension to property disputes, its only extant use today. Ignoramus is not really in enough danger to use the *haro*, and, of course, he is not in Normandy or the Channel Islands.

11

'Dazel'd Thus with Height of Place': An English Lyric in Two Latin Versions

English: Henry Wotton (1568–1639); Latin: Anonymous [Georg Weckherlin (1584–1653)?]

Victoria Moul

Introduction

One particularly intriguing feature of early modern literary bilingualism is the translation not only of Latin poetry (whether classical or post-classical) into English verse, but the movement also in the reverse direction: from English into Latin. This latter phenomenon, though a marked feature especially of the manuscript record, has received relatively little critical attention. In some cases, such as the published translations of Edmund Spenser's *Shepherds' Calendar* and John Milton's *Paradise Lost* into Latin verse, translations of this kind appear to have been intended to increase the potential readership of a work and raise its profile in the rest of Europe. Many surviving manuscript examples, however – which include, for instance, Latin translations of parts of William Shakespeare, John Dryden, Ben Jonson and Abraham Cowley – do not appear to have been intended to replace the English original for readers without English, but rather as a supplement. Such translations typically circulate in manuscript in bilingual presentations, with the original text and Latin translation, or sometimes several Latin translations, alongside one another. In cases of this sort, which are distinctive products of literary bilingualism, the Latin translation was apparently intended to be read and appreciated alongside and in direct conversation with the English originals.

One particularly interesting and widely circulated example of this phenomenon is the distinctive 'double' translation of the English lyric, 'Dazel'd thus with height of place', now usually considered to be by Sir Henry Wotton (1568–1639). Although not printed until 1651, Wotton's poem circulated widely in manuscript in the earlier part of the seventeenth century: Peter Beal records ten copies in the *Catalogue of English Literary Manuscripts*. The poem was probably originally written about the spectacular fall in 1616 of Robert Carr, the Earl of Somerset, a royal favourite, who, with his wife Frances, was charged with and convicted of the murder by poison of Sir Thomas Overbury, who had opposed their marriage. Overbury, who had been close to Carr, knew of how the relationship had begun while Frances was still married to Robert Devereux, the Earl of Essex, and had attempted to persuade his friend not to pursue the marriage. Wotton's poem often appears in manuscript miscellanies, however, with a generalizing title (such as 'On the sudden restraint of a favourite'), and it was quickly applied to the fall of other prominent individuals, such as Walter Raleigh (imprisoned for an illegal marriage in 1591 and later executed for treason in 1618), Francis Bacon (convicted of taking bribes in 1621), George Villiers, Duke of Buckingham (impeached in 1626 and eventually assassinated in 1628), and even, in two manuscripts now in Bradford, to William Davison (made a scapegoat for the execution of Mary, Queen of Scots, in 1587).

In four extant manuscripts (a relatively large number for this period) the poem appears in a distinctive form, with the English stanzas interleaved with two parallel Latin versions, one in Sapphics (on the right) and one in Alcaics (on the left). These two Latin poems are both reproduced here. Although it is impossible to attribute authorship of the Latin translations with any degree of certainty, it is possible that they were composed by Georg Weckherlin, a German poet resident in London at the time: the copy transcribed here, which is among a collection of his papers, is a single sheet (not copied into a miscellany), and his papers include a relatively large number of bi- or multilingual poetic exercises in English, Latin and German. Moreover, both translations appear to have slightly misconstrued the second line of the English poem, a mistake perhaps more likely to have been made by a non-native speaker.

For the Classicist, both the form and the allusive details of these Latin versions are of interest. Wotton's poem is an accomplished example of a form, the 'moralizing lyric', which was already traditional in English verse and which, though not a fashionable element of modern anthologies of Renaissance poetry, is found widely in manuscript and print miscellanies of the period. (Similar poems include Wotton's 'How Happy Is He Born and Taught' and Thomas Campion's 'The Man of Life Upright') There is nothing obviously 'classical' about the English lyric from a modern perspective, either in form or content. Nevertheless, the translator's choice of two markedly Horatian Latin lyric forms, both of which additionally include reminiscences of both Horace and Senecan choruses, suggests that the poem was read at the time within a Horatio-Senecan tradition of moralizing lyric that comments upon political power and the dangers of high office. Whereas Horatian lyric is mostly associated in modern criticism with relatively personal poetry, early modernity emphasized the moralizing and philosophical qualities not only of Horace himself, but also of the post-Horatian Latin lyric tradition (including Seneca, Boethius and many Neo-Latin poets). In this case, the translator's choices of an overtly Horatian form for his translation open up to modern view a literary field existing in both Latin and English, which was of great importance in early modern England, but which – due partly to modern patterns in the study and appreciation of classical poetry – has now become very difficult to discern.

An additional area of interest is the relationship between the two poems. Since they circulate exclusively together, and in a parallel presentation, they are probably, though not certainly, by the same person: multiple translations of the same passage or poem are found frequently in this period and are often evidence of a single author trying different approaches to a passage, though sometimes they are clearly the result of a group exercise, with attempts shared among friends. Nevertheless, the two versions have a different feel: the second version is, on average, slightly further removed from the English in the details of the translation, though conversely it more often achieves something close to the suggestive and quotable generality of the English lyric. It is possible that the second version is a second attempt.

Bibliography

Burke, P. (2007), 'Translations into Latin in Early Modern Europe', in P. Burke and R. Po-chia Hsia (eds), *Cultural Translation in Early Modern Europe*, 65–80, Cambridge [on early modern translation into Latin].

Forster, L. (1970), *The Poet's Tongues: Multilingualism in Literature*, Cambridge, 35–37 [on Georg Weckherlin].

Gaisser, J. H. (2017), 'Lyric', in V. Moul (ed.), *A Guide to Neo-Latin Literature*, 113–130, Cambridge [on Neo-Latin lyric as a whole].

Moul, V. (2017), 'Horace, Seneca and the Anglo-Latin "Moralising" Lyric in Early Modern England', in K. Winter, M. Stöckinger and T. Zanker (eds), *Horace and Seneca: Interactions, Intertexts, Interpretations*, 345–69, Berlin [brief discussion of this poem within its wider generic context].

Pebworth, T.-L. (1977), 'Sir Henry Wotton's "Dazel'd Thus, with height of Place" and the Appropriation of Political Poetry in the Earlier Seventeenth Century', *The Papers of the Bibliographical Society of America*, 71: 151–69 [on the English poem].

Source of the Latin text

The two Latin poems have been transcribed from British Library Additional MS 72439, fols 149^{r-v} (the Latin text in all four extant manuscripts is almost identical; some minor changes and additions to punctuation have been made, for ease of comprehension).

English text

Dazel'd thus with height of place,
Whilst our wits our hopes beguile,
No man markes the narrow space
'Twixt a prison, and a smile.

5 Then, since fortunes favours fade,
You, that in her armes doe sleep,
Learne to swim, and not to wade;
For, the Heart of Kings are deepe.

But, if Greatness be so blind,
10 As to trust in towers of Aire,
Let it be with Goodness lin'd,
That at 'least, the Fall be faire.

Then though darkned, you shall say,
When Friends faile, and Princes frowne,
15 Vertue is the roughest way,
But proves at night a Bed of Downe.

All things fall that stand by art
Nought remains from fume of sway
One man acted ill his part
20 Let another mend the play.

Latin versions

Latin version 1: Alcaics

Declive dum nos attonitos iugum
Et spes inanes vis facit ingens,
   Nescitur os blandum tyranni
      Quam prope sit rigidis catenis.

Cum sors nitentem nubibus implicet   5
Vultum, benigno quem gremio fovet
   Natare cauta discat arte,
      Mens etenim latet alta regum.

Confidat at si caeca potentia
Fallace tectis aëre conditis,   10
   Virtute firmetur, nigranti
      Ut niteat decus in ruina.

Tunc lapsus alto culmine gloriae
Dum cauta fallit turba clientium
   Et rex minatur, 'Dura', cantet,   15
      'Dulce parat pietas cubile.'

Quod arte constat corruit, haud levem
Fumum relinquit pompa superstitem
   Turbavit inconstans theatrum
      Ille, agat hic meliore plausu.   20

Latin version 2: Sapphics

Dum loci splendor ferit obstupentem
Spemque deludunt studia; haud videtur
Quam parum fallace ab honore distat
    Carceris horror.

5 Cumque declinet favor, in benigno
Qui cubant sortis gremio, natare
Cautius discant, etenim profunda
    Pectora regum.

Caeca si vero iuvenum potestas
10 Aërem audaci penetret volatu
Tota Virtutem colat, ut decoro
    Corruat ictu.

Tunc amicorum fugiat corona
Et necem princeps rigido minetur
15 Ore, cantabit, 'Placidum est cubile
    Ardua virtus'.

Arte quod constat ruit et favore
Nec levis fumus superest. Inepto
Egit hic partes, agat aptiore
20   Ille cothurno.

Commentary

Latin version 1

1 Rather compressed Latin, borrowing *facit* from the following line. *Declive
. . . iugum* (literally a 'sloping mountain ridge') is the subject of the clause; the
phrase suggests both the 'height' of the English poem and also its precarious
steepness.

2 Literally, 'and [while] great power makes our hopes vain'; a somewhat
different meaning from that of the English poem. The line is metrically
irregular, but all four of the extant copies preserve the same reading. For this
reason I have not proposed any emendation, which would alter the sense of
the line.

The English line 'Whilst our wits our hopes beguile' is, due to the lack of
inflection in English, ambiguous: it could refer to wits beguiling hopes, or
hopes beguiling wits. The context and larger meaning of the poem, however,
which is concerned as a whole with the dangers of excessive ambition and the
inevitability of reversals in fortune, means that the latter interpretation
('hopes [such as of high office] beguiling wits [as in, good sense]') is much
more likely, even though it is a more unusual (and indeed, Latinate) word
order in English. The second translation (see below) reveals a similar
misunderstanding. This mistake could be taken as further evidence in support
of Weckherlin's authorship, since he was not a native English speaker. In the
version here, the *vis . . . ingens*, which makes hopes vain, may be taken to refer
in general to the power and inevitability of fate; though when juxtaposed with
the *tyranni* of the following line, the phrase may be felt to have a political
connotation.

3 Note that the Latin here reproduces the idiomatic (but grammatically
confusing) transition from 'our' to the general 'no man' of the English poem.
The effect is odder in the Latin, partly because this translation introduces a
personal pronoun (*nos*, 1) in place of the English possessive adjective 'our'. *os
blandum tyranni* ('the smooth speech of a tyrant') is more explicit than the
English 'smile'. The expression *ore blando* is found at Ovid, *Metamorphoses*
13.555 (of Polymestor, King of Thrace).

4 *rigidis catenis* ('unyielding chains') stands in for the English 'prison'.

5 Literally, 'when fate envelops the shining face in clouds'. The imagery
suggests the shining face of the sun becoming concealed by cloud. In the
English poem, the language ('since fortunes favours fade') is neutral and
impersonal. The image of the sun sharpens the political tone: comparisons of

the king to the sun are a standard feature of both ancient and early modern panegyric. The Latin poem anticipates in its imagery the explicit mention of kings at the end of the stanza and hints at the possibility that the vagaries of fate (*sors*) may lead to the loss of royal approval.

6–7 *benigno quem gremio fovet* | *Natare cauta discat arte*: a somewhat free translation of 'You, that in her [fortune's] armes doe sleep, | Learne to swim, and not to wade'. The Latin means literally, 'He whom [Fortune] nurtures in her gentle lap | Should learn to swim with cautious skill'.

6 *gremio fovet* describes Dido dandling Amor, disguised as Ascanius, on her lap in Virgil, *Aeneid* 1.718 (itself echoing Venus' care of the kidnapped Ascanius, *fotum gremio*, 1.692). The allusion adds an effective note of menace, since the insidious activities of Amor lead ultimately to Dido's downfall.

7 Neither Latin translation attempts to reproduce the memorable distinction between 'swimming' and 'wading' of the English poem.

8 *Mens etenim latet alta regum*: a slightly awkward translation, literally 'for the deep mind of kings lies hidden', or, more naturally, 'for the mind of kings is hidden and deep'. The second version of the poem achieves a more effective translation at this point.

9 *caeca potentia* ('blind power') is a semi-technical term in scholastic theology and philosophy, referring to the will. The will is 'blind' because it depends upon information provided by the intellect. *potentia* translates 'Greatness', a term with clear social and political connotations. There is a kind of pun or word-play in the application of this philosophical term to high social status, but the word-play itself reflects the function of poems of this sort, to draw broader moral and philosophical conclusions from the vagaries of public life.

11–12 The alliteration of *nigranti . . . niteat* echoes that of the English ('Fall be faire').

12 *niteat* picks up *nitentem* (5). The sun-like countenance of the king may no longer shine upon you, but amid the darkness of social ruin your honour (*decus*) can still shine. Neither Latin version attempts to reproduce the hint of a metaphor in English, in which 'lin'd' suggests something intended to cushion the blow of the fall.

13–16 This stanza combines a generalized Horatian disdain for popular favour (see line 14) with a sharper reference to the horrific and personal disaster dramatized in Seneca's *Thyestes*; an awareness of Seneca's own fate is probably also evoked.

13 This line conflates two separate quotations from Seneca, *Thyestes*: lines 391–2, from the famous and much excerpted second chorus of the play (*stet quicumque volet potens | aulae culmine lubrico*, 'Let he who wishes stand in power | on the slippery peak of the court'), which suggests fall from high office, are blended with Thyestes' own speech from near the end of the play, where he describes himself as now *ex alto culmine lapsum* ('fallen from the high peak', 927).

14 *turba clientium* is borrowed from Horace, *Odes* 3.1.13, a poem also in Alcaics.

15–16 The introduction of direct speech (as also in version 2, lines 15–16) is borrowed directly from the English poem; it is a more striking feature in Latin. Punctuation has been added in these lines for clarity. The Latin preserves the essential contrast of the English ('roughest', 'Bed of Downe'; *dura pietas, dulce cubile*). Although the Latin phrase does not reproduce the hint of a pun in 'Bed of Downe' (referring to a fall downwards from a great metaphorical height), there is a pleasing and quotable concision to the Latin.

17–20 The final stanza of the English poem is probably not by Wotton (see Pebworth 1977: 161–3), but since it is included in all the manuscript versions with these Latin translations, it is also included here.

haud . . . meliore plausu: another rather free translation of the English lines 'Nought remains from fume of sway. | One man acted ill his part; | Let another mend the play'. The Latin means literally 'Pomp and pageantry [*pompa*] leaves behind not even a light smoke. That one unreliable man has disturbed the theatre [i.e. spoilt the performance]; let this one act his part to better applause'.

17 Another compressed phrase: 'what stands by art, falls [by art]'.

19–20 The motif of life (especially public life) as a theatrical production is a common one; see William Shakespeare, *As You Like It* II.7, 'All the world's a stage | And all the men and women merely players', a speech indebted in particular to Palingenius, *Zodiacus Vitae* 6.644–725, an extremely popular school text of the sixteenth and seventeenth centuries.

19 *inconstans* echoes *constat* (17); the inconstancy of fortune is a standard topic of moralizing verse.

Latin version 2

The commentary on this second version avoids repeating points valid for both texts and instead focuses upon areas of significant difference from the first translation.

1 Here is it is simply the *loci splendor* ('splendour of the place or situation') that overwhelms the observer. Like the English 'height of place', this phrase could refer to the situation the observer finds himself in (that is, the 'height' of high office or the 'splendour' of the court) rather than the more geographically literal image of the first poem (*Declive ... iugum*). If these translations are indeed by Weckherlin, this may be an example of him, as a non-native speaker of English, reflecting a more nuanced understanding of the tone and associations of the English poem in his second Latin version.

2 Like the first translation, this version also makes 'hopes' the object rather than the subject of the clause (see the discussion above). *studia* ('interests', 'enthusiasms') is slightly closer to the associations of the English 'wits' than the *vis ... ingens* of the first version; *deludunt* ('trick', 'mock', 'deceive') catches the meaning of 'beguile' fairly well.

3–4 In this version the proximity of favour and disaster is emphasized by the aural and visual similarities of the words *honor* and *horror*. In other respects, this translation is further removed from the English than the first version, since it makes no explicit mention of personal favour ('smile' in English; *os blandum tyranni* in version 1).

5 *Cumque declinet favor* is a closer translation of the English than the first version (preserving 'favour' as *favor*), but retains the sharper political edge of the first Latin poem. Whereas the English poem makes the 'favour' in question the impersonal 'fortune's favour', here it is *favor* itself that tends eventually to decline. Made the subject in this way, *favor* suggests the *favor* of a particular person, such as a patron or monarch.

7–8 Concisely effective, omitting the verb. This translation works better than that found in the first version.

9 *iuvenum* does not correspond to any feature of the English poem, though it fits with the allusion to Icarus in the following line.

10 *audaci ... volatu* replaces the English image of a high building, found also in the first version, with one of overbold flight. The phrase is borrowed from Ovid's description of Icarus (*Met.* 8.223), foreshadowing the inevitable fall.

11-12 The Latin imitates the marked alliteration of the English poem at this point: *colat . . . decoro | corruat . . . ictu.* The expression *decoro . . . ictu* (literally, 'with a seemly blow', or, here, 'with a graceful fall') is an unusual expression in Latin. There is no attempt to reproduce the metaphor of the English, 'lin'd', which suggests something intended to cushion the blow of the fall.

13 *corona* here means 'a crowd, multitude, encircling host (of friends)', as in Horace, *Epistles* 1.18.53; nevertheless, the sequence *fugiat corona* perhaps also hints at the inconstancy of power more generally.

14 *necem*: Though generally less menacing than the first translation, this is a much more specific threat than the English 'When . . . Princes frowne' or the *rex minatur* of the first Latin version.

15-16 *Placidum . . . Ardua*: The epigrammatic Latin preserves the essential contrast of the English ('roughest', 'Bed of Downe') while avoiding the metaphorical detail.

17 *favore* belongs with the following line ('not even a light smoke remains from favour'), but its positioning in this metrical line suggests too the parallel between *arte* and *favore*: one's own skill and the patronage of others are equally unreliable.

19-20 *aptiore . . . cothurno*: i.e. with greater dramatic skill.

12

A Meeting in Mauritania

John Barclay (1582–1621), *Argenis*, Book 5, Chapter 8 (9)

Jacqueline Glomski

Introduction

John Barclay's masterpiece novel *Argenis* was composed while its author was living in Rome, in the service of Pope Paul V. Barclay commenced work on *Argenis* probably some time in 1618; it appeared in print in Paris in 1621, just days after Barclay's sudden death, from fever, at the age of thirty-nine. The plot of *Argenis* has a definite political slant, Barclay's underlying thesis being that an absolute, hereditary monarchy was the most desirable form of government, and Barclay dedicated his book to King Louis XIII of France.

The story concerns the princess Argenis, the only child of Meleander, king of Sicily, who has secretly promised to marry the mysterious nobleman Poliarchus, unrecognized, to either her or her father, as the king of Gaul. But Poliarchus has fallen out of favour with her father, and so she must dissuade Meleander from arranging her marriage either to Radirobanes, the evil king of Sardinia, or to Archombrotus (another mysterious nobleman with obscure origins), until Poliarchus can reveal his true power and authority, and regain her father's good graces. Poliarchus does recover Meleander's favour, while Archombrotus is revealed not only to be the prince of Mauritania but Meleander's son by an early relationship and, therefore, Argenis' half-brother (and the nephew, not the son, of Queen Hyanisbe). Everything ends happily with Argenis marrying Poliarchus and Archombrotus espoused to Poliarchus' sister.

Barclay laced his narrative with extended conversations, voiced by the characters, that address political, philosophical and religious issues of the time, such as the advantages of a hereditary monarchy, the right of kings to raise taxes without the consent of the deputies of the people, the question of a permanent versus a standing army, methods for remedying the slowness of the judicial process, the dangers of religious dissent and the possibility of reconciling free will with divine prescience. Through these inserted conversations, Barclay, an early absolutist who was in step with his times, does not present a ruler as possessing limitless power, but as a sovereign who is subject to the interests of the state. In *Argenis*, Meleander, the king of Sicily, and Hyanisbe, the queen of Mauritania, receive the counsels of court advisers and of Poliarchus (who represents the ideal monarch), pertaining to the troubles affecting their realms.

John Barclay (1582–1621) was only ever a minor courtier, but his classical education and his general observation of the blunders of rulers enabled him to write this sophisticated political romance, which would entertain generations of readers and lend itself to multiple translations and adaptations. Barclay was born in 1582 at Pont-à-Mousson in Lorraine to a French mother and a Scottish father. His father, William Barclay, a devout Catholic and ardent monarchist, was a law professor at the Jesuit college there, where John also received his education. John followed his father to London in about 1605 and was connected to the court of James I, where he was appointed as a Gentleman of the King's Bedchamber and served as a sort of literary adviser and emissary. John's father William died in 1608, and in 1615 John himself left England, most likely because of financial need and for religious reasons, and moved to Rome.

John Barclay wrote exclusively in Latin (in both prose and verse), and his earlier writings also addressed contemporary political and religious issues. These include: *Regi Jacobo Primo carmen gratulatorium* (Paris 1603), a congratulatory poem to James I upon his coronation; *Series patefacti ... parricidii ... (Conspiratio Anglicana)* (London 1605), a narrative of the Gunpowder Plot; *Euphormionis Lusinini satyricon* (Paris 1605, 1607), a two-part satire with an anti-Jesuit slant; and *Icon Animorum* (London 1614), a treatise on the character of kings and courtiers.

When Barclay set out to write *Argenis*, no long romance of that type existed in Latin (the *Satyrica* of Petronius being extant only in fragments, not all of them known in Barclay's time). So, Barclay mixed Greek genres: his primary model was the *Aethiopica* of Heliodorus, a late-antique romance in which a princess must fend off other suitors in order to marry the man to whom she is secretly betrothed; his secondary model was Xenophon's *Cyropaedia*, a fictionalized biography of the Persian general Cyrus, dating from the early fourth century BCE, that includes discussion of generalship and statecraft. *Argenis* also contains echoes of traditional epic, with its opening *in medias res* and its motifs of shipwreck, capture by pirates and hand-to-hand combat, and of traditional drama with its division into five books. Yet, unlike these classical and late-antique genres, *Argenis* contains no supernatural elements – there are no instances of the use of magic or of prophetic dreams, for example. Barclay's work should be seen as part of the early development of the novel and can be compared to vernacular romances of the same period such as Philip Sidney's *Arcadia* (1590), Miguel de Cervantes' *Persiles y Sigismunda* (1617) and Mary Wroth's *Urania* (1621). The title of the novel, *Argenis*, has the appearance of a Greek term and is reminiscent of the titles of epic romance (such as *Aeneis* or *Thebais*). However, IJsewijn (1983) has identified it as an anagram of the Latin *regina*, and the title of the novel thus has the meaning 'the story of the princess'. Barclay's style and vocabulary can be described as a plain, classical mix, stemming mainly from Cicero and Livy. Barclay was not attempting to imitate any particular author in the way a sixteenth-century humanist might, but was creating a new, modern genre in order to communicate his political and philosophical views to an international audience in an entertaining manner.

Argenis became extremely popular immediately after its publication, with Latin reprints and further editions appearing already in 1622 and continuing throughout the seventeenth century and into the eighteenth. Translations began to appear, too, from the year after the original publication; *Argenis* had been rendered into French, English, Spanish, German, Italian, Dutch and Polish by the end of the seventeenth century, and Danish, Swedish, Russian and Hungarian translations followed in the next century. *Argenis* was abridged in translation, spun off into Latin and vernacular sequels, and served as inspiration for Latin and vernacular plays. To illustrate this popularity, a contemporary English translation is given in an appendix here.

Although Barclay did not intend to write a masked history of Europe, almost immediately after the publication of *Argenis*, readers attempted to connect the characters of the novel to historical persons, which added to the enjoyment of the book. Already in the early editions and translations of the novel, a key to the 'identity' of the characters began to be provided: Argenis represented the crown of France; Poliarchus, her betrothed and king of Gaul, was deemed to be Henri IV of France; Argenis' father, Meleander, king of Sicily, was equated with Henri III of France; and Hyanisbe, queen of Mauritania, with Elizabeth I of England. Archombrotus, Hyanisbe's presumed son (but actual nephew) was normally not assigned a specific model, but described simply either as a prince subordinate to the king of France or as a double for Poliarchus.

The excerpt that follows is taken from the climax of the novel, when Poliarchus and Archombrotus – the two rivals for Argenis' hand – meet face to face in Mauritania, at the palace of Queen Hyanisbe (the presumed mother of Archombrotus). At the opening of the story Poliarchus, the king of Gaul covertly residing in Sicily, was already secretly betrothed to Argenis, the princess of Sicily, but had fallen out of favour with her father. Poliarchus, away from court, then came across Archombrotus, the disguised heir to the throne of Mauritania, just arriving in Sicily, and the two became close friends. However, their friendship was ruined as Archombrotus, introduced at court, fell in love with Argenis and was preferred by her father, King Meleander. Poliarchus, as a result, decided to return to his country and gather his forces in an effort to come back to Sicily as a true royal with his retinue and prove to Meleander that he was worthy of Argenis' hand. While he was at sea, however, he was blown off course and ended up in Mauritania, which was being ravaged by the army of the king of Sardinia. Poliarchus took up arms for Mauritania and saved the country. In the meantime, Archombrotus received word from Queen Hyanisbe that his country was in danger and that he should return home immediately. What Hyanisbe knew (and hints at in this passage) is that Archombrotus could never be married to Argenis. He was not her own son, but the son of her sister Anna and King Meleander, and therefore the half-brother of Argenis. But, in this passage, Hyanisbe does not know why Poliarchus and Archombrotus have come to hate each other. How the situation is happily resolved constitutes the dénouement of the novel.

Bibliography

Bouchet, F. (1992), 'L'*Argénis* néo-latine de John Barclay: le premier «roman héroïque» (1621)', *XVIIe siècle*, 44: 169–88.

Collignon, A. (1902), *Notes historiques, littéraires, et bibliographiques sur l'Argenis de Jean Barclay*, Paris and Nancy; published separately as 'Notes sur l'*Argenis* de Jean Barclay', *Mémoires de l'Académie de Stanislas*, 5th ser., 19 (1902): 329–507 (http://catalogue.bnf.fr/ark:/12148/cb302579180).

Fleming, D. A. (1966), 'John Barclay: Neo-Latinist at the Jacobean Court', *Renaissance News*, 19: 228–36.

Glomski, J. (2016a), 'From Page to Stage: The Appeal of John Barclay's *Argenis* (Paris, 1621)', *Studia Aurea*, 10: 273–91.

Glomski, J. (2016b), 'Politics and Passion: Fact and Fiction in Barclay's *Argenis*', in J. Glomski and I. Moreau (eds), *Seventeenth-Century Fiction: Text & Transmission*, 49–63, Oxford.

IJsewijn, J. (1983), 'John Barclay and his *Argenis*: A Scottish Neo-Latin Novelist', *Humanistica Lovaniensia*, 32: 1–27.

Morrish Tunberg, J. (2013), 'An Old Wife and the Tale that She Tells in Barclay's *Argenis*', in S. Tilg and I. Walser (eds), *Der neulateinische Roman als Medium seiner Zeit. The Neo-Latin Novel in its Time*, 73–82, Tübingen.

Riley, M. and D. Pritchard Huber (eds) (2004), *John Barclay: Argenis*, 2 vols, Assen/Tempe (AZ).

Siegl-Mocavini, S. (1999), *John Barclays »Argenis« und ihr staatstheoretischer Kontext: Untersuchungen zum politischen Denken der Frühen Neuzeit*, Tübingen.

Walser, I. (2016), *Anton Wilhelm Ertl: Austriana regina Arabiae*, Berlin [47–53].

Source of the Latin text

The text has been established according to the most correct seventeenth-century edition of *Argenis*, by Gabriel Bugnotius (Leiden and Rotterdam, Officina Hackiana, 1664), and with reference to the most recent edition, by Mark Riley and Dorothy Pritchard Huber (2004). In the edition by Bugnotius, this passage is found in Book 5, Chapter 8; but Riley and Pritchard Huber number it Chapter 9, in agreement with the English translation by Kingesmill Long (London 1625), of which they print a modernized version.

Omissions in the original are indicated by ellipses.

Latin text

At vero Hyanisbe[1] alios prius se filio frui impatiens,[2] quamquam et mater et regina, omisit maiestatem, excessitque cubiculo, et praetextu videndi quam alacer circum filium populus esset, quamque ipse insignes (ita enim referebatur) milites ducesque haberet, ad atrium processit, indeque qua se primae palatii fores demittebant in oppidum. Et hanc procul conspicatus Archombrotus[3] descendit ex equo, maioribusque vestigiis, et alacritatis genio citatis, medium iter confecit. Ac ut primum pervenit ad matrem, stolamque extremam osculis strinxit, flens illa gaudio non distulit coram populo blanditias quae secreto debebantur. Tum illius dexteram tenens, Laudo[4] pietatem, o fili, quod tanto apparatu ad tuendam parentem venisti. Sed ne solus sis cui maternum affectum debeam, rex Galliae effecit;[5] cuius victoria[6] sumus incolumes. Ille a Mauritania tua exitium depulit; ille matrem tibi[7] servavit, quae nunc in Sardinia serviret: ipse tyrannus male tentatam[8] Africam sanguine perfudit. Omitto[9] illi regi adhuc aliquid amplius nos debere; quod[10] et ipse, et praeter me omnes ignorant. Veni, fili, neque ante[11] diis patriis lustrari propera, quam illum salutaveris adhuc ex vulneribus iacentem, quae hoc sceptrum tibi asseruerunt. Archombrotus tot beneficiorum magnitudine perculsus, subita Gallici regis charitate[12] flagrabat; saepe tamen excusans quod[13] externis principibus lentior fuisset in parentis patriaeque discrimine.

Modern English translation

But, truly, Hyanisbe,[1] unable to bear[2] others enjoying the sight of her son before herself, although both a mother and a queen, put aside her dignity and left her chamber, and on the pretext of seeing how animated the people were around her son and how he had distinguished (so, indeed, it was being reported) soldiers and leaders with him, she proceeded to the entrance hall, and from there to where the outer gate of the palace opened down towards the town. And Archombrotus,[3] having caught sight of her from a distance, dismounted his horse, and with very large steps spurred by the energy of his eagerness, crossed the ground between them. And, as soon as he reached his mother and touched the hem of her dress with kisses, she, weeping for joy, could not hold back in front of the people the signs of affection that should have been kept private. Then, taking his right hand, she said, 'I praise[4] your devotion, my son, because you have come with such great provision to the defence of your parent. But the king of Gaul has brought it about that you are not the only one to whom I owe maternal affection[5] – we are safe on account of his victory.[6] He repelled disaster from your Mauritania. He saved your mother,[7] who would now be a slave in Sardinia. The tyrant himself has steeped Africa, which he attacked wrongfully,[8] in his blood. Furthermore, I omit[9] saying that we are indebted to that king for something greater, of which[10] both he and everyone else except me are ignorant. Come, my son, and do not rush off to make offerings to your ancestral gods before[11] you have greeted him, still lying in bed from the wounds that have preserved the royal sceptre for you.' Archombrotus, struck by the greatness of so many favours, was stirred by a sudden feeling of affection[12] towards the Gallic king, while often excusing himself for[13] being slower than foreign princes in taking action during the danger to his parent and his country.

Iamque ad Poliarchum[14] praemissi, nunciaverant[15] si ipsi vacaret, reginam cum filio adfuturam.[16] Is, nisi morbo prohiberetur, se occupaturum officium respondet. . . . Avidissime exspectabat principem videre, quem Maurorum vocibus, et ipsius Hyanisbes[17] confessione, in rarissimis esse acceperat. Sed Hyempsalem[18] appellabant; vero scilicet nomine, passimque usitato. Clam enim Archombroti nomen assumpserat, dissimulando generi,[19] cum secretus, cultuque privato in Siciliam iret. . . . Sed posteaquam regina intravit, Archombrotum manu tenens, subito veluti monstro perculsa est.[20] Nam ut primum Poliarchus Archombrotum aspexit, vicissimque ab illo est cognitus (o fatum!) quae procella, quodve fulmen, celerius destinatos cursus exsequitur, quam tunc rabies, et indignatio, et avidus sanguinis furor, mutatis utriusque animis[21] vultus quoque corrupit? Ceu Medusam aspexissent steterunt immoti; mox trucibus oculis, necdum[22] tamen omnia impetui indulgentibus, a fronte ad vestigia contemplationem deduxere.[23] Stupebant fremebantque attoniti. . . . Sensim in utroque exsuperabat insania; nec aliud praeter reverentiam Hyanisbes obstabat quin[24] polluerent sanctitatem hospitii, et vel nudis manibus[25] nimis lenta arma praeverterent.

And now the men who had been sent to Poliarchus[14] told him[15] that if it were no trouble for him, the queen would come to see him with her son.[16] He replied that if he had not been prevented by his infirmity, he would have performed this courtesy first. . . . He was eagerly looking forward to seeing the prince, whom, from the reports of the Mauritanians and the confession of Hyanisbe herself,[17] he heard was among the most extraordinary of men. But they called him Hyempsal,[18] indeed by his own, true name, the one usually used. Yet, he had secretly taken the name Archombrotus in order to disguise his origin[19] when he travelled, in secret and in private dress, to Sicily. . . . But, when the queen entered, holding Archombrotus by the hand, she was suddenly struck with horror as if by the sight of a monstrous event.[20] For as soon as Poliarchus looked at Archombrotus, and in turn was recognized by him (oh, fate!), what storm or what thunderbolt executed its intended course more swiftly than their rage and anger and frenzied desire for blood then contaminated, with both their minds changed,[21] their facial expressions? They stood motionless as if they had looked upon the Medusa. Then, with savage eyes, but not yet[22] yielding completely to violence, they looked each other over from head to foot.[23] They stood stunned and, infuriated, they growled. . . . Gradually, the rage in both of them rose up; and nothing except respect for Hyanisbe blocked them from[24] violating the sacred laws of hospitality and even from bypassing their weapons, which would be too slow, and using their bare fists.[25]

Commentary

1 *Hyanisbe*: Her name is modelled on Sophonisbe (Sophoniba) (fl. 203 BCE), the daughter of the Carthaginian general Hasdrubal Gisco and the wife of Syphax, the king of western Numidia. After Syphax died as a prisoner of the Romans, Sophonisbe married Masinissa, the leader of the eastern Numidians and an ally of Rome. Rather than surrender herself to the Roman general Scipio when Masinissa could not protect her, she drank poison. See Livy, *Ab urbe condita* 30.12.10–11; 30.15.4.

2 *impatiens*: both modifies *Hyanisbe* and leads into an indirect statement.

3 *Archombrotus*: His name is an amalgamation of the Greek ἄρχων ('ruler') and βροτός ('mortal man') and so means the 'prince of mortals'.

4 *Laudo*: Hyanisbe's speech begins here and ends with *asseruerunt*.

5 *ne . . . sis*: a final (purpose) clause depending on *effecit*; the antecedent of *cui* is the unexpressed *tu*; *debeam* is an example of subjunctive by attraction.

6 *cuius*: a connecting relative; *victoria*: ablative of means.

7 *tibi*: dative of personal interest ('for you').

8 *tentatam*: perfect passive participle, from *tempto*.

9 *Omitto*: introduces an indirect statement, with accusative (*nos*) and infinitive (*debere*).

10 *quod*: refers back to *aliquid amplius*.

11 *ante*: goes together with *quam* (an example of tmesis).

12 *charitate* = *caritate*.

13 *quod*: used in constructions with *excuso*; see Cicero, *De oratore* 2.253. The subjunctive *fuisset* gives the speaker's own account of his actions: 'excusing himself for (so he said) being slower . . .'.

14 *Poliarchus*: from the Greek πόλις ('city') or πολύς ('many') and ἄρχων ('ruler'). So, the 'ruler of the city' or the 'ruler of many'.

15 *nunciaverant* = *nuntiaverant*.

16 *adfuturam*: supply *esse*, as with *occupaturum* in the next sentence (indirect statements).

17 *Hyanisbes*: genitive case (from Greek).

18 *Hyempsal*: inspired by Hiempsal I (d. *c.* 117 BCE), king of Numidia (see Sallust, *Iugurtha* 5.7; 11.3). Cicero refers to him as a king of Mauritania (*In Vatinium* 5.12). The use of disguises, including a change of name, was a common motif in biblical writing and in classical epic and drama, and is found also in late-antique Greek romance.

19 *dissimulando generi*: dative of purpose (*dissimulando* is a gerundive, agreeing with *generi*).

20 *perculsa est*: from *percello*.

21 *mutatis utriusque animis*: ablative absolute.

22 *necdum* = *neque dum*.

23 *deduxere* = *deduxerunt*.

24 *quin*: introduces a clause of prevention, after *nec aliud . . . obstabat*.

25 *nudis manibus*: ablative of means (literally 'with their bare hands').

Appendix: Second English translation, by Robert Le Grys (London 1628)

But *Hyanisbe*,[1] impatient that any should haue the satisfaction of seeing her Sonne before her self, though both a Mother and a Queene, laid aside her Maiesty, and went out of her chamber: and vnder colour of seeing how ioyfull the people were about him, and how braue Captaines and Souldiers (for so she had been informed) hee brought with him; went into the Court of the Palace, and from thence to the Gate that looked toward the Towne. *Archombrotus*[3] seeing her a good way off, leaped from his Horse, and with hasty steps spurred on by a spirit of chearefulnesse, he quickly passed the ground that was betwixt them. And assoone as he was come to his Mother, and had kissed the hemme of her gowne: she weeping for joy, did not forbeare before the people those expressions of tendernesse, which had otherwise been fitter for more priuacy. Then taking him by the right hand: I commend (said she) my Sonne, thy piety, who so brauely prouided, art come to thy Mothers defence. But that thou mayest not be the onely One, to whom I should be oblieged to beare a motherly affection, the King of Gallia hath prouided, whose victory hath preserued vs. Hee it is that hath defended thy Mauritania from destruction: He that hath saued thy Mother, who, but for him, had now been a Slaue in Sardinia. The Tyrant himselfe with his blood hath discoloured Africa, which to his misfortune he had assailed. I forbeare to speake of another obligation, wherein we are tied to this braue King, which, besides my selfe, both himselfe and all the World also are vnacquainted with. Come, my Sonne, and doe not make haste to tender thy deuotions to our Countrey Gods, before thou salute him, who now lyeth of those wounds, which he receiued in assuring this Kingdome to thee. *Archombrotus* moued with the regard of so many fauours receiued, was fired with a sudden loue of the Gallian King: often yet excusing himselfe to his Mother, that in the danger of his Countrey, and his Parent, he had been more slacke then forraine Princes.

And now some were sent before to let *Poliarchus*[14] know, that if it might not bee of trouble to him, the Queene and her Sonne would come to visit him. Hee returnes for answer, That if his indisposition had not hindred him, he would haue preuented their courtesie . . . Hee did with all eagernesse desire to see the Prince, whom by the report of the Moores, and by *Hyanisbes* owne confession, was deliuered to him for one of the most compleate in all noble parts that was to bee found. But they called him *Hiempsall*,[18] as his right name, and with which they were acquainted. For the name of *Archombrotus* he had secretly assumed, for the keeping his qualitie vndiscouered, when disguized, and in a priuat habit he travelled into Sicily. . . . But when the Queene came in, holding *Archombrotus* by the hand, she was strooken into an amazement, as with the sight of some fearefull Monster. For as soone as *Poliarchus* beheld *Archombrotus*, and was in exchange knowne by him; O the Fates! What tempest? What lightning did euen with so much celerity passe to the marke it aimed at! as then, rage, and indignation, and a blood-thirsting fury, perturbing both their altered minds, did demonstrate their effects in their lookes? As they had spied *Medusa's* head, they stood without motion: instantly with sparkling eyes (which as yet did not in euery thing yeeld to their first passion) they viewed one another from head to foot. Full of astonishment, they at once both fretted and mused. . . . By degrees their madnesse in both of them grew to the height: nor did any thing, besides the respect of *Hyanisbe*, stay them from violating the sacred Lawes of hospitalitie, and euen with their naked hands, attempt the satisfaction of their spleenes, not tarrying for other weapons.

13

The Gunpowder Plot

John Milton (1608–1674), *In Quintum Novembris*

Stephen Harrison

Introduction

This poem was written at the age of 17 in 1625–6 during Milton's undergraduate studies at Christ's College, Cambridge. Protestant and loyalist Neo-Latin hexameter poems on the sensational Gunpowder Plot of 5 November 1605, in which Catholic rebels narrowly failed to blow up the House of Lords and King James I at the State Opening of Parliament, rapidly became a literary sub-genre in Britain in the years immediately afterwards, for example in Francis Herring's 1606 *Pietas Pontifica* and Phineas Fletcher's 1611 *Locustae* (see Haan 1992 and 1996: xxix–lv). Milton's poem draws on several of these (see Haan 2012 for detailed parallels) and may well have been produced for the celebrations (stressed at the poem's end) on 5 November 1625, the twentieth anniversary of the Plot.

No doubt as a result of the subject's popularity, Milton's relatively short poem of 226 lines does not describe the Plot itself: the actual conspiracy and its detection are only narrated with extreme rapidity in the brief final section (211–26). Such an oblique approach to telling a well-known story, leaving the reader to fill in the gaps, is also a feature of the particular classical hexameter form adopted by Milton here, the 'epyllion' or single-book short epic (as in Catullus 64 or Callimachus' *Hecale*). Milton's narrative focuses on the character of Satan and his indignation with the defiantly Protestant English (1–47), and his journey to Rome to stir up the Pope to action, appearing to the latter in a dream disguised as a Franciscan friar (48–138); the Pope then goes to the allegorical cave of Murder and Betrayal, which he unleashes on England (139–69). The day is saved by the intervention of Rumour, who, urged by God, broadcasts the plot and ensures its failure (170–226). The strongly nationalistic and anti-Catholic tone is clear throughout.

The choice to concentrate on Satan and divine machinery (an element prominent but not predominant in other Plot-poems) recalls particular precedents in classical epic. The unsuccessful attack of an irate and ill-disposed deity on a divinely protected monarch and people reworks the intervention of Juno against the hero Aeneas and his Trojans in Books 1 and 7 of Virgil's *Aeneid*: in *Aeneid* 7 Juno rouses the Fury Allecto, who appears in human disguise in a dream (like Milton's Satan) to Aeneas' enemy Turnus to urge aggressive action. This is a particularly fitting parallel given that the poem endorses in its second line the post-classical tradition that the Britons were descended from the Trojans. The concentration on the role of malign divinities in causing political peril may also draw on the prelude to the civil war of Caesar and Pompey described in the hexameter poem embedded in Petronius' *Satyrica* (120–1), where the evil Pluto and Fortuna conspire to cause the conflict. The macabre cave of Murder and Betrayal (lines 139–54) and the house of Rumour (lines 172–94) recall set pieces in the *Metamorphoses* of Ovid, such as the squalid house of Envy (2.760–82), the ghastly home of Famine (8.788–808), the cave of Sleep (11.595–615) and the house of Rumour (12.39–66), together with elements from the abstract deities at the gates of Virgil's underworld (*Aeneid* 6.273–81) and his description of winged Rumour (*Aeneid* 4.173–88).

The poem's use of traditional epic divine machinery for triumphalist political invective also has classical antecedents. Claudian's vicious epic attack on the dead imperial minister Rufinus at the Christian court of Honorius at the end of the fourth century involves a full-scale pagan infernal council (*In Rufinum* 1.25–123), while Milton's celebratory final aetiology recalls Propertius' elegy 4.6; that poem connects the temple of Palatine Apollo at Rome (and probably its annual festival in October, matching 5 November) with Augustus' final civil war victory at Actium through the Homeric-style active intervention of the god in the battle. Similar uses of the classical-epic divine apparatus are also found in propagandist Neo-Latin hexameter poems from the reign of Elizabeth, which (anticipating the Plot sub-genre) attacked Catholic conspiracies and cruelty, and formed a significant part of the literary background to Milton's poem (see again Haan 1992, 1996 and 2012 for details). *Paraeus* (1585), possibly by George Peele (William Shakespeare's collaborator for *Titus Andronicus*), on the supposed plot of William Parry against the Queen, presents a similar Pluto/Satan as the author of religious discord in England, while in William Alabaster's unfinished *Elisaeis* (pre-1592), treating Elizabeth's early tribulations under her sister Mary Tudor and praised by Edmund Spenser, we find especially close parallels. There Satan gives an angry speech about the progress of the Protestant cause in England, and then goes to Rome to goad Papacy (the Church personified) into action; Papacy in turn goes to England, where she appears to the evil bishop Stephen Gardiner in a dream and inspires him to stir up Mary against Elizabeth. Some anti-Catholic details are also drawn from the anti-monastic satires of the great Scottish Neo-Latin poet George Buchanan (1506–1582: see Text 3).

In Quintum Novembris remained unpublished until 1645, when it appeared with a number of youthful Latin poems under the title *Poemata*, as a separate section of the poet's first collection *Poems of Mr John Milton* (a parallel section of shorter English and Italian poems included 'Lycidas', and *Comus* appeared in a third section). Within the *Poemata* it formed part of the *Sylvarum Liber*, which imitated the *Silvae* of Statius by including poems in varied metres; this sub-collection was matched by the *Elegiarum Liber*, which combined short Latin epigrams (including four on the Gunpowder Plot) with some longer elegiac poems. This was a redoubtably learned debut verse collection for a writer then becoming known as a prose controversialist (two of his tracts on divorce and his *Areopagitica* on free speech had been published in 1644).

The Latin style of the poem is mostly Virgilian, the standard model for hexameter composition, and the vocabulary is largely classical, with many imitations of Virgilian and Ovidian phrases (see Haan 2012 for more details) and occasional lexical coinages (see Hale 1994); pagan religious terminology is used, as regularly in Neo-Latin works, to describe Christian figures and features (cf. e.g. 8, 23 nn.), sometimes with interesting crossover between the two (cf. 3, 8, 129–30, 137, 221–6). The metre and word-order is generally elegant (cf. e.g. the artful word-distribution in lines 8, 28, 82, 99, 132 and 200, the vertical juxtaposition of parallel proper nouns in lines 2–3 and 201–2, the Greek-style hiatus in line 65, the dramatic enjambment in lines 79–80, the spondaic ending of line 201); the frequent placing of noun and epithet in agreement at the end of the two halves of the same hexameter can be a little monotonous (seventeen in the first fifty lines, including four in succession in lines 12–15, as against six in the first fifty lines of Virgil's *Aeneid* and seven in the first fifty lines of Ovid's *Metamorphoses*).

As often noted, Milton's poem presents an early version of elements of the first two books of *Paradise Lost* (1667), notoriously a work of deeply Latinate colouring; Satan's memorably voiced indignation there at his expulsion from heaven and his calling of the infernal council as a prelude to malign intervention in Eden share both vivid diabolic characterization and classical-style divine machinery with *In Quintum Novembris*. The Latin poem's two opening sentences both cover eleven lines, looking forward to the long sentences of Milton's English epic (which begins with two of sixteen and ten lines). This Neo-Latin narrative poem thus not only shows the young Milton's virtuoso adaptation of Latin epic style and technique, but also gives a fascinating foretaste of one of the great masterpieces of English poetry.

Metre: dactylic hexameter

Bibliography

Texts, translations and notes are available in Sutton 1999/2013, Haan 2012 and Carey 2007.

Carey, J. (2007), *Milton: The Complete Shorter Poems*, 2nd edn, Harlow.

Cheek, M. (1957), 'Milton's *In quintum Novembris*: An Epic Foreshadowing', *Studies in Philology*, 54: 172–84.

Haan, E. (1992), 'Milton's *In Quintum Novembris* and the Anglo-Latin Gunpowder Epic', *Humanistica Lovaniensia*, 40: 221–50.

Haan, E. (1996), *Phineas Fletcher: Locustae vel Pietas Iesuitica*, Leuven.

Haan, E. (2012), edition of and commentary on *In Quintum Novembris*, in E. Haan and B. K. Lewalski (eds), *Complete Works of John Milton III: The Shorter Poems*, lxxxi–xcix, cxviii–cxx, 453–63, Oxford.

Hale, J. K. (1994), 'Notes on Milton's Latin Word-Formation in the *Poemata* of 1645', *Humanistica Lovaniensia*, 43: 405–10.

Hale, J. K. (2001), 'Milton and the Gunpowder Plot: *In Quintum Novembris* reconsidered', *Humanistica Lovaniensia*, 50: 351–66.

Hardie, P. (2012), *Rumour and Renown: Representations of Fama in Western Literature*, Cambridge [429–37].

James, A. (2016), *Poets, Players, and Preachers: Remembering the Gunpowder Plot in Seventeenth-Century England*, Toronto [127–34].

Quint, D. (1991), 'Milton, Fletcher, and the Gunpowder Plot', *Journal of the Warburg and Courtauld Institutes*, 54: 261–8.

Schleiner, W. (1978), '*Divina Virago*: Queen Elizabeth as an Amazon', *Studies in Philology*, 75: 163–80.

Starnes, D. T. (1951), 'More about the Tower of Fame in Milton', *Notes and Queries*, 196: 515–18.

Sutton, D. F. (1998), 'Milton's *In Quintum Novembris anno aetatis 17* (1626): Choices and Intentions', in G. Schmeling (ed.), *Qui Miscuit Utile Dulci: Festschrift Essays for Paul Lachlan MacKendrick*, 349–75, Wauconda (IL).

Sutton, D. F. (1999/2013), hypertext edition of John Milton's *In Quintum Novembris* (http://philological.bham.ac.uk/milton/index.html).

Tung, M. (1978), 'Milton's Adaptation in *In quintum Novembris* of Virgil's Fama', *Milton Quarterly*, 12: 90–5.

Source of the Latin text

The Latin text has been taken from Haan 2012: 167–80, with some modifications of spelling, punctuation and paragraphing.

Latin text

Iam pius extrema veniens Iacobus ab arcto
Teucrigenas populos lateque patentia regna
Albionum tenuit, iamque inviolabile foedus
sceptra Caledoniis coniunxerat Anglica Scotis,
5 pacificusque novo felix divesque sedebat
in solio occultique doli securus et hostis,
cum ferus ignifluo regnans Acheronte tyrannus,
Eumenidum pater, aetherio vagus exul Olympo,
forte per immensum terrarum erraverat orbem,
10 dinumerans sceleris socios vernasque fideles,
participes regni post funera maesta futuros.
Hic tempestates medio ciet aëre diras,
illic unanimes odium struit inter amicos
armat et invictas in mutua viscera gentes,
15 regnaque olivifera vertit florentia pace,
et quoscumque videt purae virtutis amantes,
hos cupit adiicere imperio, fraudumque magister
temptat inaccessum sceleri corrumpere pectus,
insidiasque locat tacitas cassesque latentes
20 tendit ut incautos rapiat, ceu Caspia tigris
insequitur trepidam deserta per avia praedam
nocte sub illuni et somno nictantibus astris.
Talibus infestat populos Summanus et urbes
cinctus caeruleae fumanti turbine flammae.
25   Iamque fluentisonis albentia rupibus arva
apparent et terra deo dilecta marino,
cui nomen dederat quondam Neptunia proles
Amphitryoniaden qui non dubitavit atrocem
aequore tranato furiali poscere bello
30 ante expugnatae crudelia saecula Troiae.
At simul hanc opibusque et festa pace beatam
aspicit et pingues donis Cerealibus agros,
quodque magis doluit venerantem numina veri
sancta Dei populum, tandem suspiria rupit
35 Tartareos ignes et luridum olentia sulphur,
qualia Trinacria trux ab Iove clausus in Aetna
efflat tabifico monstrosus ab ore Typhoeus:
ignescunt oculi, stridetque adamantinus ordo

English translation

Already pious James, coming from the furthest north,
Held under his sway the peoples born of Troy
And the wide-spreading kingdoms of the men of Albion,
And already an inviolable treaty had joined
The kingdom of England with the Caledonian Scots,   5
And the peace-making ruler sat happy and prosperous
On his new throne, unconcerned for secret plots and enemies,
When the fierce tyrant who reigns over fire-flowing Acheron,
The father of the Furies, that wandering exile from heavenly Olympus,
Had chanced to stray over the measureless world of earth,
Counting his companions in crime and faithful slaves,   10
Destined to share his realm after their miserable deaths.
Here he summons terrible storms in mid-air,
There stirs up enmity between loving friends,
And turns unconquered races in arms against their own vitals,
And overturns kingdoms flourishing with the olive branch of peace.   15
And whichever lovers of pure virtue he perceives
He wishes to add to his dominion, and as the master of lies
He tries to corrupt the heart that is blocked to crime,
And lays hidden ambush and stretches concealed nets,
To catch them unawares, like a Caspian tigress   20
Pursues its trembling prey through trackless deserts
Under a moonless night and stars blinking with sleep.
With such means does the dark god, girded
With the smoking bolt of blue fire, assail peoples and cities.
    And already the land white with sea-echoing cliffs was in sight, 25
And the country loved by the god of the sea,
To which Neptune's scion had once given his name,
He who did not hesitate to cross the ocean
And challenge fierce Hercules in furious war
Before the cruel age of the sack of Troy.   30
And as soon as he saw this land rich in resources and cheerful peace,
And its fields fat with the gifts of Ceres,
And, which grieved him more, its people who revered
The holy power of the true God, at last he burst out in sighs
Which stank of the fires of Tartarus and its yellow sulphur,   35
Just like those that fierce Typhoeus, shut up by Jupiter
In Sicilian Etna, breathes out monstrously from his pestilential mouth.
His eyes were aflame, and the adamantine row of his teeth

dentis ut armorum fragor ictaque cuspide cuspis.
40 Atque 'pererrato solum hoc lacrimabile mundo
inveni', dixit, 'gens haec mihi sola rebellis
contemptrixque iugi nostraque potentior arte.
Illa tamen, mea si quicquam tentamina possunt,
non feret hoc impune diu, non ibit inulta.'
45 Hactenus, et piceis liquido natat aëre pennis:
qua volat, adversi praecursant agmine venti,
densantur nubes, et crebra tonitrua fulgent.
      Iamque pruinosas velox superaverat Alpes
et tenet Ausoniae fines: a parte sinistra
50 nimbifer Appenninus erat priscique Sabini
dextra veneficiis infamis Etruria nec non
te furtiva Tibris Thetidi videt oscula dantem.
Hinc Mavortigenae consistit in arce Quirini.
Reddiderant dubiam iam sera crepuscula lucem,
55 cum circumgreditur totam tricoronifer urbem,
panificosque deos portat, scapulisque virorum
evehitur. Praeeunt summisso poplite reges
et mendicantum series longissima fratrum,
cereaque in manibus gestant funalia caeci
60 Cimmeriis nati in tenebris vitamque trahentes.
Templa dein multis subeunt lucentia taedis
(vesper erat sacer iste Petro) fremitusque canentum
saepe tholos implet vacuos et inane locorum
qualiter exululat Bromius Bromiique caterva
65 Orgia cantantes in Echionio Aracyntho
dum tremit attonitus vitreis Asopus in undis,
et procul ipse cava responsat rupe Cithaeron.
      His igitur tandem solemni more peractis,
Nox senis amplexus Erebi taciturna reliquit
70 praecipitesque impellit equos stimulante flagello:
captum oculis Typhlonta Melanchaetemque ferocem
atque Acheronteo prognatam patre Siopen
torpidam et hirsutis horrentem Phrica capillis.
Interea regum domitor, Phlegethontius haeres
75 ingreditur thalamos (neque enim secretus adulter
producit steriles molli sine pellice noctes).
At vix compositos somnus claudebat ocellos
cum niger umbrarum dominus rectorque silentum
praedatorque hominum falsa sub imagine tectus

Clashed like the crashing of weapons and the smash of spear on spear,
And he said: 'I have wandered the world and found   40
Only this miserable turf, only this people to resist me
And scorn my dominion, superior to all my subtlety.
But, if my efforts can accomplish anything,
It will not escape with this unpunished, it will not get off unchastised.'
So far he spoke, and plunged through the clear air on pitch-black pinions;   45
Where he flew, enemy winds ran before him in a hostile line,
The clouds grew dense, and frequent thunderbolts flashed.
    And already he had rapidly crossed the frosty Alps,
And reached the bounds of Italy: on his left
Was cloud-bearing Appeninus, and the Sabines of old,   50
On his right was Etruria infamous for poisonings, and further
He could see you, Tiber, giving secret kisses to Thetis' sea.
Here he stopped on the citadel of Romulus, the son of Mars.
The late day's gloom had made the light uncertain,
When the bearer of the tiara walked about the whole city   55
And carried his gods made of bread, portered
On men's shoulders; kings precede him on bended knee,
And the lengthiest line of begging brothers,
And they bear wax tapers in their hands in their blindness,
Born in Cimmerian darkness, dragging out their lives.   60
Then they approach sanctuaries that shine with many torches
(That evening was sacred to Peter), and the clamour of singers
Often filled the empty domes and vacant spaces, just as Bacchus and his
    horde wail,
Chanting their rituals on Theban Mount Aracynthus,
While the river Asopus trembles in shock in its glassy waters,   65
And Cithaeron itself echoes at distance from its hollow rocks.
    And so, when these actions were ceremoniously completed,
Silent Night left behind the embrace of old Erebus
And drove on her horses to speed with the spur of her whip: 70
Typhlon, bereft of sight, fierce Melanchaetes,
And sluggish Siope born from an infernal sire
And Phrix bristling with a mane full of hair.
Meanwhile the tamer of kings, the heir of Hell,
Entered the bedchamber: he, the secret adulterer,   75
Does not spend his nights fruitlessly without a soft mistress.
But hardly was sleep closing his eyes in rest,
When the dark lord of the shades and ruler of the silent,
The predator of men, concealed under a false appearance,

80 astitit. Assumptis micuerunt tempora canis,
    barba sinus promissa tegit, cineracea longo
    syrmate verrit humum vestis pendetque cucullus
    vertice de raso et, ne quicquam desit ad artes,
    cannabeo lumbos constrinxit fune fallaces
85 tarda fenestratis figens vestigia calceis.
    Talis uti fama est vasta Franciscus eremo
    taetra vagabatur solus per lustra ferarum
    silvestrique tulit genti pia verba salutis
    impius atque lupos domuit Libycosque leones.
90   Subdolus at tali serpens velatus amictu
    solvit in has fallax ora execrantia voces:
    'Dormis, nate? Etiamne tuos sopor opprimit artus,
    immemor o fidei, pecorumque oblite tuorum,
    dum cathedram, venerande, tuam diademaque triplex
95 ridet Hyperboreo gens barbara nata sub axe
    dumque pharetrati spernunt tua iura Britanni?
    Surge, age, surge piger, Latius quem Caesar adorat,
    cui reserata patet convexi ianua caeli:
    turgentes animos et fastus frange procaces
100 sacrilegique sciant tua quid maledictio possit
    et quid apostolicae possit custodia clavis,
    et memor Hesperiae disiectam ulciscere classem
    mersaque Iberorum lato vexilla profundo
    sanctorumque cruci tot corpora fixa probrosae
105 Thermodoontea nuper regnante puella.
    At tu si tenero mavis torpescere lecto
    crescentesque negas hosti contundere vires
    Tyrrhenum implebit numeroso milite pontum
    signaque Aventino ponet fulgentia colle:
110 reliquias veterum franget flammisque cremabit
    sacraque calcabit pedibus tua colla profanis
    cuius gaudebant soleis dare basia reges.
    Nec tamen hunc bellis et aperto Marte lacesses,
    (irritus ille labor), tu callidus utere fraude:
115 quaelibet haereticis disponere retia fas est.
    Iamque ad consilium extremis rex magnus ab oris
    patricios vocat et procerum de stirpe beatos,
    grandaevosque patres trabea canisque verendos:
    hos tu membratim poteris conspergere in auras

Stood by him; his temples shone with sham white hair,   80
A lengthy beard covered his bosom, his ash-coloured dress
Swept the ground with its long train, and a hood hung
From his shaved head, and lest his arts be in any way deficient,
He bound his lying loins with a rope of hemp,
Fastening his slow feet with windowed sandals.   85
Such, so goes the story, was Francis in the great desert
When he wandered alone through the foul lairs of beasts,
And brought the holy words of salvation to the people of the woods,
Though himself impious, and tamed wolves and the lions of Libya.
The subtle serpent, concealed in such dress   90
Deceitfully opened his mouth of curses with these words:
'Are you asleep, my son? Has sleep overcome even your limbs,
Forgetful of your faith, heedless of your flock,
While the barbarian race born under the far northern sky
Laughs, venerable one, at your throne and triple diadem,   95
And while the Britons with their quivers scorn your power?
Come, arise, arise, sluggish one, whom Latin Caesar worships,
For whom the gate of arched heaven is unbolted and open:
Overcome your slow spirits and extravagant disdain,
And let the sinners know the power of your curse,   100
And the power of the guardianship of the apostle's key,
And, mindful of the Western land, avenge the scattering of its fleet
And the standards of Spain sunk in the broad deep,
And so many saints' bodies nailed to the cross of shame
When the Amazonian maid was lately reigning.   105
But if you prefer to lie inert in your soft bed
And refuse to beat back the growing power of your enemy,
He will fill the Tyrrhenian sea with a mass of men
And set his shining standards on the Aventine hill:
He will smash the relics of the ancients and burn them with flames,   110
And tread on your holy neck with his profane feet,
Your neck, whose feet kings used to joy to kiss.
Yet do not provoke him with war and open conflict –
That is a vain labour – but be cunning and use guile:
It is lawful to stretch any net before heretics.   115
And now the great king is calling his nobles to council
From his farthest shores, and the wealthy of high stock,
And the senators of great age, to be revered for their purple dress and grey
    locks.
These you will be able to scatter limb from limb to the winds

120 atque dare in cineres nitrati pulveris igne
     aedibus iniecto qua convenere sub imis.
     Protinus ipse igitur quoscumque habet Anglia fidos
     propositi factique mone: quisquamne tuorum
     audebit summi non iussa facessere Papae?
125 Perculsosque metu subito casuque stupentes
     invadat vel Gallus atrox, vel saevus Iberus:
     saecula sic illic tandem Mariana redibunt,
     tuque in belligeros iterum dominaberis Anglos.
     Et necquid timeas, divos divasque secundas
130 accipe, quotque tuis celebrantur numina fastis.'
     Dixit, et ascitos ponens malefidus amictus
     fugit ad infandam, regnum illaetabile, Lethen.
       Iam rosea Eoas pandens Tithonia portas
     vestit inauratas redeunti lumine terras
135 maestaque adhuc nigri deplorans funera nati
     irrigat ambrosiis montana cacumina guttis,
     cum somnos pepulit stellatae ianitor aulae,
     nocturnos visus et somnia grata revolvens.
     Est locus aeterna septus caligine noctis
140 vasta ruinosi quondam fundamina tecti,
     nunc torvi spelunca Phoni, Prodotaeque bilinguis
     effera quos uno peperit Discordia partu.
     Hic inter caementa iacent semifractaque saxa
     ossa inhumata virum et traiecta cadavera ferro;
145 hic Dolus intortis semper sedet ater ocellis,
     Iurgiaque et stimulis armata Calumnia fauces,
     et Furor atque viae moriendi mille videntur
     et Timor exsanguisque locum circumvolat Horror
     perpetuoque leves per muta silentia manes
150 exululant, tellus et sanguine conscia stagnat.
     Ipsi etiam pavidi latitant penetralibus antri
     et Phonos et Prodotes, nulloque sequente per antrum,
     antrum horrens, scopulosum, atrum feralibus umbris
     diffugiunt sontes, et retro lumina vertunt.
155 Hos pugiles Romae per saecula longa fideles
     evocat antistes Babylonius, atque ita fatur:
     'Finibus occiduis circumfusum incolit aequor
     gens exosa mihi; prudens natura negavit
     indignam penitus nostro coniungere mundo.
160 Illuc, sic iubeo, celeri contendite gressu,

And consign them to ashes, setting the fire of gunpowder 120
In the depths of the house where they have met.
And so warn forthwith all England's faithful
Of the plan and deed: which of your people
Will dare not to execute the orders of the supreme Pope?
And when they are stricken by sudden fear and numb with disaster 125
Let the fierce Frenchman invade or the savage Spaniard:
So then at last shall the age of Mary return,
And you will once more exercise mastery over the warlike English.
And so that you have no fear, know that the gods and goddesses
Favour you, and all the divine powers celebrated in your calendar.' 130
So he spoke, and deceitfully laying aside his assumed dress
He fled to unspeakable Lethe, that joyless kingdom.
    Now the rosy wife of Tithonus, opening the gates of the East,
Clothed the golden lands with returning light,
And still grieving for the sorrowful death of her dark-hued son, 135
Soaked the mountain heights with her immortal tears,
When the doorkeeper of the starry hall drove away sleep,
Pondering his nocturnal visions and welcome dreams.
There is a place enclosed by the eternal mist of night,
Once the vast foundations of a ruined building, 140
Now the cavern of cruel Murder and two-tongued Betrayal
Whom wild Discord bore together in a single birth.
Here amidst rubble and smashed stones lie
The unburied bones of men and bodies stabbed with steel;
Here dark Guile always sits with crooked eyes, 145
And Quarrels, and Calumny, her jaws armed with spikes,
And Madness and a thousand routes to death are visible,
And Fear and blood-draining Horror fly around the place,
And insubstantial spirits forever wail through the speechless silence,
And the guilty surface pools with blood. 150
Murder and Betrayal themselves lurk fearful in the depths of the cave,
And none pursues them through the cavern, a cavern
Horrid, rocky and dark with shades of death,
As they flee in guilt, and turn their eyes to the back.
These prize-fighters for Rome, faithful through long ages, 155
Are called upon by the high priest of Babylon, who spoke as follows:
'A people hateful to me inhabits the sea surrounding
The western bounds; nature in its wisdom has refused
To join this deeply unworthy race to our world.
There, so I command, hasten with speedy step, 160

Tartareoque leves difflentur pulvere in auras
et rex et pariter satrapae, scelerata propago;
et quotquot fidei caluere cupidine verae
consilii socios adhibete, operisque ministros.'
165 Finierat, rigidi cupide paruere gemelli.
Interea longo flectens curvamine caelos
despicit aetherea dominus qui fulgurat arce
vanaque perversae ridet conamina turbae
atque sui causam populi vult ipse tueri.
170   Esse ferunt spatium, qua distat ab Aside terra
fertilis Europe et spectat Maeotidas undas.
Hic turris posita est Titanidos ardua Famae
aerea, lata, sonans, rutilis vicinior astris
quam superimpositum vel Athos vel Pelion Ossae:
175 mille fores aditusque patent, totidemque fenestrae
amplaque per tenues translucent atria muros.
Excitat hic varios plebs agglomerata susurros
qualiter instrepitant circum mulctralia bombis
agmina muscarum aut texto per ovilia iunco
180 dum Canis aestivum coeli petit ardua culmen.
Ipsa quidem summa sedet ultrix matris in arce,
auribus innumeris cinctum caput eminet olli
quis sonitum exiguum trahit atque levissima captat
murmura ab extremis patuli confinibus orbis;
185 nec tot Arestoride servator inique iuvencae
Isidos, immiti volvebas lumina vultu,
lumina non unquam tacito nutantia somno,
lumina subiectas late spectantia terras
(istis illa solet loca luce carentia saepe
190 perlustrare etiam radianti impervia soli)
millenisque loquax auditaque visaque linguis
cuilibet effundit temeraria veraque mendax
nunc minuit, modo confictis sermonibus auget.
     Sed tamen a nostro meruisti carmine laudes,
195 Fama, bonum quo non aliud veracius ullum,
nobis digna cani, nec te memorasse pigebit
carmine tam longo: servati scilicet Angli
officiis, vaga diva, tuis, tibi reddimus aequa.
Te Deus aeternos motu qui temperat ignes,
200 fulmine praemisso alloquitur terraque tremente:

And let there be blown in infernal dust to the light breezes
The king and his lords together, an accursed stock,
And use those who are warm in desire for the true faith
As comrades in your plan and servants of the enterprise.'
He had finished, and the cruel twins eagerly obeyed.   165
Meanwhile, as he turned the skies in their long curve,
The lord who thunders from the citadel of heaven
Looks down and laughs at the vain effort of the perverse mob,
And wills to protect personally the cause of his own people.
They say there is a space where fertile Europe stands apart   170
From the land of Asia and looks over the waters of Maeotis.
Here is placed the lofty tower of the Titan Rumour,
Brazen, wide, resounding, nearer to the ruddy stars
Than Athos or Pelion when placed on Ossa:
Its thousand doors and entrances lie open, and as many windows,   175
And its ample halls shine through its insubstantial walls.
The people gathered here engender various murmurs,
Just as hosts of flies make noise with buzzing around milk-pails
Or through sheep-pens of woven rushes,
As the Dog-star seeks the heights of heaven at its summer zenith. 180
Rumour herself sits at the height of the citadel, her mother's avenger:
Her head protrudes, wrapped with ears innumerable,
With which she gathers the least sound and picks up the lightest murmurs
From the furthest bounds of the widespread world.
Not so many were the eyes you rolled in your unrelenting face,   185
Argus, cruel watcher of Isis when she was a heifer,
Those eyes that never nod in silent sleep,
Eyes that gaze far and wide at the lands that lie below:
With these she is wont to survey regions lacking light,
Even those impassable to the rays of the sun,   190
And freely voluble she pours out to all at random
What she has seen or heard with her thousand tongues,
And deceptively now she plays down the truth,
Now she exaggerates it with invented stories.
But you, Rumour, have deserved praise of my poem,   195
You a benefit more truthful than any other, worthy of my song,
Nor will I regret telling of you in such a long poem:
We the English, saved indeed by your services,
Wandering goddess, pay a fair return to you.
The God who rules the eternal fires in their motion
Addressed you, sending a thunderbolt first and as the earth quaked: 200

'Fama, siles? An te latet impia Papistarum
coniurata cohors in meque meosque Britannos,
et nova sceptrigero caedes meditata Iacobo?'
Nec plura: illa statim sensit mandata Tonantis
205 et satis ante fugax stridentes induit alas
induit et variis exilia corpora plumis;
dextra tubam gestat Temesaeo ex aere sonoram.
Nec mora: iam pennis cedentes remigat auras
atque parum est cursu celeres praevertere nubes:
210 iam ventos, iam solis equos post terga reliquit
et primo Anglicas solito de more per urbes
ambiguas voces incertaque murmura spargit,
mox arguta dolos et detestabile vulgat
proditionis opus nec non facta horrida dictu,
215 auctoresque addit sceleris nec garrula caecis
insidiis loca structa silet. Stupuere relatis
et pariter iuvenes pariter tremuere puellae,
effetique senes pariter, tantaeque ruinae
sensus ad aetatem subito penetraverat omnem.
220 Attamen interea populi miserescit ab alto
aethereus pater et crudelibus obstitit ausis
papicolum: capti poenas raptantur ad acres.
At pia tura Deo et grati solvuntur honores,
compita laeta focis genialibus omnia fumant,
225 turba choros iuvenilis agit: quintoque Novembris
nulla dies toto occurrit celebratior anno.

'Rumour, are you silent? Or are you unaware of the impious host
Of the Papists in conspiracy against me and my Britons,
And the unprecedented murder planned against James who wields the
    sceptre?'
No more he spoke: she at once recognized the instructions of the Thunderer,
And though apt enough to fly before, put on whirring wings   205
And clothed her slender body with multi-coloured feathers;
In her right hand she carried a sounding trumpet of Bruttian bronze.
Without delay she now surges through the yielding breezes with her pinions;
It is too little for her to surpass the swift clouds in speed:
Already she leaves the winds and the horses of the Sun in her wake,   210
And first in her usual manner she spreads through the cities of England
Dubious utterances and uncertain whisperings,
Next, clear and shrill, she broadcasts the plottings,
The hateful enterprise of treason, and the deeds foul to relate,
And adds the leaders of the crime, and in her chatter   215
Is not silent about the place laid out for the unseen ambush.
All were stunned at the news, youths and maidens trembled together,
Together with worn-out old men, and at once the apprehension
Of such a great disaster had penetrated to every age.
But then the heavenly father took pity on his people from on high   220
And stood in the way of the cruel enterprises of the Papists:
The criminals were captured and haled off to fierce punishments.
But dutiful incense and grateful thanks were paid to God,   ·
All the crossroads smoked in joy with fires of celebration,
The youthful throng turned to dances; and no day comes round   225
In all the year more to be fêted than the fifth of November.

Commentary

1–6 The introduction refers to the accession of James VI of Scotland as James I of England in 1603, uniting the two crowns.

1 Both James's piety and his role as the destined royal heir from abroad recall Aeneas, hero of Virgil's *Aeneid*.

2 *Teucrigenas* refers to the story that the Britons were descended from Brutus the Trojan, supposed grandson of Aeneas (cf. Geoffrey of Monmouth's twelfth-century *Historiae Regum Britanniae* 1.3; Teucer was an ancestor of Aeneas), but also suggests that they reprise in this poem the Trojans' role in the *Aeneid* as divine favourites. The name itself is not classical but appears in Renaissance dictionaries of synonyms for 'Trojan' available to Milton (e.g. the sixteenth-century *Synonymorum Sylva* of Simon Pelegromius).

5 *pacificus* alludes to James's 1604 treaty with England's old enemy Spain.

7 *Acheronte*: a river of Hell in Virgil (*Aen.* 6.107), usually sluggish; *ignifluo* seems to conflate it with Virgil's fiery infernal river Phlegethon (6.550–1, cf. line 74 here), but also recalls the 'lake of fire' into which Satan is cast in Revelation (19:20; 20:14).

8 *Eumenidum pater*: 'father of the Furies', Pluto according to Virgil (*Aen.* 7.327), here his Christian analogue Satan. *aetherio vagus exul Olympo* refers to Satan's expulsion from Heaven (Revelation 12:9) by echoing Virgil's account of Saturn's expulsion from Olympus by Jupiter (*Aen.* 8.319–20: *aetherio ... Olympo | ... exul*, 'an exile from heavenly Olympus').

13–14 Satan's capacity to sow dissension echoes that of Virgil's fury Allecto at *Aeneid* 7.335–6 (she can drive brothers to battle and divide houses with hatred); *viscera* ('vitals') recalls the striking metaphor of civil war as evisceration of the state at *Aen.* 6.833.

18–20 Cf. 1 Peter 5.8 (KJV): '... your adversary the devil, as a roaring lion, walketh about, seeking whom he may devour'; for the tigress-simile see Statius, *Thebaid* 10.288–9 (again *Caspia tigris*); Milton, *Paradise Lost* 4.403–8 (of Satan assailing Eve).

23 *Summanus* was the Etruscan god of nocturnal thunder (Pliny, *Natural History* 2.138), here appropriately designating the infernal Satan as a dark storm-deity.

27–30 Albion, son of Neptune, earlier called Ialebion (Apollodorus, *Bibliotheca* 2.5.10) or Alebion (Pomponius Mela 2.78), later seen as the eponymous hero of Albion (England), was said to have fought with and been killed by Hercules on his western adventures; Spenser, Milton's likely source, mentions the story at *Faerie Queene* 4.11.16.

28 *Amphitryoniaden*: i.e. Hercules (Amphitryon was his reputed mortal father).

31–44 Satan's frustration at England's prosperity, which leads to his monologue and destructive intervention, is closely parallel to Juno's reactions to the good fortune of the hated race of Trojans at Virgil, *Aen*. 7.287–322 and to Envy's reactions to the splendours of Athens at Ovid, *Met*. 2.787–96; Satan's envy of England is a topos already in Plot-poetry before Milton (see Haan 2012: 455).

36–7 These lines (an appropriately impious simile) recall Ovid's account of the imprisonment of Typhoeus under Mount Etna at *Met*. 5.346–53 (see also Virgil, *Aen*. 3.578–82; 9.716).

48 *Iamque pruinosas velox superaverat Alpes* reworks Lucan 1.183, *iam gelidas Caesar cursu superaverat Alpes*, with Satan now playing the destructive role of Lucan's Caesar as Alp-crossing mover of civil war.

51 *veneficiis infamis Etruria*: Ferdinando I de' Medici (1549–1609) was rumoured to have poisoned his brother in order to succeed him as Grand Duke of Tuscany (*Dux Magnus Etruriae*) in 1587.

52 Ostia, the port of Rome, where the river Tiber meets the sea.

53, 55 *Mavortigenae* and *tricoronifer* are probably Miltonic coinages on ancient models (Hale 1994), referring to Mars's ancestry of the Romans as father of Romulus and the three-tiered mitre (tiara) of the Pope respectively (cf. *diademaque triplex*, 94).

54–67 A highly invidious evocation of Catholic ritual in Rome on the evening of the feast of St Peter (29 June; this date is symbolically linked with the Papacy, not a realistic chronology of the Plot, in planning since 1604). Note the negative comparison to wild and noisy Bacchic revels (*Bromius* = 'thunderer', a common epithet of Bacchus) in the god's home region of Thebes (the location of the mountains Aracynthus and Cithaeron and the river Asopus), drawing on a similarly negative Bacchic simile at Virgil, *Aen*. 7.385–96. The setting is emphasized by the (unEnglish) dome, characteristic of St Peter's and other churches in Rome.

56 *panificosque deos* refers contemptuously to the Catholic doctrine of transubstantiation, the presence of the body of Christ in the bread of the

Mass (Milton re-etymologizes *panificus*, usually active, 'bread-making', as passive, 'made of bread').

60 Cimmeria was a region of legendary darkness north of the Black Sea (Cicero, *Lucullus* 61; Ovid, *Epistulae ex Ponto* 4.10.1); the adjective was used loosely of any deep darkness (e.g. [Tibullus] 3.5.24).

65 The Grecizing hiatus before *Aracyntho* echoes that at Virgil, *Eclogues* 2.24: *Actaeo Aracyntho*.

69 Night was mother of Aether and Day by her brother Erebus, god of darkness, according to Hesiod (*Theogony* 123–5).

71–3 The catalogue of Night's four horses recalls the four horses of the Sun at Ovid, *Met.* 2.153–5; like those of Ovid's chariot-team, Milton's horses have names which play via Greek etymologies on their (appropriate) characteristics: Typhlos 'blind', Melanchaetes 'dark-haired', Siope 'silence' and Phrix 'bristling'.

75–6 A standard propaganda attack on Catholic priestly celibacy, echoing George Buchanan's *Franciscanus* 549–50 (published 1566): *cum pellice noctes | ducere* ('spend nights with a mistress').

80–5 The description of Satan's monkish disguise (employing post-classical vocabulary) again draws on details from the hard-hitting anti-Franciscan satires of Buchanan; see Haan 2012: 457 (as she notes, other Plot-poems present Satan disguised as a Jesuit).

86–9 An invidious version of the austere wandering life and communion with animals of St Francis of Assisi (1181–1226); the destructive wolf of Gubbio was tamed by Francis, according to the fourteenth-century *Little Flowers of St Francis*, but the lion-taming may look rather to the story of St Jerome and the lion with a thorn in its foot (narrated e.g. in the thirteenth-century *Golden Legend*).

86 *vasta*: The feminine gender of *eremus* follows that of Greek *eremos* (sc. *chora*), 'empty space', a standard use in Latin patristic literature.

90 Cf. Genesis 3:1 (KJV): 'Now the serpent was more subtle than any beast of the field' (Satan in Eden).

92–3 These lines echo Virgil's two dream-vision appearances of Mercury to stir Aeneas to action in Carthage (92 ~ *Aen.* 4.560; 93 ~ *Aen.* 4.267); line 97 likewise recalls Aeneas' similar dream-vision of the river-god Tiberinus (*Aen.* 8.59).

96 *pharetrati* suggests barbarian archers from the edge of civilization, as at Horace, *Odes* 3.4.35, *pharetratos Gelonos* ('the quiver-wearing Geloni'), as well as the long-standing English reputation for archery.

97 Invidiously suggests the supposed domination of the Pope over the Holy Roman Emperor; cf. similarly line 112.

98, 101 Cf. Matthew 16:19 (KJV) (Christ to Peter): 'And I will give unto thee the keys of the kingdom of heaven'. Peter's keys were an emblem of the Popes, his spiritual successors, and represented his role as the gate-keeper of heaven.

102–5 allude to the wreck of the Spanish Armada off Britain's shores in 1588 and to Elizabeth's subsequent persecution of suspect Catholics (rhetorically substituting saintly crucifixion for her burnings and hangings). Thermodon is a river in Thrace linked with the female warrior Amazons (cf. *Aen.* 11.695), to whom Elizabeth could be compared at the time of the Armada as England's notional military leader (see Schleiner 1978); the epithet *Thermodoonteus* appears in classical literature only at Propertius 3.14.14, *Thermodoonteis . . . aquis*, in editions of Milton's time (modern editions read *Thermodoontiacis . . . aquis*).

108–12 Satan's rhetorical projection of an Italian expedition by James I is very improbable.

111–12 recalls Joshua 10:24 (KJV): 'Come near, put your feet upon the necks of these kings'.

112 A normal mode of greeting the Pope in Milton's time, invidious from a Protestant perspective.

118 refers to the House of Lords in their peers' robes (*trabea* is a purple cloak).

127 *saecula . . . Mariana* suggests a Catholic monarch for England after the model of Queen Mary I (1553–8); the plotters had planned to place James's nine-year-old daughter Elizabeth on the throne and force her to reign as a Catholic.

129–30 A neat conjunction of Roman polytheism with an allusion to the particular prominence and multiplicity of saints and their festivals in the Catholic tradition.

132 Artful Virgilian word-order with 'parenthetic apposition': cf. e.g. *Ecl.* 1.57, *raucae, tua cura, palumbes* ('hoarse doves, your concern').

133–6 Alludes to the mythological sorrow of the goddess Aurora (Dawn) for her Aethiopian son Memnon, killed at Troy by Achilles (cf. e.g. Propertius 2.18.15–16; Ovid, *Amores* 1.13.3–4).

137 *stellatae ianitor aulae*: i.e. the Pope as door-keeper of heaven (cf. 98, 101 n.); the phrase picks up Ovid's description of the door-god Janus (*Fasti* 1.139) as *caelestis ianitor aulae* ('the door-keeper of the heavenly hall').

139 *est locus* is the standard classical formula beginning a formal description (cf. e.g. Virgil, *Aen.* 1.530; 3.163; 7.563). The macabre and fragmented locale described here suits Rome, city of catacombs and ruins.

141–2 The twin birth of Murder and Betrayal alludes verbally to the triple birth of the similarly fearsome Furies at Virgil, *Aen.* 12.845–7.

157–8 Cf. Virgil, *Aen.* 1.67 (Juno): *gens inimica mihi Tyrrhenum navigat aequor* ('a race hateful to me is sailing the Tyrrhenian sea'): the Pope, like Satan (see Introduction), replays Juno's Virgilian role of intervening malign deity.

162 *satrapa* refers technically to provincial governors in the Persian Empire ('satrap'), but here describes the members of the House of Lords as regional overlords in Britain.

170–1 The tower of Rumour is here located at 'the meeting of Europe and Asia', following Ovid's location of his house of Rumour (see Introduction) in the middle of the world (*Met.* 12.39). The text here, therefore, at line 171 adopts the conjecture *Maeotidas* (Starnes 1951; seen as possible by Haan 2012: 461) for the 1645 edition's *Mareotidas*, which would indicate an inappropriate location in Egypt (Virgil, *Georgics* 2.91); *Maeotis* refers to the Sea of Azov, opening into the Black Sea (Ovid, *Epistulae ex Ponto* 3.2.59; Lucan 3.227–8), which fits the required geographical position much better.

172 *Titanidos*: Earth is the mother both of Rumour and of the Titans Coeus and Enceladus in Virgil (*Aen.* 4.178–80).

173 Ovid's house of Rumour is similarly made of (resounding) bronze (*Met.* 12.46).

174 For Mount Athos in northeastern Greece as a simile for large size, cf. Virg. *Aen.* 12.701; for the impious piling of the Thessalian mountains Pelion on Ossa to attack Olympus by giants rebelling against Jupiter, cf. Virg. *Geo.* 1.281.

175 Ovid's house of Rumour similarly has *innumerosque aditus ac mille foramina* ('innumerable approaches and a thousand openings', *Met.* 12.43).

178–80 The simile of flies buzzing around a milk-pail is famously Homeric (*Iliad* 2.469–71; 16.641–3; 17.570–2); it is found in the Plot-poem of Phineas Fletcher (*Locustae*, first published 1629) and also used of Satan at *Paradise Regained* 4.15–17 (see Haan 2012: 462).

181 *ultrix matris* refers to Servius' ancient commentary on Virgil, *Aen.* 4.178–80, which suggests that Earth bears her daughter Rumour to take her revenge for her Titan sons (172 n.), killed in the Titanomachy, by broadcasting the misbehaviour of their victors, the Olympian gods.

182 *olli*: archaic/poetic form of *illi*.

185–8 These lines allude artfully to the Ovidian story of the vigilant hundred-eyed Argus, son of Arestor, vainly guarding the princess/heifer Io, subsequently the goddess Isis, at Ovid, *Met.* 1.625–723; 182 picks up its start, *centum luminibus cinctum caput* ('a head girt with a hundred eyes', 1.625), the anaphora of *lumina* in 186–8 its end, *in tot lumina lumen* ('light divided into so many eyes', 1.720).

191–3 For Rumour's propensity to distortion cf. similarly Virgil, *Aen.* 4.178 and especially Ovid, *Met.* 12.56–8 (her exaggeration and suppression of the truth).

194–8 The Plot was revealed after the receipt of a letter warning a peer not to attend the State Opening of Parliament, here seen as a form of Rumour.

204–9 The description of Rumour and her actions draws again on Virgil (*Aen.* 4.180–8). This is a very rapid and general account of events and public reaction which has little specific historical reference. Note the neat verbal balance of God's terse instruction and Rumour's rapid fulfilment of it (*nec plura*, 204; *nec mora*, 208).

207 *Temesaeo* refers to Temese, a town in Bruttium, southern Italy, well known for its copper mines, and is a learned poetic epithet used several times by Ovid.

221–6 James's government instituted extensive annual celebrations on 5 November (for details in Milton's time see Hale 2001). The description here combines the traditional bonfires (still kindled today in Britain) with Roman modes of thanksgiving (for *pia tura* and the offering of incense see Tibullus 2.2.3 and Ovid, *Amores* 3.3.33; for smoking altars see Virgil, *Ecl.* 1.43).

222 *papicolum* is a Miltonic coinage, according to Hale 1994.

14

A Frost Fair on the Thames

William Baker, *Descriptio Brumae, et intensissimi Ianuario mense frigoris, quo Thamesis omnino congelata fuit* (1634/5)

George Pounder

Introduction

William Baker's poem on the occasion of the freezing of the Thames, dated January 1634, is a charming example of the ongoing conversation between Neo-Latin and classical Latin literature during the early modern period. There are other examples of poems commemorating the Thames freezing over from this period, and Baker's poem engages with this tradition (see Reed 2002: 10–12). Frequent suggestive references to classical authors show off the poet's erudition, and his use of contemporary Neo-Latin vocabulary and deft touch bring his observations to life. Written in stylish Latin hexameters in a pastiche of high Roman epic, this poem provides a somewhat generalized and often light-hearted vision of the Thames frost fairs. Between 1600 and 1814 Britain was gripped by a 'Little Ice Age', and the Thames regularly froze hard enough for entrepreneurs to set up stalls on the ice (see Beaver 1980). On offer were markets, pubs and other attractions; it was even said that an elephant was brought to one fair (see thamesleisure.co.uk). The medieval London Bridge, built in 1209 and replaced in 1831, held a number of shops and stalls. The irregularly spaced arches allowed slabs of ice to form in the relatively slow-flowing river, which would become jammed up against the piers, creating further pile-ups, and eventually a solid raft of ice (see historic-uk.com). The frozen surface was far from smooth as a result, and it made the normally straightforward movement over the river difficult and dangerous; one of the initial enterprises involved boatmen laying planks over the ice to allow travellers to cross, for a fee; other enterprises followed. It was, of course, a risky undertaking and the ice would regularly break (see Reed 2002: 31). One story from 'towards the end of the frost' of 1608 involved a man walking his dogs. He became stranded on a piece of ice, to the horror of the terrified onlookers. Eventually, resigned to his fate, he started to pray, and his iceberg was driven against the bridge. He scrambled up one of the arches, his dogs followed, and he was saved (see Arber 1877: 97–9). While the lack of landmarks in this poem makes it impossible to identify exactly where along the Thames the poem is set, various accounts from the period seem to have similar events upstream of London Bridge (Reed 2002).

The poem divides into three broad sections: the description of the various folk working on the river (stallholders and their customers, the boatmen and the hunters); a rough football match complete with snowball fight; and the creation of terrifying snow beasts. Throughout, we get a lively account of how the people behave: they take the day off work, go to the pub, play games with each other and generally enjoy the snow.

The poem appears in two MSS: one from State Papers held at the National Archives in Kew (MS TNA: SP 16/282, fols 284–5); the other in the Bodleian Library in Oxford (MS Selden supra 108, fols 193–4). The second appears in a collection of letters made by the legal and classical scholar John Selden. Both are in what looks like the same hand, and the MSS are very similar. The Selden collection has been assembled chronologically for the most part (Hunter 2009: 46–7). This therefore enables us to date the letter to between 8 September 1634 and February 1635. The main system for dating in England at this time set the beginning of the year at 25 March (Lady Day). The dating system that made 1 January the start of the year was introduced by Pope Gregory in 1582, but this was not officially adopted in England until 1752. There was a winter severe enough to make the Thames freeze over in 1635, so, even considering the potential difficulty with the calendar during this period, it would appear to refer to a specific event; indeed, it seems like the poet is writing at the time, rather than looking back too far into the past (Hunter 2009: 45–6). We can therefore be confident that this poem refers to the very hard winter of 1634/5, despite the date on the poem being 1634 (see Kington 2010). There is no obvious connection with the rest of the volume, which seems to be nearly all correspondence (there are letters either side of the Baker poem, which are in Greek). The volume was re-bound, perhaps in the nineteenth century, but the original foliation has been retained, and this corresponds to a list of contents at the front of the volume, apparently compiled by Sir Matthew Hale. 'Baker's verses on the freezinge of Thames' duly appears in the list at fol. 193.

We know very little about William Baker. The fact that we have two versions in the same hand suggests that the poet felt suitably pleased with his work to send it round to his friends, including Selden. A William Baker is the author of two epigrams in elegiac couplets, found in Selden's *Jani Anglorum*

Facies Altera, which are dedicated to Selden. Even more tantalizing is the will from 1656 belonging to a William Baker from Oxfordshire (National Archives, Kew: PROB 11/260/172, 'Will of William Baker of Rotherfield Grays, Oxfordshire', dated 3 November 1656), containing bequests of various scholarly works, though unfortunately nothing that connects Baker with Selden. It is therefore more than possible that this is the same man.

As an educated man, Baker would have been able to write Latin poems as a leisure activity, and Selden would undoubtedly have enjoyed reading this one. It is unlikely the Thames will freeze over in the same way, or that people would be allowed to set up stalls like this today, but what is particularly enjoyable is the modern resonance: snow days then and now are little different.

Metre: dactylic hexameter

Bibliography

Arber, E. (1877), *An English Garner*, London.

Beaver, S. H. (1980), 'Famous British Frosts and Frost Fairs, Part 1, 1564–1684', *Journal of Meteorology*, 5.45: 1–9.

Hunter, M. (2009), *Editing Early Modern Texts: An Introduction to Principles and Practice*, Basingstoke.

Kington, J. A. (2010), *Climate and Weather*, London.

Reed, N. (2002), *Frost Fairs on the Frozen Thames*, London.

https://www.thamesleisure.co.uk/the-curious-story-of-river-thames-frost-fairs/ [accessed 1 October 2018].

https://www.historic-uk.com/HistoryUK/HistoryofEngland/The-Thames-Frost-Fairs/ [accessed 1 October 2018].

Source of the Latin text

The Latin text follows the version in the State Papers held at the National Archives in Kew (MS TNA: SP 16/282, fols 284–5).

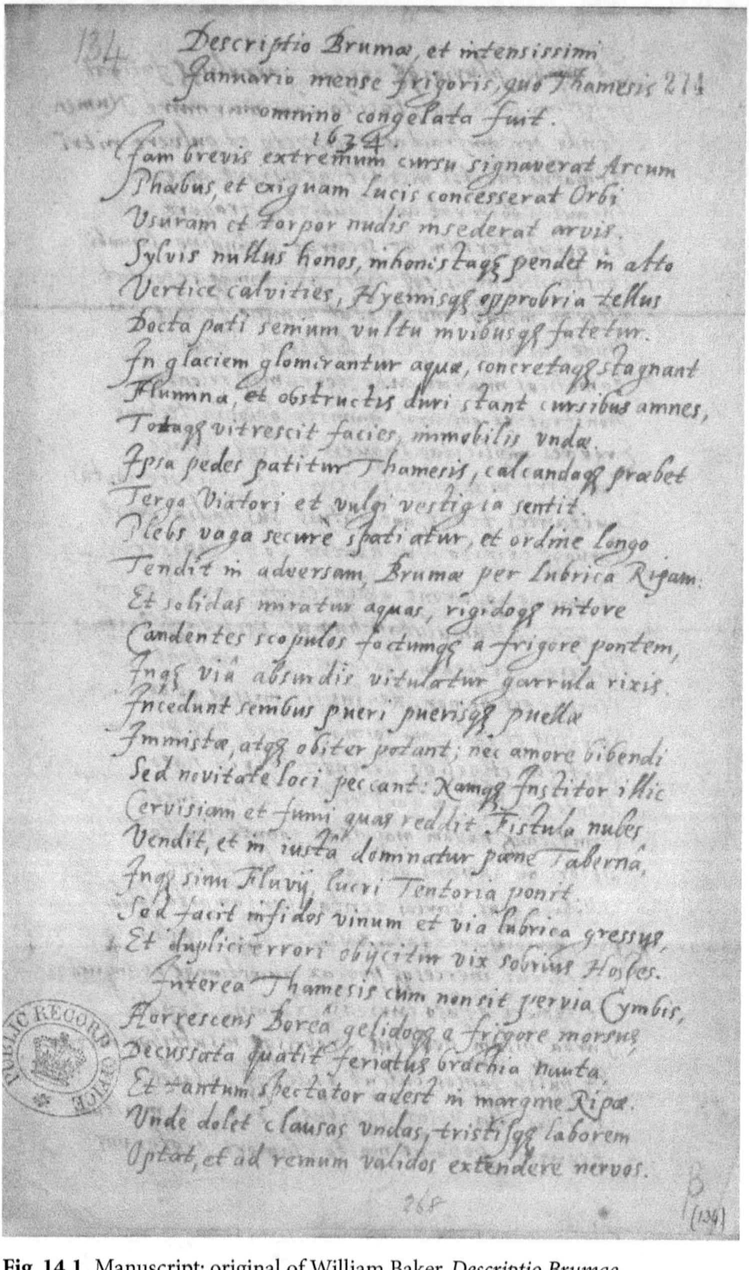

Fig. 14.1 Manuscript: original of William Baker, *Descriptio Brumae*, The National Archives, Kew (State Papers, MS TNA: SP 16/282, fol. 284r).

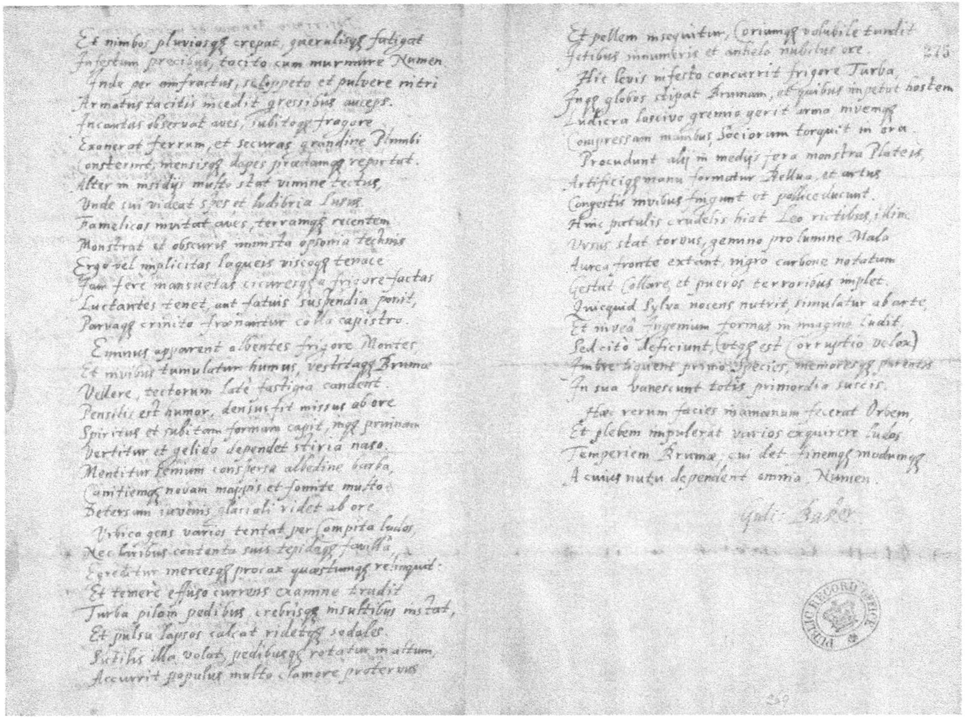

Fig. 14.2 Manuscript: original of William Baker, *Descriptio Brumae*, The National Archives, Kew (State Papers, MS TNA: SP 16/282, fols 284v–5r).

Latin text

Descriptio Brumae, et intensissimi Ianuario mense frigoris, quo Thamesis omnino congelata fuit. 1634

Iam brevis extremum cursu signaverat arcum
Phoebus et exiguam lucis concesserat orbi
usuram et torpor nudis insederat arvis.
sylvis nullus honos, inhonistaque pendet in alto
5 vertice calvities, hyemisque opprobria tellus
docta pati senium vultu nivibusque fatetur.
in glaciem glomirantur aquae, concretaque stagnant
flumina, et obstructis duri stant cursibus amnes,
totaque vitrescit facies, immobilis undae.
10 ipsa pedes patitur Thamesis, calcandaque praebet
terga viatori et vulgi vestigia sentit.
plebs vaga secure spatiatur, et ordine longo
tendit in adversam, brumae per lubrica ripam:
et solidas miratur aquas, rigidoque nitore
15 candentes scopulos factumque a frigore pontem,
inque via absurdis vitulatur garrula rixis.
incedunt senibus pueri puerisque puellae
immistae, atque obiter potant; nec amore bibendi
sed novitate loci peccant: namque institor illic
20 cervisiam et fumi quas reddit fistula nubes
vendit, et in iusta dominatur paene taberna,
inque sinu fluvii, lucri tentoria ponit.
sed facit infidos vinum et via lubrica gressus,
et duplici errori obicitur vix sobrius hospes.
25 interea Thamesis cum non sit pervia cymbis,
horrescens Borea gelidoque a frigore morsus,
decussata quatit feriatus brachia nauta,
et tantum spectator adest in margine ripae.
unde dolet clausas undas, tristisque laborem
30 optat, et ad remum validos extendere nervos.
et nimbos pluviasque crepat, querulisque fatigat
infestum precibus, tacito cum murmure numen.
inde per amfractus, scloppeto et pulvere nitri
armatus tacitis incedit gressibus anceps.
35 incautas observat aves, subitoque fragore

English translation

The description of the Winter and the most bitter freeze, during which the Thames completely froze over, in January 1634

Now Apollo's short-lived sun had traced its final path in its course and had given a tiny gift of light to the world, and numb idleness had settled upon the bare fields. The woods have no dignity, unseemly baldness hangs on the 5 treetops, and the earth, which has learned to endure the insults of winter, declares its old age through its features and the snow. The water hardens into ice, the rivers lie still and solid, and the streams stand firm, their flow stopped. The whole surface of the motionless wave is as glass.

The Thames herself grants footfall, she offers her surface as a walkway to 10 the traveller, and she feels the footsteps of the crowd. The wandering folk stroll about in safety, and in a long line they go towards the opposite bank, over winter's slippery ways. And they are amazed by the solid water, the rocks glistening with their stiff whiteness, the bridge forged by the cold, and on 15 the path, chattering, they celebrate with rough brawls. The lads fall upon the older men; the girls, in among them, fall upon the boys, and they drink on the way; it's not because of a desire for a tipple, but because of the novelty of their surroundings, that they misbehave. For the enterprising fellow there sells 20 beer and the clouds of smoke which the pipe gives off, and lords it in the almost honest tavern, and at the bend of the river he pitches his profitable stall. But wine and the slippery path make steps unreliable, and the half-cut punter is sent flying, afflicted by a double wandering.

Meanwhile since the Thames allows no way through for boats, the sailor 25 on his day off, shivering with the North Wind and bitten by the icy chill, shakes his unfolded arms, and he can only watch from the edge of the bank. From there he laments that the river is blocked, and sadly longs for work, and 30 to strain his strong muscles at the oar. And he rebukes the clouds and the rain, and wears out with his silent grumbling a god hostile to prayers of complaint. Then along the winding river, equipped with a musket and gunpowder, he advances uncertainly on his silent course. He watches the careless birds, and 35

exonerat ferrum, et securas grandine plombi
consternit, mensisque dapes praedamque reportat.
alter in insidiis multo stat vimine tectus,
unde sui videat spes et ludibria lusus.
40 famelicas invitat aves, terramque recentem
monstrat et obscuris immista opsonia technis
ergo vel implicitas laqueis viscoque tenace
iam fere mansuetas cicuresque a frigore factas
luctantes tenet, aut fatuis suspendia ponit,
45 parvaque crinito frenantur colla capistro.
eminus apparent albentes frigore montes,
et nivibus tumulatur humus, vestitaque brumae
vellere, tectorum late fastigia candent.
pensilis est humor, densus fit missus ab ore
50 spiritus et subitam formam capit, inque pruinam
vertitur et gelido dependet stiria naso.
mentitur senium conspersa albedine barba,
canitiemque novam mappis et fomite multo
detersam iuvenis glaciali ridet ab ore.
55 urbica gens varios tentat per compita ludos
nec laribus contenta suis tepidaque favilla,
egreditur mercesque procax quaestumque relinquit:
et temere effuso currens examine trudit
turba pilam pedibus, crebrisque insultibus instat,
60 et pulsu lapsos calcat ridetque sodales.
sutilis illa volat, pedibusque rotatur in altum,
accurrit populus multo clamore protervus
et pellem insequitur, coriumque volubile tundit
ictibus innumeris et anhelo nubilus ore.
65 hic levis infesto concurrit frigore turba,
inque globos stipat brumam, et quibus impetat hostem
ludicra lascivo gremio gerit arma, nivemque
compressam manibus, sociorum torquit in ora.
procudunt alii in mediis fera monstra plateis,
70 artificique manu formatur bellua, et artus
congestis nivibus fingunt et pollice ducunt.
hinc patulis crudelis hiat leo rictibus, illinc
ursus stat torvus, gemino pro lumine mala
aurea fronte extant, nigro carbone notatum
75 gestat collare, et pueros terroribus implet.
quicquid sylva nocens nutrit, simulatur ab arte,

with a sudden crack he fires his musket, lays low the heedless creatures with a hail of lead, and brings back as his prize a feast for his table. Another stands hidden behind a covering of many osiers from where he can see the hopes and targets for his sport. He tempts the hungry birds, he shows the fresh 40 ground and the bait buried in hidden traps. Then he either holds them as they struggle, tied in a noose and with mistletoe that grips, and now nearly tame and docile from the cold, or inflicts hanging on the silly creatures, their little 45 necks held in a fur halter.

In the distance appear the mountains white with cold, and the ground is heaped with snow; and, clad in winter's fleece, the gables of the houses far and wide are white. The dampness hangs about, the breath emitted from the mouth becomes heavy, and taking a sudden shape, changes into frost; and an 50 icicle hangs from the frozen nose. A beard, specked with whiteness, feigns old age; and the young man laughs at the new whiteness, wiped away from his icy face by rags and a great load of kindling.

The city folk play various games at the crossroads and, not content with 55 their own household gods and their warm embers, out they go; cheekily they forget the benefits of earning a living. Running around at random in a chaotic scrum the crowd kicks a ball. They press on with repeated assaults, and 60 trample and mock their companions who have fallen in the shoving. The ball, stitched together, flies and is whirled on high by their feet; the eager players run forward with a great cry and chase after the leather pill. They kick the flying leather with countless blows, and a cloud forms from their breath.

Elsewhere the frivolous crowd joins battle on the treacherous ice, and 65 they pack the snow into balls. So they can use these to attack the enemy, they carry their playful arsenal in their impudent bosoms, and they hurl the snow, compacted by their hands, at the faces of their friends.

Some build terrible monsters in the middle of the streets: a beast is made 70 with their skilful hands, fashioning limbs out of packed snow and shaping them with their thumbs. Over here a cruel lion opens his jaws wide, while over there stands a wild bear, a pair of golden apples on its face for his two eyes, and sporting a collar marked out with black coal: it fills the small boys 75 with terror! Whatever harmful creature the forest feeds is created in art;

et nivea ingenium formas in imagine ludit.
sed cito deficiunt, (utque est corruptio velox)
imbre liquent primo species, memoresque parentis
80 in sua vanescunt totis primordia succis.
haec rerum facies inamoenum fecerat orbem,
et plebem impulerat varios exquirere ludos
temperiem brumae; cui det finemque modumque
a cuius nutu dependent omnia, Numen.

and artfulness makes playful shapes in snowy statue. But quickly they disappear, and (just as corruption is swift) their appearance melts with the first rain, and, remembering their parent, they seep into their original form 80 with all their moisture.

Such an appearance of things had made the world an inhospitable place, and had driven people to try out various forms of entertainment as an antidote to temper [the harshness of] winter. To the winter too may He grant an end and a limit – He on whose will everything depends, God Himself.

Commentary

1–3 Enjambment across these three lines mirrors the sweeping course of Apollo through the sky and suggests the idea that the ice is everywhere.

1 *Iam brevis extremum*: This formula appears to be used in monumental inscriptions of the period (e.g. *cum brevis extremum clauderet hora diem*, 'when the short hour puts an end to the final day': George Bolles [d. 1632], in W. Maitland et al., *The History and Survey of London from its Foundation to the Present Time, Vol. 2*, London 1756: 1184). The reference to Apollo finishing his course across the sky, short because it is winter, sets the time of day: this is late afternoon.

arcum: *arcus, -us* (m) is often used of the rainbow (e.g. Virgil, *Aeneid* 5.88; Ovid, *Metamorphoses* 6.63). Here, a flash of colour contrasts with the chill whiteness of the frozen Thames.

2 *Phoebus*: The strong caesura shifts focus on to the power of the gods. The *numen* mentioned through the poem may not be pagan, but there is a definite sense of the classical divine in this icy world. The separation of *brevis* ... *Phoebus* is ironic: the day may be short, but the poetic description is less so.

3 The lethargic spondees in this line reflect the torpid mood that has come over the frozen countryside.

4–6 *nullus honos, inhonista ... calvities, ... opprobria tellus ... fatetur*: Focus on the negative shows the destructive force of the winter and its unseemly and insulting behaviour.

4 *sylvis nullus honos* (*sylvis = silvis*): for the usage, compare Virgil, *Georgics* 2.404: *silvis Aquilo decussit honorem* ('the North Wind has shaken the glory from the woods') and Horace, *Epodes* 11.6: *December ... silvis honorem decutit* ('December ... shakes the glory from the woods').

4–5 *inhonista ... calvities*: 'unseemly baldness' (*inhonista = inhonesta*). Cf. Petronius 108.1: *spoliati capitis dedecus superciliorum etiam aequalis cum fronte calvities* ('the disgrace of our shaven heads, our eyebrows were as bald as our pates'). The personified trees add a humorous touch to the otherwise dead landscape.

5 *hyemis = hiemis.*

5–6 *tellus docta*: 'the earth, which has learned'.

7–8 *in glaciem glomirantur aquae, concretaque stagnant | flumina* (*glomirantur = glomerantur*): The harsh sounds in these lines echo the hardness of the ice. Also, the parallel word order in the two clauses makes for a neat tautology.

8–9 Heavy spondees in line 8 convey the motionless solidity of the river. The conglomeration of words conveying lack of movement (*glomirantur, concreta, stagnant, obstructis, duri, stant*) enhances this idea, which contrasts nicely with the enjambment of *stagnant flumina*: the meandering line is stopped in its tracks by the ice. *immobilis undae* follows a strong caesura and describes perfectly the unnatural stillness in a usually constantly flowing and unstoppable river.

10 *ipsa ... Thamesis*: The river is personified, as if providing a service to the people. *patitur* ('suffers, tolerates') suggests the river is not entirely happy about this.

11 *vulgi*: The might of the river is debased by having the common people walking on it. This unnaturalness is further evoked by the ugly repetition of the 'v' and 'i' sounds in this line.

12 *plebs vaga ... spatiatur*: *plebs* echoes the sense of *vulgus* in the previous line. Their aimless wandering is emphasized by *vaga ... spatiatur*.

ordine longo: the long line formed by the people nicely juxtaposes the disorder created by the winter with man's desire to conform to nature's power. Here, though, the people in great numbers aimlessly follow each other along in their confusion at the strangeness of the frozen river. This image is reminiscent of Virgil's description of the souls of the dead in the Underworld crowding by the banks of the Styx (Virg. *Aen.* 6. 313–4: *stabant orantes primi transmittere cursum,* | *tendebantque manus ripae ulterioris amore*).

13 *brumae*: cf. Virgil, *Geo.* 1.211: *brumae intractabilis* ('rough, unmanageable, uninhabitable winter').

lubrica: *lubricus, -a, -um* = slippery. But cf. Virg. *Aen.* 11.716, where it carries the sense of 'deceitful'. Walking on the ice is not only slippery, it will catch you out (cf. line 23).

14–15 The singular verb *miratur* shows how the people to a man are amazed at the sights before them. They see the solid water and glistening rocks, but most of all they are impressed by the bridge forged by the chill: their own engineering skills are bettered by nature.

16 The focus on nature switches to the responses of the people, presenting the absurdity of human behaviour. It is as if they are on holiday (*vitulatur*, again singular because they are all of the same mind).

rixis: cf. Juvenal 3.288 (and *ebrius ac petulans* ['the drunkard looking for a fight'], 278): they behave boisterously, drunkenly and violently like street thugs.

17 *incedunt*: 'fall upon'. The change to the plural indicates the disorderly nature of the people; no longer do they act as one, now they are individuals *en masse*. The confusion is further emphasized by the polyptoton *pueri puerisque*, the parallel word order (*senibus pueri puerisque puellae*) and the enjambment into *immistae*: this scene is indecent, vulgar and certainly against the natural order of things.

18 *immistae* = *immixtae* (*immisceo, -ere, -ui, -mixtum*): here, 'in among them'.

19–22 *institor, vendit, taberna, lucri, tentoria*: The language of the marketplace is reminiscent of the frost fairs that took place during this period. There is always a way to make a quick profit, particularly with everyday things in unusual situations.

19 *peccant*: 'they misbehave'. For the usage compare Horace, *Satires* 1.2.63: *ancilla peccesne togata* ('whether you sin with a maid or a prostitute'): their drunken misbehaviour may not be merely innocent horseplay (*amore* in line 18 is suggestive of more than drinking). In the context perhaps it simply means 'they lose their footing'.

institor, -is (m): 'vendor', 'pedlar' (cf. Juvenal 7.221).

illic: 'there, in that place'. It is in the novel surroundings that the enterprising fellow sets up.

20 *cervisia, -ae* (f): 'beer'. This (or something similar) was known to Pliny the Elder (Pliny, *Natural History* 22.82) and appears to have been widespread across the Mediterranean, including Gaul, Spain and Egypt.

fumi quas reddit fistula nubes: 'the clouds of smoke which the pipe gives off' are presumably tobacco.

et in iusta dominatur paene taberna: a perplexing phrase. Selling beer and tobacco without the proper licence was against the law. The situation is novel, however, so the seediness is overlooked; and there may have been local bylaws which tolerated such carnival type events. It could also be that *taberna* is a technical word, distinguishing alehouses (for lower classes) from 'taverns' that sold wine to the urban élites. *iusta* might even suggest 'honest' rather than 'licensed' premises, where the *institor* is not overcharging his customers. *paene* is interesting: he almost manages to lord it in a legal establishment. Perhaps *paene* is also a comment on the establishment: it is almost *iusta*.

22 *sinu fluvii*: It is impossible to locate this point with any accuracy, but it was presumably upstream of London Bridge (see Introduction). Much of the Thames seems to have frozen solid on such occasions in the seventeenth century.

23 *lubrica*: cf. 13 n. Their way is treacherous where it looks safe.

24 *duplici errori . . . vix sobrius*: Barely sober, the people are doubly affected by their drunken walking on the slippery ice. The pronounced and awkward elision in *duplici errore obicitur* helps to emphasize the meaning.

25 *non sit pervia*: cf. Francis Bacon, *Historia Naturalis*, Leiden 1638: 422, and Anton Deusing, *Oeconomus Corporis Animalis*, Groningen 1661: 33. This phrase had been used in contemporary philosophical and scientific works. Perhaps Baker had this in mind when depicting the sailor reluctant to get back to work.

cymbis: *cymba, -ae* (f) = 'small boat', 'skiff' (cf. Virg. *Aen.* 6.303: Charon's boat). The reference conjures up images of the lifeless Styx (see 81 n.).

26 *morsus*: a strong word describing the biting chill, but cf. Cicero, *Tusculan Disputations* 4.20.45: *morderi est melius conscientia* ('reproach is a stronger check than conscience'): perhaps the sting of conscience is greater.

27 Mention of the grumpy sailor is delayed: we are all shivering in the cold, but our eyes focus eventually on the *nauta*.

28 *tantum spectator*: The conditions are such that the sailor cannot do his job; he is merely a *spectator* on the riverbank.

31 *crepat*: *crepo, -are, -ui, -itum* = 'rattle', 'crack', 'make a noise'. This form appears in both MSS. In Plautus, F 162 Lindsay, *neque leges crepo* ('and I don't care much for the laws'), the verb means 'to make much ado about', and it seems to derive from a Sanskrit word meaning to lament. It is likely that the poet has in mind *increpo, -are* as in Virg. *Aen.* 10.830–1: *increpat ultro | cunctantis socios* ('he rebuked his comrades as they hung back'). The compound form would not fit the metre, so the poet has shortened it to *crepat*. The three words of complaint in this line (*crepat, querulisque, fatigat*) emphasize the strength of the complaint about the bad weather.

32 *tacito cum murmure*: The paradox is striking. But at the end of it all, the sailor is subject to the power of God, notably placed at the end of the line (as in line 84).

33 *amfractus*: *amfractus, -us* (m) = 'bend', 'turn'. The word carries the meaning of a tortuous or circuitous route (Caesar, *Bellum Gallicum* 7.46), perfect for a river.

scloppeto: *scloppetum, -i* (n) = 'musket'

pulvere nitri: *pulvus nitri* = 'gunpowder'.

34 *tacitis . . . gressibus*: 'on his silent course'. The experienced hunter makes no noise, but, *anceps* ('uncertain'), he is finding the conditions challenging.

35 The two references to 'silent' in quick succession (*tacito* and *tacitis*, 32 and 34) make *subito . . . fragore* all the more striking and shocking.

36 *ferrum*: 'weapon'. *plombi* = *plumbi* (*plumbum, -i* [n]: 'lead'). The hail of lead refers to the shot fired from the musket. *grandine plombi*: cf. Virg. *Geo.* 1.449: *horrida grando* ('bristling hail') and Hor. *Odes* 3.1.9: *non verberatae grandine vineae* ('the vines are not pummelled by hailstones'). *grando* is associated with wintry weather and is cleverly applied here, cf. the description of storm and its consequences at Virg. *Aen.* 4.161: *insequitur commixta grandine nimbus* ('rain mixed with hail follows').

37 In spite of his uncertainty (*anceps*, line 34), once he sees his prey, the hunter does what he knows best. The short sentences convey his businesslike professionalism; and he takes home his supper.

38 *vimine*: *vimen, viminis* (n) = 'osier', 'pliant twig'.

39 *sui . . . ludibria lusus*: 'targets for his sport'. Hunting was recreational as well as practical. The alliterative quality of this phrase is notable.

40–5 These lines are reminiscent of Homer, *Odyssey* 22.468–73, where the housemaids are grimly compared to birds caught in a snare as they are strung up in a noose: ὡς δ' ὅτ' ἂν ἢ κίχλαι τανυσίπτεροι ἠὲ πέλειαι | ἕρκει ἐνιπλήξωσι, τό θ' ἑστήκῃ ἐνὶ θάμνῳ, | αὖλιν ἐσιέμεναι, στυγερὸς δ' ὑπεδέξατο κοῖτος, | ὣς αἵ γ' ἑξείης κεφαλὰς ἔχον, ἀμφὶ δὲ πάσαις | δειρῇσι βρόχοι ἦσαν, ὅπως οἴκτιστα θάνοιεν. | ἤσπαιρον δὲ πόδεσσι μίνυνθά περ οὔ τι μάλα δήν ('Just as when long-winged thrushes or doves fall into a snare which is set in a bush, as they try to reach their resting-place, and hateful is the bed that receives them, even so the women held their heads in a row, and nooses were around the necks of all of them, so that they might die most piteously. And they struggled for a time with their feet, but not very long').

40 *famelicas*: *famelicus, -a, -um* = 'hungry'. This word is often found in classical comedy and satire (e.g. Plautus, *Stich.* 575; Juvenal 14.146).

41 *obscuris . . . technis*: lit. 'hidden devices', i.e. 'snares', 'traps'.

opsonia: *obsonium, -i* (n) [standard form] = 'that which is eaten with bread', 'meats'; here, 'bait'.

42 *visco*: *viscum, -i* (n) = 'mistletoe', 'birdlime' (e.g. Virg. *Geo.* 1.139): sticky substance from mistletoe berries used to trap birds, hence its description as *tenace*.

43 *fere*: the pun on *ferus* ('wild') is clever: the birds are not quite tame in their traps.

mansuetas: *mansuetus, -a, -um* = 'tame'. *cicures*: *cicur, cicuris* = 'tame' (synonymous with *mansuetus* and opposite of *ferus*). The pleonasm creates an interesting *figura etymologica*.

44 The spondaic *luctantes* contrasts with the busy flapping conveyed by the light dactyls of the previous line. The birds' struggle has changed.

45 *crinito . . . capistro*: 'fur halter', 'muzzle'.

46-8 Note the abundance of words depicting the pictorial whiteness of the frozen landscape. In addition, this is everywhere and abundant (*eminus, tumulatur, late*). The metaphor of *vestita . . . brumae vellere, tectorum . . . fastigia* is somehow comforting: the snow is harsh, but it also embraces.

albentes frigore montes: could we be looking at Hampstead Heath?

49 *pensilis*: lit. 'hanging down', here: 'the dampness (*humor*) hangs about'. Cf. Horace, *Satires* 2.2.121, where *pensilis uva* is hung for preservation through the winter. Note also the heavy spondees in this line, which, along with the repeated sibilance, recreate the heavy breathing of the people in the bitter cold.

50 *pruinam*: *pruina, -ae* (f) = 'frost'.

51 *stiria*: *stiria, -ae* (f) = 'icicle'.

52-4 The lines create an amusing optical illusion (the neuter noun *senium*, 'old age', is the object of *mentitur*): the young man's beard, normally dark, has become white with all the snow in it. The normal colour returns when the whiteness is wiped away (*canitiem . . . detersam*) by a handkerchief or melted by the warmth of a fire (hence the bundle of kindling).

55-7 *urbica gens*: The move into the city is indicated by the more domestic language (*ludos, laribus, favilla, merces*). *per compita*: *compitum, -i* (n) = 'crossroads'. In Roman times *compita larum* were cult centres, often used for dividing up the city. *tepida . . . favilla* reminds us of the religious aspect of worship of the *lares*. The juxtaposition *compita ludos* (akin, perhaps, to playing games in a church) again shows the irreverent departure from the traditional norm. *nec laribus contenta . . . tepidaque favilla* ('not content with their own household gods and their warm embers'): The wintry conditions are such as to make folk want to leave the fireside to go out and play.

57 That the people are *procax* ('bold', 'shameless', 'impudent') makes them ignore their responsibilities. In a nicely symmetrical line (verb-noun-adjective-noun-verb) their impudence is enhanced by being the centre of their actions. The verbs (*egreditur, relinquit*) describe a lack of care, and the nouns (*merces, quaestum*) are technical words for making money. The singular *urbica gens* (line 55) shows that their behaviour is unanimous.

58 This football match is a disorganized kickabout, emphasized by the accumulation of words describing disorganization: *temere effuso currens examine* ('running around at random in a chaotic scrum'). The spondees characterizing the crowd like a swarm in this line contrast strikingly with the quicker dactyls in the next.

examine: *examen, -inis* (n) = 'swarm, crowd'; cf. Horace, *Odes* 1.35.31–2: *iuvenum . . . examen* ('army of young men') and Virgil, *Geo.* 4.21 (of bees).

59 *turba pilam pedibus*: The juxtaposition of these words paints a picture of a rough close-quarters game, and the harsh sounds echo the kicking of the ball.

60 *calcat*: *calco, -are* = 'trample upon', 'oppress' (cf. Juvenal 10.86: *hostem*), 'scorn' (cf. Propertius 2.8.20: *insultetque rogis, calcet et ossa mea* ['let her jump about on my pyre, and trample on my bones']). The fallen player is subjected to the frequent derision of his friends; such is the nature of this kickabout.

61–4 The poet gives a striking sensory description of this game. Note the change from long vowel sounds in *coriumque volubile tundit* (63) to the shorter *ictibus innumeris* (64): the sharp kicks are mixed with the dull thud of the heavy leather ball. We are left with the highly sensory image of the cloud formed by their breath, softened by the nasal and liquid diction *anhelo nubilus ore* (64). The adjective *nubilus* describes the *populus*, creating an interesting image: the people are cloudy with the breath from their mouths.

61–3 *volat . . . rotatur . . . accurrit . . . insequitur . . . tundit*: Words conveying swift movement and the lively dactylic rhythm keep up the pace.

61 *sutilis*: 'sewn', 'stitched'. By metonymy, this must refer to the leather ball. *illa volat*: cf. Virg. *Aen.* 12.855, where Jupiter sends a Fury to confront Juturna as an omen on the battlefield. The reference to a battle from epic poetry creates an amusing sense of bathos.

62 *protervus*: 'wild', 'violent', 'vehement'. Not as extreme as *procax* (57), but perhaps used for variation.

63 *corium*: *corium, -i* (n): 'leather', 'skin', 'hide'.

65 The transition from football to snowballs is marked by a golden line: *hic levis infesto concurrit frigore turba* (*levis* with *turba*, *infesto* with *frigore*, with *concurrit* at the centre). The contrasting word placement is also significant: *levis* contrasts with *infesto*, and of course the *turba* is cold!

66–8 The short sentences and frequent verbs convey the playfully quick dynamics of the snowball fight. The military vocabulary (*hostem . . . arma . . . sociorum*) creates amusing bathos (as in line 61), as does the oxymoron created by *ludicra . . . arma. torquit* (= *torquet*) is the word often used to describe the launching of a missile in battle (e.g. Virg. *Aen.* 10.585); here it is a snowball.

69 *procudunt*: corrected in the Bodleian MS from *incudunt*. Cf. Virg. *Geo.* 1.261–2: *durum procudit arator . . . dentem* ('the ploughman forges a hard blade'). *alii*: Other folk are making snowmen (or snow beasts).

fera monstra: ironic: these are not even alive, yet they scare the little boys.

plateis: *platea, -ae* (f) = 'street'. Note the mimetic word order in *mediis fera monstra plateis*: on a verbal level, too, the 'terrible monsters' are 'in the middle of the streets'!

The art imagery creates some striking echoes and consequently some humorous bathos. Cf. Virg. *Aen.* 6.847–8: *excudent alii spirantia mollius aera | (credo equidem), vivos ducent de marmore vultus* ('others [I can well believe] will hammer out more gently breathing bronze and will fashion living features in marble'), *Geo.* 4.57: *excudunt ceras et mella tenacia fingunt* ('they form wax and fashion sticky honey'), and even the Pygmalion scene in Ovid, *Metamorphoses* 10, with the reference in 285 to his *pollice*: Roman statuary, beehives, and dream girls are all fashioned in the lines of these great classical poets, and our poet follows them with snow beasts.

70 *bellua*: The MSS have *bellua*: this form is retained for metrical purposes.

71 *pollice ducunt*: 'they fashion with their thumbs'. Cf. Claudian, *De Raptu Proserpinae* 1.53: *seriem fatorum pollice ducunt* ('they trace out the order of the fates with their thumbs'). The bathos in this allusion is striking: the joyous creation of a snowman against the charting of the course of the fates.

72 The snow beasts appear everywhere you look (*hinc . . . illinc*). The words frame the line neatly, and the enjambment suggests the sweep of our eyes as we scan this scene. The elegant chiastic word order in *crudelis hiat leo . . . ursus stat torvus* reinforces the image of being surrounded by terrible beasts.

73 *gemino . . . lumine*: reminiscent of Catullus 51.10–11: *gemina . . . lumina*.

73–4 *mala aurea*: *malum* ('apple') can be used to describe many fruits, including oranges. The fact that these are *aurea* is suggestive of oranges. Oranges were considered something of a luxury in the seventeenth century, having only recently been brought into Europe from China in the previous century. These snow creatures are therefore quite special.

74 *carbone*: *carbo, carbonis* (m) = 'coal'.

75 *pueros terroribus implet*: The subject of the verb is both the *leo* and the *ursus*. The singular form gives each statue a life of its own: they do not simply frighten the boys, they fill them with terrors.

76 *nocens*: a clever transferred epithet: it is unclear whether it is *sylva* (= *silva*) or *quicquid* that is harmful; here understood as *quicquid nocens*, 'whatever harmful creature'.

78 *cito deficiunt*: The moment passes quickly. The next sentence outlines the fragility of the snow statues as they melt away. In spite of their terrifying appearance, the fragility of their existence is highlighted as they start to disappear fast.

corruptio: *corruptio, -onis* (f) = 'a spoiling', 'a corruption'. This strongly loaded word makes a moral point: just as all flesh passes away in corruption, so the snow creatures melt (cf. 1 Corinthians 15:53: δεῖ γὰρ τὸ φθαρτὸν τοῦτο ἐνδύσασθαι ἀφθαρσίαν καὶ τὸ θνητὸν τοῦτο ἐνδύσασθαι ἀθανασίαν, 'for the perishable must put on the imperishable, and the mortal must put on immortality').

79 The juxtaposition of *species, memoresque* develops the idea of transience: credible sight quickly fades into distant memory. The water is personified by *parentis*: it is the creator of the statues.

80 *totis primordia succis* (= *sucus, -i* [m]: 'moisture'): cf. Ovid, *Met.* 15.67: *magni primordia mundi* ('the primal origin of this great world'), where the Samian sage Pythagoras tells of the origins of the world, and goes on (line 69) to describe where the snow comes from (*unde nives*): obviously appropriate in a poem about a hard winter.

81 *rerum facies*: again reminds us of the illusions created by the snow: it is not real and makes the people seek out ways to alleviate the harshness through *ludos*.

inamoenum ... orbem: cf. Ovid, *Met.* 10.15: *inamoenaque regna* ('joyless kingdom'), the description of the Underworld when Orpheus visits. The *locus amoenus*, a charming place (e.g. Cicero, *Fin.* 2. 107), refers to the literary *topos* of an idyllic landscape, typically containing trees and shade, a grassy meadow, running water, song-birds and cool breezes. Homer's description of Calypso's cave (*Odyssey* 5.55ff.), Virgil's *Eclogues* and Theocritus' *Idylls* all contribute to this idea, as does the Golden Age ideal of the Elysian Fields. This wintry place therefore stands as the polar opposite, more akin to the lifelessness of Ovid's underworld.

84 *nutu*: *nutus, -us* (m) = 'nodding', 'nod'. The decisions of the gods are often executed by their nodding, cf. e.g. Virg. *Aen*. 9.106: *nutu tremefecit Olympum* ('with his nod he made Olympus tremble') and Hom. *Iliad* 1.526–7: οὐ γὰρ ἐμὸν παλινάγρετον οὐδ᾽ ἀπατηλὸν | οὐδ᾽ ἀτελεύτητον ὅ τί κεν κεφαλῇ κατανεύσω ('no word of mine can be recalled, nor is it false, nor unfulfilled, to which I bow my head'). Reassuringly, it is God (*Numen*) who finally provides an end and a limit in the prayer that completes the poem.

15

The Beauty and Horror of the Mountains

Thomas Burnet (*c.* 1635–1715),
Telluris theoria sacra 1.1.9 (pp. 66–8)

William M. Barton

Introduction

Thomas Burnet (*c.* 1635–1715) published the first part of his *Telluris theoria sacra* ('*The Sacred Theory of the Earth*') in 1681. By 1689 it had been expanded to include a second volume and now comprised four books: *De Diluvio, De Paradiso, De conflagratione mundi* and *De futuro rerum statu* ('On the Deluge', 'On Paradise', 'On the Conflagration of the Earth' and 'On the Future Condition of Things'). The original Latin volumes were followed by English editions of the work produced by the author himself in 1684 and 1689 respectively.[1] *The Sacred Theory* was the first in a series of attempts at theoretical cosmogenesis that appeared in England at the end of the seventeenth century. It thus belongs among the most debated and controversial works in English natural philosophy of the period.

Burnet's theory attempted to combine the biblical account of the earth's history with Cartesian physics. He had a smooth, egg-shaped earth emerge out of chaotic matter. This pristine globe was composed of several layers with fire at the centre, and then strata of earth and water before the final upper crust. Burnet's *ovum mundanum*, 'earthly egg', was mankind's paradisiacal home before Noah's Flood, but its smooth surface, without water or hills to offer cooling moisture or shade, started to heat up under the sun's glare. The water under the crust began to boil and, as the earth's surface cracked, the Flood ensued – *decreto tempore*, 'at the time that God decreed' – to coincide with the climax of man's sinfulness. For Burnet, the broken face of the earth after the Flood thus bore the marks of God's punishment of mankind, and the crumpled, uneven landscapes of Europe's mountains were, from his theoretical standpoint, the ruins of the former, perfect earth. His personal responses to these rugged landscapes were, however, somewhat at odds with this view, and the ambiguity thus introduced into his account would become one of the several points of interest for his contemporary and later readership. That Burnet could both praise the mountain landscapes' restorative effects and label them horrible wastelands in one sentence is a particularly striking example of this fascinating ambiguity (*Et quanquam revera semper horreant loca montana, et tesqua, ut iam diximus; non deest tamen in tanta varietate, quod recreet animum*: 'And while, in truth, mountainous areas are always horrible and wastelands, as I have already said, there is nonetheless something in such great variety which restores the mind').

Soon after the work's publication, responses to Burnet's natural philosophy, as well as to his aesthetic position and writing style, quickly followed. Already by 1698, Oxford mathematician John Keill had taken Burnet to task on his calculations for the volume of water required for the Flood in his *Examination of Dr. Burnet's Theory of the Earth* (Oxford 1698), while the charge of deism (the then-heretical idea that, after God had set the world into motion, he no longer subsequently interferes with his creation) was levelled against Burnet by Herbert Croft, Bishop of Hereford, in his *Some Animadversions upon a Book Entitled the Theory of the Earth* (London 1685). Meanwhile, on the Continent – perhaps the obvious target market for Latin versions of the *Theory* – Burnet's ambiguous aesthetic position towards the mountain, often strongly expressed throughout his work (as in the passage below), came particularly under fire. In the universities of Germany and Austria, for example, doctoral candidates whose disputations focused on natural philosophical questions surrounding the mountain frequently came to the defence of the beauty of their native Alpine landscapes when dealing with questions over the creation and use of the mountains in God's design of the earth.

If responses to Burnet's *Theoria* were, then, in large part critical of his natural philosophy and its consequences for his interpretation of the Bible, his work nonetheless fuelled a large number of competing theorists in formulating their own accounts of the earth's history. These texts similarly combined the results of contemporary science and key moments of Moses' account. In Britain, William Whitson's *A New Theory of the Earth from the Original to the Consummation of Things* (London 1696) and John Woodward's *An Essay toward a Natural History of the Earth and Terrestrial Bodies* (London 1695) are particularly well-known examples of this sort of theoretical method for natural history. Moreover, Burnet's inventive approach and striking baroque prose style certainly garnered him admirers. His frequent elaborate lists of numerous detailed features after a more vague introductory phrase have been singled out as a particularly noteworthy aspect of his baroque Latin style (see e.g. passages from the second paragraph of the text below: *nova illa atque horrida rerum facies, magnae rupes undique, et saxa, et praecipitia, et squalor et vastitas* . . .; and *plurimi montes plane saxei sunt, silicei, marmorei, cretacei, aut aliter lapidei* . . .). Scholars have also commented on his repeated use of antithetical constructions as another prominent feature of his literary style (see e.g. also in the second paragraph: *quidam molliter assurgunt, et leniori clivo; alii asperitate, et praecipitiis plane impervii sunt*). Indeed, prominent essayist Joseph Addison wrote a Latin ode on the work to celebrate the publication of its second volume in 1689, and Samuel Taylor Coleridge proposed to turn the *Theoria* into blank verse out of admiration for its grand style (Coleridge jotted a note to this effect in his notebooks from 1833–4). Burnet's skilful and atmospheric expressions of his almost bewildered responses to the mountain landscape in the *Theoria* have been highlighted in the work of literary historians as pioneering articulations of an emerging feeling for 'the sublime'.

Note

1 On these vernacular publications Burnet noted 'The English edition is the same in substance with the Latin, though, I confess, 'tis not so properly a translation, as a new composition upon the same ground': T. Burnet, *Sacred Theory of the Earth*, 3rd edn, London 1697, Preface. The English translation provided here follows the Latin original.

Bibliography

Addison, J. (1698), *Ad insignissimum virum dominum Thomam Burnettum sacrae theoriae telluris auctorem*, in *Examen poeticum duplex, sive Musarum anglicanarum delectus alter*, 49–54, London.

Barton, W. M. (2016), *Mountain Aesthetics in Early Modern Latin Literature*, Abingdon.

Davies, G. L. (1969), *The Earth in Decay: A History of British Geomorphology, 1578–1878*, New York.

Gould, S. J. (1987), *Time's Arrow, Time's Cycle: Myth and Metaphor in the Discovery of Geological Time*, Cambridge (MA).

Haller, E. (1940), *Die barocken Stilmerkmale in der englischen, lateinischen und deutschen Fassung von Dr. Thomas Burnets Theory of the Earth*, Bern.

Nicolson, M. H. (1959), *Mountain Gloom and Mountain Glory: The Development of the Aesthetics of the Infinite*, Ithaca (NY).

Ogden, H. V. S. (1947), 'Thomas Burnet's *Telluris Theoria Sacra* and Mountain Scenery', *English Literary History*, 14: 139–50.

Poole, W. (2010), *The World Makers: Scientists of the Restoration and the Search for the Origins of the Earth*, Witney.

Source of the Latin text

Thomas Burnet, *Telluris theoria sacra: Orbis nostri originem et mutationes generales, quas aut iam subiit, aut olim subiturus est, complectens* [*The Sacred Theory of the Earth: Containing an Account of the Original of the Earth and of All the General Changes Which It Hath Already Undergone, or Is to Undergo*], 3rd edition, 2 vols (London: Benjamin Took, 1702), vol. 1, book 1, chap. 9, pp. 66–8.

Latin text

De montibus: eorum magnitudine, forma, situ irregulari, et origine

Cum vero magnarum rerum, licet incultarum, non iniucunda sit speculatio, redeamus iterum ad Alpes nostras: et iactatis oculis in omnes partes, istarum ruinarum[1] differentias et deformitates paululum contemplemur.

Siquem fingeremus somno aut vino obrutum, ex patria campestri subito translatum, relictumque in mediis montibus, et ruinis Alpium; cum expergiscenti astaret nova illa atque horrida rerum facies, magnae rupes undique, et saxa, et praecipitia, et squalor et vastitas; extra fines orbis habitabilis se proiectum crederet;[2] aut in istum angulum universi protrusum, ubi natura, perfecto reliquo opere, materiam inhabilem congesserat. Mihi, cum haec contemplabar,[3] venit in mentem infamis pugnae Gigantum,[4] cum, montibus in montes aggestis,[5] omnia susque deque verterentur. Omnium materiarum atque formarum est hic quaedam confusio; plurimi montes plane saxei sunt, silicei, marmorei, cretacei, aut aliter lapidei; quidam terrei: quanquam id rarius in magnis montibus. Quoad interiora, pauci pleni sunt, plurimi cavi: ubi latibula ferarum et serpentum: amnes subterranei repunt, crescunt fossilia,[6] et metalla aggregantur. In forma externa nulla constantia, aut aequabilitas: quidam praegrandes crassitie et altitudine, alii mediocres:[7] quidam bicipites aut tricipites, atque (mirum dictu)[8] aeterna canitie venerandi, cum ab omni hominum memoria, tecta nive capita, soli licet propius admota, et ex omni parte exposita, aestate et hyeme ostentarint;[9] alii e contra fumos et flammas vomunt. Quidam exterius solidi, corpore integro et unito; alii laceri, fracti, et multifidi. Quidam solitarii (quanquam id rarissime in magnis montibus;) alii conglomerati, aut in longos, et tortuosos tractus exporrecti.[10] Quidam sensim acuminantur, et desinunt in apicem; alii eiusdem fere ambitus sunt, radice, medio et summo; quandoque etiam planitiem in fastigio habent instar mensae. Quidam molliter assurgunt, et leniori clivo; alii asperitate, et praecipitiis plane impervii sunt. Innumerae denique sunt formae, et situs harum molium, ut solet esse ruinarum. Et quanquam revera semper horreant loca montana, et tesqua,[11] ut iam diximus; non deest tamen in tanta varietate,

English translation

On mountains: their size, shape, uneven position and origins

Since it is by no means unpleasant to look at large, or even rugged, things, let us return once again to our Alps and, after taking a look all around, briefly consider the characteristics and defects of these ruins.[1]

If we imagine someone overcome with sleep or wine suddenly transported out of the plains of his homeland and left in the middle of the mountains and ruins of the Alps, he would think himself hurled out of the limits of the habitable world when he woke up faced with that new and bristling appearance of things, the huge cliffs everywhere, rocks and peaks, and their repulsive, desolate nature.[2] Or he would think himself flung into some corner of the universe where nature, her other work completed, had heaped up her intractable material. For me, when I was considering this part of the world,[3] the notorious battle of the giants came to mind,[4] when everything was turned upside down with mountains heaped on mountains.[5] There is a certain confusion here of all materials and forms; many mountains are completely made of rocks, of limestone, marble, chalk or other stones; some are earthy, although this is more seldom in higher mountains. As for their insides, few are filled and many are hollow, where wild beasts and snakes have their dens. Here underground rivers also creep along, fossils grow,[6] and metals are accumulated. There is no consistency or evenness in their external form: some are of colossal density and altitude, others are moderate;[7] some have two or three peaks and some (extraordinary to relate)[8] are to be revered for their perpetual whiteness, since for the whole of human memory they have displayed their summits capped with snow both in summer and winter,[9] and this even though they are raised up very near to the sun and exposed on all sides. In contrast, others spew out smoke and flames. Some are solid on the outside, in an unbroken and unified body; others are mangled, broken and splintered. Some stand on their own (although this is very rare in the high mountains), while others are collected together or spread out in long, tortuous expanses.[10] Some rise up gradually and finish in a sharp peak; others of them are of almost the same circumference at the bottom, middle and top; and sometimes they also have a plateau on their summit, just like a table. Some rise up softly and with a gentler slope; others are plainly impassable with jaggedness and cliffs. There are, thus, innumerable forms and countless structures of these heaps, as is usually the case with ruins. And while, in truth, mountainous areas are always horrible and wastelands,[11] as I have already said, there is nonetheless

quod recreet animum: Atque saepe loci ipsius insolentia, et spectaculorum novitas delectat magis, quam venustas in rebus notis et communibus. Iucundum est ex profunda valle prominentia montium supercilia, et impendentes moles suspicere:[12] quae tristi umbra involvunt subiectos populos, solemque et coelum, maximam partem, adimunt. Id tantillum vero, quod illis superest, coeli,[13] cum montium summitates utrinque contingere videatur, suppositae valli tecti instar apparet, aut coerulei laquearis: haerent, hinc illinc, in media via montis, aut lente serpunt nubes, nec elatum cacumen attingere possunt; et ruit saepe per declive latus, ex nivis resolutione ortus, praeceps et spumosus torrens; squalidis montanis potus insaluberrimus.[14]

Ex montis fastigio alia se aperit rerum facies: coelo liberiori hic fruimur;[15] aspectu vero propter multitudinem montium assurgentium, et perturbatum ordinem, interruptissimo.[16] Etiam ex mari mediterraneo[17] non ingratus est aspectus Alpium et Apenninorum: cum praeternavigantibus multiplices vertices et latera ostentant, quandoque nuda, quandoque urbibus et oppidis ornata.[18]

Siquod vero natura nobis dedit spectaculum in hac tellure, vere gratum, et philosopho dignum, id semel mihi contigisse arbitror; cum ex celsissima rupe speculabundus[19] ad oram maris mediterranei, hinc aequor caeruleum, illinc tractus Alpinos prospexi; nihil quidem magis dispar aut dissimile,[20] nec in suo genere, magis egregium et singulare. Hoc theatrum ego facile praetulerim Romanis cunctis, Graecisve; atque id quod natura hic spectandum exhibet,[21] scenicis ludis omnibus, aut amphitheatri certaminibus. Nihil hic elegans aut venustum,[22] sed ingens et magnificum, et quod placet magnitudine sua et quadam specie immensitatis. Hinc intuebar maris aequabilem superficiem, usque et usque diffusam quantum maximum oculorum acies ferri potuit; illinc disruptissimam terrae faciem, et vastas moles varie elevatas aut depressas, erectas, propendentes, reclinatas, coacervatas, omni situ inaequali et turbido. Placuit, ex hac parte, naturae unitas et simplicitas, et inexhausta quaedam planities; ex altera, multiformis confusio magnorum corporum, et insanae rerum strages:[23] quas cum intuebar,[24] non urbis alicuius aut oppidi, sed confracti mundi rudera, ante oculos habere mihi visus sum.

something in such great variety which can restore the mind. Moreover, the unfamiliarity of the place itself and the novelty of its sights often delights more than beauty in familiar and ordinary things. It is pleasant to admire from the deep valley the jutting peaks of the mountains and overhung boulders,[12] which envelop the people underneath them in gloomy shade and obscure the sun and sky to a great extent. But this tiny part of the sky, which is above them,[13] since it seems to meet the mountain peaks on both sides, appears similar to a roof over the valley below, or to a blue ceiling panel. Here and there clouds cling together in the middle of their way through the mountains, or they slowly edge through, but they cannot touch the very high summit. There often runs a headlong, frothing torrent on the downward facing slope, born out of the melting of the snow; a most unhealthy draught from the filthy mountains.[14]

From the mountain peak another appearance of things opens up: here we enjoy a freer sky,[15] but with a very interrupted view because of the crowd of rising mountains and their confused order.[16] The view of the Alps and the Appennines from the Mediterranean Sea[17] is not unpleasant either, since they reveal numerous peaks and slopes to people passing by, sometimes bare and sometimes decorated with cities and towns.[18]

But if nature has given us some spectacle on this earth which is truly pleasing and worthy of the philosopher, I think that it befell me on one occasion: when I was looking out[19] from a very high cliff towards the shore of the Mediterranean Sea, I saw the blue sea on one side and the expanse of the Alps on the other; there is certainly nothing more disparate or diverse,[20] nor more extraordinary and unique in its kind. I would easily set this theatre above all those of the Romans and Greeks. Moreover, I would easily set that which nature offers here for us to observe[21] above every performance on the stage or every contest in the amphitheatre. There is nothing elegant or graceful here,[22] but rather enormous and magnificent, and that which delights does so in its magnitude and a certain appearance of immeasurableness. On one side I was admiring the smooth surface of the sea spreading out on and on continuously, as far as the gaze could reach. On the other, I could look at the very broken face of the earth, its vast heaps variously raised or sunken, upright, overhung or sloping backwards and crowded together, every section disordered and uneven. On the first side, the unity and simplicity of nature, a kind of unending levelness, was delightful, while on the other, it was the confused mess of shapes in these huge masses, their wild disarray.[23] When I was observing these things,[24] I seemed to have the ruins of a broken world before my eyes, not the remains of some town or city.

Commentary

1 *ruinarum*: In earlier classical Latin prose the word *ruina* followed more closely its verbal root (*ruo*) and described 'a fall', 'falling', 'downfall' or 'collapse', almost synonymous with *casus* or *lapsus*. In Augustan poetry (e.g. Ovid) and post-Augustan prose (e.g. Pliny the Elder) the abstract term gained a concrete meaning – like its cognate today in English – and could now describe the results of a collapse or 'ruins': cf. *Oxford Latin Dictionary*; *Thesaurus Linguae Latinae*, s.v. In the Latin editions of Burnet's *Theoria* the word *ruina* is used to describe both the process of collapse and its results (compare e.g. two early occurrences: 1.46, 'collapse', and 1.48, 'ruins'). Similarly, in Burnet's English version, the word 'ruine' is used with both of these senses (compare 1.21 and 1.47). In both the English and the Latin texts, the context of the passages in which the word occurs leaves it reasonably clear to the reader which of these meanings is intended. The three occurrences of the word in the passage above are to be taken with the physical meaning, 'ruins', as reflected in the translation. The more common translation of the Latin word, 'collapse', does not fit the context here.

2 *Siquem fingeremus . . . se proiectum crederet*: Note the use of the imperfect subjunctive (*fingeremus*; *crederet*) in this clause expressing a hypothetical condition. The verb *astaret* is also imperfect subjunctive, but here following *cum*. The dative present participle *expergiscenti* in this passage picks up on the person imagined in *siquem* at the beginning of the paragraph. The dative case follows the verb *astaret* (lit. 'the new face of things was standing near (awaiting) him awaking').

3 *cum haec contemplabar*: Burnet visited the Alps while on the Grand Tour in 1671 with Charles Paulet, Earl of Wiltshire, later Duke of Bolton. He even suggests elsewhere in the *Theoria* that the inspiration for writing the book came to him on his travels while crossing Europe's imposing mountain chains: *Certe animum meum non parum tetigit, et ad cogitandum de iis rebus stimulavit, cum per Alpes et Apenninos, semel atque iterum iter faciens, eorum vastitatem, confragositatem et magnitudinem, multas provincias, et ingentes terrae tractus pervadentium intuebar* ('Indeed, my mind was deeply affected and encouraged to consider these issues when I observed the desolation, wreckage and size of the mountains which sweep through numerous regions and vast stretches of land, while travelling to and fro through the Alps and Apennines', 1.85).

4 *venit in mentem*: Note the use of the phrase *venire in mentem* with a genitive (*pugnae*), most likely on the model of the verbs *memini*, *recordor*, *reminiscor* and their antonym *obliviscor*, which are normally construed with

the genitive. We can either assume that the phrase *venire in mentem* was simply considered a synonym of these other verbs and therefore followed by a genitive as standard, or that a subject for the verb *venire* was understood (e.g. in this sentence [*memoria*] *pugnae*).

pugnae Gigantum: Descriptions of the gigantomachy, which saw the Olympian gods defeat the *Gigantes*, offspring of Gaia and Uranus, are well attested in ancient literature (see also Text 13, line 174 with note). Among classical authors, Apollodorus' detailed account of the myth (*Bibl.* 1.6.1–2) and that of Ovid in his *Metamorphoses* (1.151–62) are perhaps the most significant. The Olympians' battle with the giants was frequently conflated in literary treatments with the similar Titanomachy as well as with Zeus' struggle against Typhon, among others. Many of these mythological events involved manipulation of geophysical or other natural phenomena by the gods, giants or Titans: Enceladus (a giant) was said to be buried under Mount Etna, and the volcano's activity was thus often attributed to his movements (e.g. Virgil, *Aen.* 3.378–94), for example, and Typhon was said to be imprisoned under the same mountain (Pindar, *Olympian* 4.6–7). These literary images reached a pinnacle in the late-antique *Gigantomachia*, a Greek poem of Claudian, where the earth's surface is imagined to have been altered vastly by these godly contests (*Gig. Gr.* 62–73). By describing the confusion and destruction he saw in Europe's mountainous regions with reference to this well-known mythological and literary episode, Burnet undoubtedly left his readers a clear image of the ruinous scenes he perceived.

5 *montibus in montes aggestis*: Note the use of polyptoton. Burnet's employment of the literary technique that sees the repeated use of words from the same root fittingly emphasizes the chaotic piling up of mountains he imagines here.

6 *crescunt fossilia*: The systematic study of fossils grew to prominence in early modern natural philosophy. In Britain, Burnet's contemporaries, John Ray (1627–1705) and Hans Sloane (1660–1753), both Fellows of the Royal Society, were prominent proponents of the now accepted view that fossils are the remains of living organisms. The traditional view, which saw fossils as the results of natural anomalies, *lusus naturae*, where a stony object had 'grown' by means of an inner plastic virtue (as conceived in Aristotle's teleological conception of nature) was still, however, prevalent at the time of the *Theoria*'s publication.

7 *In forma externa . . . alii mediocres*: Note the omission (common in Latin of all periods) of the verb *esse*, 'to be', in this phrase. We should read, for example: *nulla constantia, aut aequabilitas* [*est*]; *alii mediocres* [*sunt*].

8 *(mirum dictu)*: The fossilized archaic use of the second supine with an adjective (particularly widespread with the verb *dicere*, 'to say') is frequently to be found in Neo-Latin literature, as in other periods.

9 *hyeme ostentarint*: Note the alternative spelling of *hieme* ('winter') as well as the syncopated perfect subjunctive form *ostentarint* (following *cum*) from *ostentaverint*, having dropped the approximant [v] and contracted the vowel.

10 *Quidam exterius solidi . . . tractus exporrecti*: In these sentences, as earlier (see n. 7), the reader should understand *esse*: *Quidam exterius solidi [sunt]*; *Quidam solitarii [sunt]*, etc.

11 *tesqua*: on this word see Text 17, line 21 with note.

12 *Iucundum . . . suspicere*: In this passage Burnet touches on an idea which would become an aspect central to aesthetic theory from the eighteenth century onwards, namely that of 'distancing'. The concept in aesthetics sees special significance laid on the effect of distancing, be it psychical, emotional or, as here, physical, for aesthetic perception. In Burnet's text this means that, while the mountains 'are always horrible and wastelands' when under close inspection, as we read two sentences earlier, he is prepared to admit here that 'it is pleasant to admire from the deep valley the jutting peaks of the mountains and overhung boulders'. In Britain, the abstract idea of 'distancing' – particularly the effect of physical distance for aesthetic perception – would find one of its earliest and clearest theoretical expressions in Edmund Burke's *Philosophical Enquiry into our Ideas of the Sublime and the Beautiful* (London 1757), where the Irishman wrote: 'When danger or pain press too nearly, they are incapable of giving any delight and are simply terrible; but at certain distances, and with certain modifications, they may be, and they are delightful' (2nd edition, 1759: 60). Burnet's passage illustrates Burke's abstract explanation with a fitting concrete example.

13 *coeli*: Note the partitive genitive, dependent on *id tantillum*, 'this tiny part'.

14 *potus insaluberrimus*: Burnet's apparent disgust at the Alpine melt water may sound somewhat surprising to modern ears – indeed, it was certainly rather unusual within the early modern tradition of writing about the mountains. The famous Swiss polymath Conrad Gessner, whose descriptions of his native Alps form an important part of the Neo-Latin literature on the mountain, expressed very different ideas about the peaks' melt water in his *Descriptio montis Fracti* (Zurich 1555). Gessner recounts his walk up the mountain (known today as Mount Pilatus) near Lucerne, where, on approaching the summit, the path becomes steep and somewhat challenging. Here, the

author and his group encounter a stream, *cuius purissima gelidissimaque aqua a lassitudine, siti, et aestu mirifice refecti sumus* ('by whose very pure and very chilled water we were wonderfully restored of our tiredness, thirst and the heat'). Moreover, in classical literature, even Theocritus' Cyclops knew the value of Etna's melt water for a cooling drink in the summer heat (*Idylls* 11.47–8).

15 *Ex montis . . . fruimur:* While evaluation of views *of* the mountains in early modern descriptions often depended on an author's background, theoretical natural philosophical position or the effect of 'distancing' (as noted above, n. 12), views *from* the mountain were regularly praised by authors from numerous periods and fields of interest. The appreciation of views from the mountain could range from the information viewers were able to gain about the surrounding regions, be that geographical, tactical, scientific or otherwise, but observers also enjoyed the change in perspective a mountain-top view could offer, be that literal or figurative, just as Burnet does in this clause. Moreover, views were also often appreciated from an early point in the tradition of writing about mountains on purely aesthetic grounds: for the pleasing variety they could offer, the surprising patterns, shapes and colours that were observable, as well as for the effect of the impressive size and expanse of the available sights. Burnet moves into this mode of engagement with the mountain-top view in the next paragraph (see n. 23). For the phrase *coelo liberiori hic fruimur,* 'here we enjoy a freer sky', cf. Claudian XX (LII).10: *adspectu fruitur liberiore poli.*

16 *aspectu . . . interruptissimo:* Notice how the arrangement of this sentence reflects the idea of the 'very interrupted view' described: the words *aspectu . . . interruptissimo* – dependent on each other grammatically – find themselves at opposite ends of the phrase.

17 *mediterraneo:* A typographical error has *miditerraneo* in the original printed text. The word is otherwise spelled correctly elsewhere in this edition as well as in earlier editions.

18 *urbibus et oppidis ornata:* Mountains belong to the most outstanding features of the 'natural' environment and studies of their appearance in historical literatures rightly emphasize the mountain's part in the development of attitudes towards nature more generally. Concentration on the mountain as a part of the 'natural' world and its separation from human society as a part of the 'wilderness', however, was not a theme of particular interest for Burnet nor for early modern writers more generally. Authors writing descriptions of their trips to the mountain would often comment on the pleasing views of the towns, cities and other symbols of human society they saw below (see F. Calzolari, *Iter Baldi civitatis Veronae montis,* Venice 1571, or B. Aretius,

Stocchornii et Nessi descriptio, Zurich 1561, for example), and the 'cityscape' would become a popular subject in its own right both in literary and artistic works in the period (see, for example, G. Braun and F. Hogenberg, *Civitates Orbis Terrarum*, 6 vols, Cologne 1572–1618).

19 *speculabundus*: Note the use of the suffix *-bundus*, employed to derive an adjective with a transitive meaning (thus giving the word the force of a participle) from a verb form. Other frequently encountered examples include, for example, *moribundus*, 'dying', and (especially in later Latin) *vagabundus*, 'wandering'. The present example from *speculor*, 'I watch, observe', can be found in classical authors.

20 *dissimile*: The reader should again understand *esse*, 'to be': *dissimile* [*est*].

21 *id quod natura hic spectandum exhibet*: The form *spectandum* (lit. 'that which is to be observed') is a neuter gerundive referring to *id quod*.

22 *venustum*: The reader should again supply *est* here.

23 *Placuit ... strages*: In this sentence Burnet sums up the atmospheric, ambiguous and almost paradoxical reactions to the mountain landscape as a whole that he has developed throughout the last paragraph: he enjoys the apparent 'unity' of nature which he sees revealed from the mountain's summit, but he also perceives a 'confused mess' in 'wild disarray'. Moreover, this confusion at once delights him (as in this sentence) while at the same time (as noted above) he finds these mountainous 'ruins' horrid and almost 'outside of the habitable world'. Burnet's imaginative and ingenious attempt to match the developments of his contemporary science with the scriptural account of the earth's history stirred up much debate over its natural philosophical issues. Equally stimulating for contemporary readers, however, were these examples of Burnet's complex aesthetic responses to the natural world, expressed in a magnificent baroque Latin prose, which strongly influenced attitudes towards nature in the decades that followed.

24 *quas cum intuebar*: *quas* picks up the feminine plural *strages* in the previous sentence.

16

A Satire on the Bishop of Salisbury

Anonymous (Thomas Brown?),
In Episcopum Quendam (*c.* 1689)

Victoria Moul

Introduction

One aspect of later seventeenth-century Latin literary culture that has attracted almost no scholarly attention, and barely even an acknowledgement, is the surprising popularity of a range of Latin forms on the boundary between prose and verse, including a very large number of texts, such as the one presented here, which are best described as 'free verse'.

This satiric poem on Gilbert Burnet (1643–1715), Bishop of Salisbury, is preserved in at least ten manuscript copies, most of which appear to date from shortly after Burnet's consecration as Bishop of Salisbury in 1689. Such a large number of extant examples suggests a wide circulation; since there is no whole or even partial catalogue of Latin verse of this period in manuscript, it is very likely that further copies remain to be identified. The poem refers to Burnet's self-imposed exile on the Continent during the reign of the Catholic James II (1685–1688) as well as to his Scottish origins. Burnet was a close personal friend and advisor of King William III, who deposed James II in 1688. The poem presented here is plainly satirical, or even invective in tone, excoriating Burnet for his disloyalty to King James II (who was a Roman Catholic), in contrast to his vigorous defence of the royal authority of Charles II.

Although it appears without attribution in all extant manuscript examples, the poem was printed in eighteenth-century posthumous editions of the works of Thomas (or Tom) Brown (1662–1704), a popular satiric poet in both Latin and English, active in the later seventeenth century. This is a plausible attribution, though far from a certain one: since the poem circulated widely, and Brown was particularly interested in Anglo-Latin verse satire, it is not surprising that he had a copy among his papers – in the absence of further evidence, this does not necessarily prove that he was the author.

The form, described here as free verse, is clearly lineated as verse in all the surviving copies, but is not divided into stanzas, not even into the stanzas of irregular length often found in Latin and English 'Pindarics' of this period. The poem does not systematically use any conventional poetic structuring device, whether quantitative, stress-based or in terms of regular rhyme or alliteration. The various surviving manuscript copies are all similar in overall visual impression, and all contain the same elements, but variations in word order between them are common, and several lines appear in some but not all of the copies. The fairly large degree of variance between the surviving copies suggests that they are not closely related to one another, but evidence of a much larger number of contemporary circulating versions.

The poem ends by comparing Burnet to Cardinal Mazarin (1602–1661), Chief Minister to both Louis XIII and Louis XIV of France. Both Burnet and Mazarin were senior clergymen who acted as close advisors to the monarch, but the link is poetic as well as political. Most of the earliest examples of satiric free verse of this kind circulating in English manuscripts are examples of the so-called 'Mazarinades' against Mazarin, produced in profusion in France in the late 1640s and early 1650s, or poems responding satirically to his death in 1661. In this poem, we see the domestication of that French form for a similar satiric purpose, aimed this time against a Scottish bishop.

Latin free verse was not, however, an exclusively satiric mode: the emergence of the form is probably related also to what Stefan Tilg has described as the 'literary inscription' (texts laid out like inscriptions, and usually centred, though in many cases with no evidence that they were ever inscribed or intended for inscription); he has traced the popularity of this Latin form, which is sometimes panegyric and sometimes satiric, in Germany from the first half of the seventeenth century. It can be hard in some cases to determine whether texts of this sort were considered to be poetry or prose, though in a relatively large number of cases either the title of the text (such as '*carmen lapidarium*', 'lapidary poem', 'poetic inscription') or an accompanying English version plainly in verse, strongly suggests that they were understood as poetry, not prose.

The popularity of Latin free verse in the second half of the seventeenth century is probably also related to the fashion for 'irregular' Pindarics, in both Latin and English. Such 'irregular' Pindarics, made famous in English by Abraham Cowley's *Pindarique Odes* in the 1650s, though certainly traceable to earlier experiments in Neo-Latin verse, usually include clear stanza divisions, albeit between stanzas of irregular length and shape. Nevertheless, the metrical freedoms of this form no doubt encouraged the composition of Latin free verse more generally.

Metre: free verse

Bibliography

There has been almost no scholarship on Latin experimental and free verse in the English seventeenth century, despite the large quantities of extant evidence for the practice.

Bradner, L. (1940), *Musae Anglicanae: A History of Anglo-Latin Poetry, 1500–1925*, New York and London, 109 [a very brief discussion of Latin 'free verse' from this period].

Brown, T. (1720), *The Remains of Mr. Tho. Brown, Serious and Comical, in Prose and Verse. In one Volume. Collected from scarce Papers and Original Mss. Which makes his Works compleat*, London: Sam. Briscoe, 1720, 36–7 [for the text attributed (posthumously) to Thomas Brown].

Greig, M., 'Gilbert Burnet', *Oxford Dictionary of National Biography* [https://doi.org/10.1093/ref:odnb/4061].

Moul, V. (2019), 'Neo-Latin metrical practice in English manuscript sources, *c.* 1550–1720', in S. Tilg and B. Harter (eds), *Neulateinische Metrik. Formen und Kontexte zwischen Rezeption und Innovation*, 257–75, Tübingen [on the overall patterns found in English manuscript sources (including a brief discussion of this poem)].

Moul, V. (forthcoming), 'Neo-Latin Metre', in J. Lidov and A. S. Becker (eds), *Oxford Handbook to Greek and Latin Metre*, Oxford [on Neo-Latin metre as a whole, with a brief discussion of metrical innovation and experiment].

Tilg, S. (2019), 'Die "argute" Inschrift als barocke Form des freien Verses', in S. Tilg and B. Harter (eds), *Neulateinische Metrik. Formen und Kontexte zwischen Rezeption und Innovation*, 133–47, Tübingen [on 'literary inscriptions'].

Source of the Latin text

The extant manuscript versions of this poem so far known are quite varied, both in the precise wording and in the lineation of the poem, though all show a similar variety in line length and the use of indentation. The text below is based upon that found in Oxford, Bodleian MS Rawlinson D. 383, fol. 136ʳ, which is probably one of the earliest versions identified so far. In a few cases, readings have been adopted from other manuscripts.

Latin text

In Episcopum Quendam

E Scotia Presbyter Profugus
In Angliam ad bene mentiendum
Reipublicae causa aliquando venit
Ibi primum Dominum suum
5   Deinde Regem
Tandem patriam et Ecclesiam prodidit.
Egregius mehercule simulator,
      omnium horarum homo,
Proteus nullo (nisi quem meruit)
10   nodo tenendus
Pro regibus aliquando disputavit
      Nunc contra Regem suum
Cristas suas erigit Episcopales.
      Hic rebellionis Antistes
15 Olim ad miseriam damnavit
      et Gehennam seditiosos:
Nunc Caelum et Terram
Presentia et futura
      Iisdem promittit,
20 Homo crudeliter misericors.
Anglia Exul, ad exteras se contulit Regiones
Ut male falleret taedium Conscientiae
      Sed frustra haeret lateri
          Lethalis Arundo.
25 Caelum non animum male sibi conscium
      Aliis Machinantem
Mutavit trans mare Currendo.
Veram ubique (si fas est credere)
      Quaesivit Religionem
30 Parisiis, Romae, Genevae,
      Amstelodami
Sed nullibi invenit, ne quidem in Anglia
   nisi in Ecclesia Sarisburiensi
      Cathedra

English translation

Against a Certain Bishop

A fugitive priest from Scotland
Once came to England to do some good lying
In the cause of the Republic.
There he betrayed first his own Lord
Then the King   5
And at last his country and the Church.
Goodness me, what an extraordinary dissimulator!
This man for all seasons
A Proteus held by no knot (except one he'd bought himself)   10
He once argued for Kings
And now against his own King
He has raised his Bishop-y crest.
This highpriest of Rebellion
Once condemned to the misery   15
Of Gehenna all seditious types:
Now to those same types he promises
Heaven and Earth,
The present and the future!
A man whose mercy is cruelty,   20
An exile from England, he has borne himself off to foreign regions
In the hope of wickedly concealing the queasiness of his Conscience:
But in vain, for the lethal reed sticks fast in his side.
For by running across the sea   25
He has changed the weather, not his own heart:
Bereft of self-knowledge, he simply goes on plotting against others.
Everywhere (if it is right to believe it)
He has sought true religion
At Paris, Rome, Geneva,   30
Amsterdam –
But he finds it nowhere, not even in England
Except in the Cathedral Church of Salisbury

35 Ubi nunc magnifice sedet
          in sui Gloriam
      Ecclesiae Regnique Dedecus
    Bonorum omnium Tristitiam.
    De moribus suis corrigendis parum Sollicitus
40   Precibus publicis in melius
            (Si placet) reformandis
                Totus incumbit.
    Rogandus est, ut inter alias novas
        Quas meditatur formulas
45 Hanc precatiunculam secundum usum Sarum
              Interseri curaret:
    'Hic in Templo negociator.
    Da mihi fallere, da Justum Sanctumque
    videri noctem peccatis et fraudibus objice nubem.'
50 Vivit nobis, Vae nobis in Anglia
            vivit Mazarinus,
    Alterum vidimus triumphare fugitivum
            Et regnare exulem.

Where he now sits magnificently,   35
To the glory of himself
To the shame of the Church and the Kingdom
And to the sorrow of all good men.
Too little concerned about correcting his own habits
He puts all his energy into reforming for the better   40
(If you please) public prayers.
We must ask him how it is that, among the other
Novel forms he has in mind,
He is so particularly keen to see inserted
This little prayer   45
According to the Sarum Rite:
'Here in the Temple grant me, as your chief agent,
The right to cheat, the right to seem Just and Holy;
And cast the darkness of night around my sins, and a cloud of obscurity
    around my deceptions.'
He lives for us; alas, for us in England   50
Mazarinus lives,
A second Mazarin, whom we have seen triumph as a fugitive
And reign as an exile.

Commentary

Regarding the title *In Episcopum Quendam*, 'Against a certain Bishop': This is the title given to the poem in Bodleian MS Rawlinson D. 383. The reader's process of identification is part of the satiric effect. Some manuscript copies give the more explicit title *In Episcopum Sarisburiensem* ('Against the Bishop of Salisbury'). In one case, the poem is titled 'Scott upon Scott', suggesting that the author of the poem (or the person believed to be the author) was either also Scottish or called 'Scott'.

1 *E Scotia*: Burnet was born in Edinburgh and educated at the University of Aberdeen. After travels on the Continent, he became a prominent clergyman and academic in Scotland before coming to London in 1674.

Presbyter: 'Priest', though here a kind of joke, since Burnet, a Scot who accepted a prominent English bishopric, was certainly not a Presbyterian (a form of Protestant church governance that does not include bishops).

4 *Dominum suum*: One manuscript copy of the poem glosses this as 'Duke Lauderdale', that is, John Maitland, the second Earl of Lauderdale, Charles II's secretary of state in Scotland. Lauderdale was a friend and patron of Burnet's for around a decade from 1663, but Burnet fell out of his favour in 1674; from that point on the two men were enemies.

5 *Regem*: When the Catholic King James II came to the throne in 1685, Burnet went into exile on the Continent and spent time at the court of William, Prince of Orange, at The Hague. William was married to Mary, the daughter of James II. William and Mary acted as godparents at the christening of Burnet's son, William, in April 1688. Although Burnet was unaware of William's plans to invade England and depose King James, after the invasion went ahead successfully in November 1688, Burnet was closely involved in the arrangements for the coronation of William III and Mary II as king and queen. He preached their coronation sermon in April 1689 and was appointed as Bishop of Salisbury later that year. The *Rex* referred to here, whom Burnet is accused of having betrayed, is therefore King James II, who fled into exile.

8 *omnium horarum homo*: This phrase is included in Erasmus, *Adagia* (I.iii.86).

9 *Proteus*: The mythical Proteus could change shape at will, transforming from one creature to another, making him almost impossible to catch. In William Shakespeare's *Henry VI Part III*, Richard, Duke of Gloucester, who will go on to usurp the throne, uses the image of Proteus to boast of his own political opportunism: 'I can add colours to the chameleon, | Change shapes

with Proteus for advantages' (III.ii.193–4). The myth is put to similar use here.

11 *Pro regibus aliquando disputavit*: Earlier in his career, under Charles II, Burnet had frequently defended the principle of royal supremacy in church affairs.

12 *contra Regem suum*: referring once again to King James II. Whereas Burnet had been a staunch defender of the principle of obedience to a sovereign monarch under Charles II, he became an enthusiastic supporter of the armed deposing of James II in 1688.

13 *Cristas suas erigit*: The image is of a male bird, such as a cockerel or peacock, raising its crest in pride. It is typically used satirically: to indicate the absurdity of someone who has no real reason to feel pride, for instance because they are being shamelessly flattered (as in Juvenal, *Satires* 4.69–70: *quid apertius? et tamen illi | surgebant cristae*). The wording here is, however, closer to medieval and early modern examples; in the preface to his *Praise of Folly* (*Moriae encomion* 3), for instance, Erasmus uses the phrase *cristas erigit* ('raises his crest') in his justification of the moral and satiric effect of praising that which deserves no praise.

14 *Antistes*: an 'overseer' or 'high priest'; used in Christian authors for 'bishop'.

15–19 *Olim . . . Nunc . . . promittit*: Again, this contrasts Burnet's defence of the authority of King Charles II with his support for the deposition of King James II. Earlier in his career, while in Scotland, Burnet had defended the principle of royal authority in church matters. Later, during the crisis created by the rumours of a so-called 'Popish Plot' against King Charles II in 1678, Burnet, though at least somewhat sceptical about the plot itself, did not hesitate to exploit the situation politically. In other words, he was quick to condemn sedition against Charles II, but actively supported the deposition of the Roman Catholic James II.

16 *Gehennam*: transliteration of a Hebrew place name, referring to a valley near Jerusalem where children were sacrificed to Moloch; used to mean by extension, in both the Vulgate and early Christian authors, 'hell'.

20 *misericors*: As a senior clergyman, Burnet ought to be compassionate and merciful, though in fact he is *crudeliter misericors* ('cruelly merciful'), a paradox suggesting that he shows compassion to the wrong people or in the wrong way, resulting in suffering.

23–4 *Sed frustra haeret lateri | Lethalis Arundo*: These lines quote Virgil, *Aeneid* 4.73. In that passage Dido, struck by Cupid with a fatal passion for

Aeneas, is compared to a deer shot by an arrow. The use of the expression here implies that Burnet was unable to shake off the charge of disloyalty to his rightful monarch (that is, James II), despite going into exile. The Virgilian simile indicates that the inception of Dido's passion for Aeneas leads directly to her death; the allusion may therefore be meant to suggest that Burnet's reputation will not recover.

25–7 *Caelum non animum . . . Mutavit trans mare Currendo*: a rephrasing of a much-quoted passage from Horace, *Epistles* 1.11.27 (*caelum, non animum mutant qui trans mare currunt*; 'men who run away across the sea change the weather, not their heart'). Here *animum* is expanded with the phrases *male sibi conscium Aliis Machinantem* standing in apposition, to indicate that Burnet takes his guilty conscience and his habit of plotting against others with him into exile.

28–32 *Parisiis, Romae, Genevae,* | *Amstelodami*: Burnet travelled extensively in 1685–6. After two months in Paris, he travelled on to Switzerland and then to Rome, where he was offered an audience (which he declined) with Pope Innocent XI. He spent several months in Geneva in the winter of 1685–6 and returned to the Netherlands, via Germany, in the spring of 1686. In 1687 Burnet published as a single volume five letters he had written to Robert Boyle during this period of travel (*Some Letters, Containing an Account of what seemed Most Remarkable in Switzerland, Italy, etc*). This markedly anti-Catholic work became one of Burnet's most popular publications. The phrase *si fas est credere* (28) is probably intended to imply that his account of his travels may not be entirely reliable.

32 *nullibi*: adverb, 'nowhere', a post-classical word.

40–1 *Precibus publicis . . . reformandis*: Burnet was an energetic bishop, concerned particularly with education of the clergy. Since this poem, however, almost certainly dates from very shortly after his consecration as Bishop of Salisbury, the point here seems to be simply to draw a contrast between Burnet's concern for the conduct of others and his neglect of his own conduct.

45 *precatiunculam*: in classical usage, 'a minor request', though here playing upon the usage of *precatio* (for 'prayer'); thus meaning 'a trifling little prayer'. The diminutive is satiric: Burnet's 'little prayer', which he hopes to slip in unnoticed, is of almost demonic self-importance.

usum Sarum: The 'Sarum rite' ('Sarum' means Salisbury, as it was originally established in that diocese) was the form of worship used throughout England and Wales up until the Reformation. Here the familiar phrase *usus Sarum*, 'the Sarum rite', is used satirically to refer to Burnet's particular devotional and liturgical practice, imagining him inserting into the liturgy a prayer to protect his own duplicity (47–9).

47 *negociator = negotiator*: a 'factor', 'agent', 'dealer' or 'trader'; the connotation is strongly secular. This is the person entrusted with the transaction of a particular business.

48–9 *Da mihi ... nubem*: almost a quotation of Horace, *Epistles* 1.16.61–2 (*da mihi fallere, da iusto sanctoque videri, | noctem peccatis et fraudibus obice nubem*). In both texts this is direct speech: in Horace, the lines are an example of a hypocrite at prayer.

50 *Vivit nobis*: lit. 'he lives for us'. The phrase 'he lives for us', or variants of it, occurs frequently in a devotional context referring to Christ, especially in commemorations of the Resurrection. Here Burnet is a kind of resurrected Cardinal Mazarin (d. 1661, see n. on 51).

51 *Mazarinus*: At this point the comparison to Mazarin is made explicitly; Cardinal Mazarin, first minister of state for Louis XIV, was the subject of a large quantity of popular satiric verse and song (the 'Mazarinades') during the 'Fronde' rebellion (1648–53). In England, several popular Latin poems, written in a free verse form very similar to that we see here, circulated widely both during his lifetime and immediately following his death. In this sense, the link to Mazarin is established by the form, style and tone of the poem before we reach the explicit comparison in the closing lines.

52–3 *fugitivum ... exulem*: referring once again to Burnet's period on the Continent during the reign of James II; perhaps also alluding to the fact that, after losing the favour of Lauderdale, the secretary of state for Scotland, in 1674, Burnet resigned his professorship at Glasgow and never returned to his native country.

17

A View of the Scottish Highlands

James Philp (1656/7–c. 1713), *Grameid* 3.10–36

L. B. T. Houghton

Introduction

James Philp's *Grameid* (in Latin *Grameis*, the epic of Graham [*Gramus*]), composed around 1691, is an incomplete Latin epic of just over five books on the Jacobite rising of 1689, led by John Graham of Claverhouse, 1st Viscount Dundee. The poem traces events from the birth of a son to James II and VII and his wife Mary of Modena, through the ensuing 'Glorious Revolution', which brought William III and Mary II to the throne, to the campaign of 1689, but breaks off before Dundee's victory and death at the Pass of Killiecrankie. Combining the resonant imperial proclamations of Virgil's *Aeneid* with the darker descriptions of civil conflict found in the epic of Lucan, the *Grameid* gives strident expression to its author's allegiance to the Stuart dynasty and his hostility to the Presbyterian party in Scottish religious politics.

This passage, taken from the beginning of Book 3 of Philp's epic, is part of a description of the hardships endured by Dundee's troops during their march through the Highlands (perhaps an imitation in reverse of Cato's march through the hot and dry Libyan desert in Book 9 of Lucan's *Bellum civile*). The account of an arduous winter journey had distinguished precedent in Neo-Latin literature, notably in one of Erasmus' letters (*Epistulae* 82, February 1497) in which the humanist paints a vivid picture of the rigours he faced on a stormy ride through a wintry landscape. Philp's treatment of the theme offers an instructive illustration of the imitative techniques of Neo-Latin verse, drawing on a wide range of poetic models both ancient and modern; this inherited material is tempered with details reflecting local circumstances (for a map of the locations mentioned, see Fig. 17.1).

James Philp (or Philip, 1656/7–c. 1713) of Almerieclose in Arbroath, who wrote under the name 'Panurgus Philo-caballus Scotus' (i.e. James Philip the Scot), was related to the leader of the rising through his mother's family. Educated at the University of St Andrews in the 1670s, the poet joined his

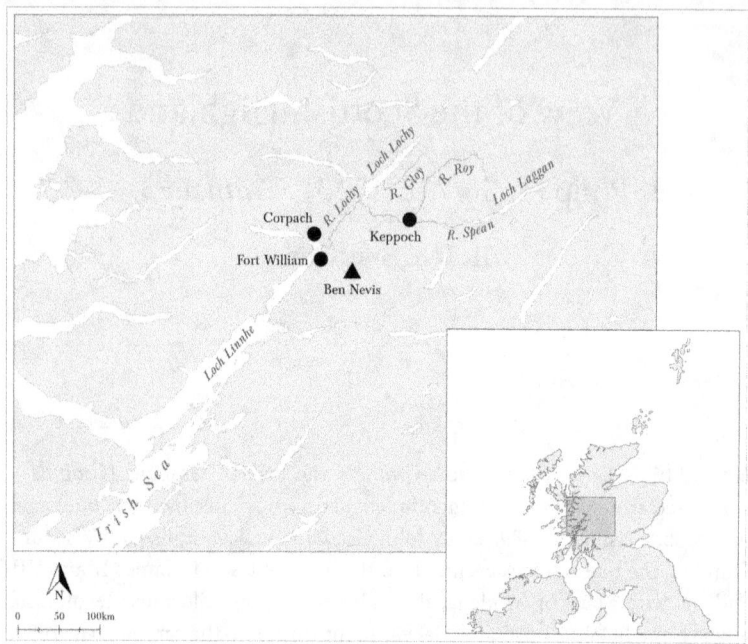

Fig. 17.1 Map of the Scottish Highlands: designed by Matilde Grimaldi.

kinsman's campaign and claims to have served as his standard-bearer, comparing himself to the Roman poet Ennius (239–169 BCE, author of the historical epic *Annales* and other works), who was said to have accompanied Scipio Africanus the Elder on his military expeditions. Shortly afterwards Philp began work on the *Grameid*, which survives in several manuscripts (to Murdoch's list add Glasgow University Library, MS Gen. 367 and NLS, MSS 100 and 318) – though enquiries to the National Library of Scotland reveal that the autograph manuscript (Murdoch's A) has been lost, probably since before 1923. Philp also produced a number of shorter Latin pieces, among them a paraphrase of Virgil's fourth Eclogue in celebration of the birth of the Prince of Wales in 1688.

Murdoch (1888: 80–1 n. 3) quotes an eighteenth-century verse translation by John Drummond of the final nine lines of this passage (see *Memoirs of Sir Ewen Cameron of Locheill, Chief of the Clan Cameron*, Edinburgh 1842: 239).

Metre: dactylic hexameter

Bibliography

Houghton, L. B. T. (2012), 'Lucan in the Highlands: James Philp's *Grameid* and the Traditions of Ancient Epic', in L. B. T. Houghton and G. Manuwald (eds), *Neo-Latin Poetry in the British Isles*, 190–207, London.

Houghton, L. B. T. (2017), 'The Scottish Fourth Eclogue', in S. J. Reid and D. McOmish (eds), *Neo-Latin Literature and Literary Culture in Early Modern Scotland*, 74–99, Leiden and Boston.

Murdoch, A. D. (ed.) (1888), *The Grameid: An Heroic Poem Descriptive of the Campaign of Viscount Dundee in 1689, and Other Pieces by James Philip of Almerieclose, 1691*, Edinburgh.

Pittock, M. G. H. (1994), *Poetry and Jacobite Politics in Eighteenth-century Britain and Ireland*, Cambridge [39–42].

Source of the Latin text

The Latin text has been taken from Murdoch 1888: 79–80, corrected and checked against manuscripts in Edinburgh and Glasgow.

Latin text

(10) Iam Boreae rigidis tentoria cana pruinis
egressi, lustrant nemora, et pernice pedum vi
scandunt nimbiferi praerupta cacumina clivi,
et iuga celsa petunt, unde omnis rite videri
5 (14) iam poterit regio; qua Kapocha respicit Austrum,
Corpocha spumosum vel qua glacialis Ierne
vergit ad Oceanum, vel qua Balnavius ingens
emicat, et salebris, durique crepidine saxi
arduus, et magna attollens fastigia mole
10 (19) exsurgentem apicem stellanti immittit Olympo;
quaque lacus liquido diffunditur amne Spaini;
et qua magna Gluae, vallisque sonantia Roae
flumina non uno currunt in caerula cornu;
quaque pruinosis Boream secat Abria saxis
15 (24) cernere erat, camposque oculis haurire patentes.
Iam scopulos super assurgentes aetheris oras,
atque cavas tacito permensi lumine valles,
quocunque ingenti torserunt ora rotatu,
nil praeter montes et saxa amnesque lacusque
20 (29) collustrant, spinisque et vepribus obsita densis
tesqua patent, raris et rura habitata colonis.
Frigoribus durescit humus, concreta rigebant
arva gelu, assiduis algetque aquilonibus aer,
horrebantque rubis late omnia, et undique sentes,
25 (34) dumique et tribuli incultis dominantur in arvis.
Vestit erica solum, montes nixque alta tegebat,
pigraque ferratis concrescunt flumina crustis.

English translation

Now, leaving their tents white with the North Wind's hard frost, they go through the woods, and by the swift force of their feet they climb the jagged peaks of the cloud-capped height, and they make for the lofty ridges, from where the whole area can now be seen properly: where Keppoch faces the   5
south, or where Corpach slopes down towards the foaming sea of chilly Ireland, or where vast Ben Nevis flashes out, steep with its rough places and projection of hard rock, and lifting up its summit with mighty bulk raises its   10
towering peak to starry heaven; and where the loch is poured out by the flowing current of the Spean, and where the great streams of the Gloy and the sounding streams of the valley of the Roy rush into the ocean, not by a single branch; and where Lochaber parts the North Wind with its frosty cliffs – all   15
this they could see, and take in with their eyes the spreading plains. Now, scanning with silent gaze crags rising above the regions of the air and hollow valleys, wherever they turn their faces in a vast circle they survey nothing but mountains and rocks and rivers and lakes; and wastes overgrown with thick   20
thorns and brambles stretch before them, and country inhabited by farmers few and far between. The ground is hard with frost, the fields were frozen stiff with ice, and the air is chilled by constant blasts from the north; everything far and wide bristled with brambles, and everywhere briars, thorn bushes and   25
thistles hold sway in the untended fields. Heather cloaks the soil, deep snow covered the mountains, and the sluggish rivers congeal with shells hard as iron.

Commentary

1 The language of this line displays several points of contact with Jacopo Sannazaro, *Eclogae piscatoriae* 2.65–6: **Boreae** *extremo damnata sub axe* | *stagna petam et* **rigidis** *numquam non* **cana pruinis** . . .? ('Shall I make for the pools cursed beneath the North Wind's furthest clime and forever white with hard frost . . .?'). The eclogues of the Neapolitan poet Sannazaro (1458–1530) were among the most influential works of Neo-Latin pastoral poetry following their publication in 1526. For the expression *tentoria* . . . *egressi* ('leaving their tents': *tentoria* is the accusative object of the participle), see Lucan, *Bellum Civile* 5.510–11: *tentoria* . . . *egressus*.

2 Note the abrupt effect of the monosyllabic line-ending, perhaps reflecting the scramble of the ascent; the line-ending is found at Lucretius, *De rerum natura* 5.253 (where *multa pulsata pedum vi*, 'beaten by the frequent force of feet', creates the same alliteration as in Philp's line). The Lucretian expression had previously been adopted by Maffeo Vegio at *Aeneidos liber XIII*, line 52.

3 For the rare and stylistically elevated compound adjective *nimbifer* (here 'cloud-capped'; lit. 'cloud-bearing', hence 'stormy'), see Ovid, *Epistulae ex Ponto* 4.8.60, where it is used of the fire of Jupiter's thunderbolt.

4–5 For the expression see Virgil, *Aeneid* 8.604–5: *celsoque omnis de colle videri* | *iam poterat legio* ('and from the lofty hill the whole troop could now be seen'). The change of tense from Virgil's imperfect *poterat* to future *poterit* is probably conditioned by the narrative present *petunt* (they *are* making their way now, and when they reach the top, they *will be able* to see). Take *omnis* – emphasized, as in the Virgilian passage, by its early position (the *whole* region can be seen) – with *regio* in the following line.

5 *Kāpŏcha* is Keppoch (Gaelic *Ceapaich*), seat of Clan MacDonald of Keppoch, an estate at the confluence of the rivers Spean and Roy (see lines 11–13 of this passage). The castle had been destroyed in 1663 following the infamous Keppoch Murders. *qua* begins a catalogue of geographical areas and features, which runs through the next few lines: the repetition *qua* . . . *vel qua* . . . *vel qua* . . . *quaque* . . . *et qua* has the effect of a panoramic sweep across the landscape from the height on which the observers are standing, moving from one point to the next in a broad arc.

6 *Cŏrpŏcha* is Corpach (Gaelic *A' Chorpaich*), a little to the north of Fort William at the northern end of Loch Linnhe. Murdoch (1888: 80 n. 1) locates the viewpoint somewhere near Roy Bridge, with Corpach lying to the west in the direction of the Irish Sea (from which it is in fact some distance).

spumosum must be taken with *Oceanum* in the following line, while *glacialis* is most naturally taken with *Ierne*, as confirmed by the occurrence of this phrase in Claudian's panegyric on the fourth consulship of the Emperor Honorius, line 33, quoted by George Buchanan (see Text 3) in his *Historia* (for discussion see C. J. Classen, 'The References to Classical Authors in Buchanan's *Rerum Scoticarum Historia*', in I. D. McFarlane [ed.], *Acta conventus neo-Latini Sanctandreani*, 3–29, Binghamton 1986, at 9–10, 22–3).

7 The continuation of the sentence on to the following line with *vergit* possibly mirrors the meaning of the verb. *Balnavius* is Ben Nevis (Gaelic *Beinn Nibheis*), the highest mountain in Britain at 1,345 m (4,411 ft) above sea level. Philp once again uses this Latinized name for the mountain at *Grameid* 4.509; one of the nearest settlements to Ben Nevis is Banavie.

8 The sudden appearance of Ben Nevis as the gradual panoramic sweep comes round to it is nicely conveyed by the enjambment of *emicat* at the start of the line. For the line-ending *crepidine saxi*, see Virgil, *Aen.* 10.653.

9 *arduus*: another enjambment, emphasizing the adjective. The long vowels in the middle of the line evoke the immense mass (*magna . . . mole*) of the mountain; *magna*, which must be taken with *mole* rather than *fastigia*, elides into *attollens* (enhancing the thrust of the line by elision over the main caesura, the principal metrical break in the middle of the line) and is emphasized by its position. Murdoch prints *magno*, but *moles* is always feminine, and the reading *magna* is confirmed by the manuscripts: here *moles* refers primarily to the 'bulk' of the mountain, but there may also be a hint of personification – the mountain strains to raise its peak 'with great effort'.

10 *exsurgentem* elides into *apicem* and *stellanti* into *immittit*: once again, the sequence of long vowels (the line is spondaic except for *apicem* and the fifth foot) conveys the awesome grandeur of Ben Nevis, lifting its peak hyperbolically to heaven. The cosmic hyperbole is arguably made even more emphatic by the position of *Olympo* as the final word of the line. For the expression *stellanti . . . Olympo* ('starry Olympus'), see Cicero, *De divinatione* 1.12.19. There is a possible suggestion of personification here too, in *apicem . . . immittit*: Ben Nevis is like a giant, raising his head to heaven – and in view of the common military use of *immitto* ('launch at', 'despatch against'), it is perhaps not too fanciful to see in *immittit Olympo* undertones of gigantomachy, as the Scottish mountain delivers a passionate Glasgow kiss to the realm of the gods.

11 *lacus* is Loch Laggan, from which the River Spean (here *Spainus*) flows westward to join the River Lochy in the Great Glen. The alliteration *lacus*

liquido might be taken to suggest the lapping of the lake. *Spăīnī* at the end of the line must be scanned as three syllables.

12 *Glŭa* is the River Gloy, which flows through Glen Gloy before emptying into Loch Lochy at Inverlochy; *Rōa* is the River Roy, which runs almost parallel to the Gloy and joins the Spean at Roybridge. *flumina* in the following verse should be taken with both halves of this line, agreeing with both *magna* and *sonantia*, and with both genitives *Gluae* and *vallis . . . Roae* dependent on it.

13 The parallel character of the two rivers is implied by the balance of the previous line and shared noun *flumina*, but here their courses to the sea (*caerula*, neuter plural) are differentiated (*non uno* is emphasized by its position and its separation from *cornu*). The closest parallel to the expression of this line is perhaps to be found at Marco Girolamo Vida, *Christiad* 1.31: *turbidus haud uno dum rumpat in aequora cornu* ('until it [the river Po], in confusion, bursts into the sea, through more than one [literally 'not a single'] branch': the end of the first simile of Vida's Christian epic [1535]); for *cornu* as the branch of a river, see also Ovid, *Metamorphoses* 9.774: *septem digestum in cornua Nilum* ('the Nile divided into seven branches'). Murdoch (1888: 80 n. 2) notes: 'The idea is that they reach the salt water together, but in different ways, the Gloy falling into Loch Lochy, the Roy into the Spean, which, falling into the Lochy, there meets the waters of the Gloy, and both flow together into Loch Eil'. The line ends with marked alliteration.

14 *Abria* had been used by George Buchanan (see Text 3) in his history and by Andrew Melville in his *Scotiae topographia* as the Latin name for the district of Lochaber.

15 *cernere erat* ('it was possible to see') perhaps comes as a surprise: the reader is likely to have taken the various descriptions introduced by *qua* as proceeding from *regio* in line 5. The postponement may be intended to reinforce the sense of the previous lines as an uninterrupted panorama experienced by Dundee's men from their viewpoint. For the expression (often in the context of ekphrastic descriptions) see Virgil, *Aen.* 6.596; 8.676; Statius, *Thebaid* 5.256; 7.61.

16 *scopulos . . . assurgentes* has been taken here as the object of *permensi*, with *oras* as accusative after *super*, as being in keeping with the sublimity of the passage. If *scopulos* is accusative with *super*, and *oras* the object of *permensi*, the translation would read: 'Now, scanning with silent gaze the regions of the air rising above the crags' (or 'above the rising crags'). Possibly the ambiguity is deliberate: the precise configuration of sky and rock can scarcely be distinguished. *assurgentes* might also be nominative, forming a

pair with the nominative plural participle *permensi* and connected with it by *atque*. In this case, *aetheris oras* would need to be taken in apposition to *scopulos* (*super*): 'Now, rising up above the crags, the regions of the air, and scanning ...' (thanks to Daniel Hadas for this suggestion). Note the awe-inspiring long syllables of *assurgentes* (recalling *exsurgentem* in line 10), displacing the main caesura. The phrase *aetheris oras* is from Lucretius, *De rerum natura* 5.681 (who in turn may have taken it from Ennius, *Saturae*, F 3, *Fragments of Republican Latin*, Loeb).

17 Murdoch concludes the sentence after *valles*, which leaves it without a main verb (unless we understand *sunt* with *permensi*). The participle *permensi* (from *permetior*) refers to the subject of *torserunt* ('they', i.e. Dundee's men). The pleasingly symmetrical arrangement of adjectives and nouns around *permensi*, and the return to a regular main caesura, may imply a gentler landscape than the rugged grandeur of the preceding line.

18 The line is wholly spondaic apart from the fifth foot, as the observers' gaze pans slowly round the imposing prospect that surrounds them; *quocunque* elides into *ingenti*, leaving the first half of the line without a break and suggesting the continuous sweep of the view. *ingenti* ('vast') is emphasized by its position before the caesura and ahead of its (rare) noun *rotatu*.

19 The spondees continue, reflecting the scene of desolation on every side. Note the polysyndeton (multiple conjunctions) in *et ... que ... que* (and continued in *spinisque et*) as the viewers' eyes take in one feature after another in a seemingly unending sequence. For the line-ending see Ovid, *Metamorphoses* 7.197 (also part of a catalogue).

20 Yet more long syllables (though the second half of the line breaks the run of spondees), with *collustrant* reflecting the slow scrutiny of the onlookers as they survey every detail. Take *densis* with both *spinis* and *vepribus*. Some manuscripts (unmetrically) have *vel* ('or') for *et*.

21 On the unusual word *tesqua* (or *tesca*) see J. N. Adams, *The Regional Diversification of Latin 200 BC – AD 600*, Cambridge 2007: 181, quoting the *Oxford Latin Dictionary*, s.v. *tesquum*: 'by non-technical writers interpreted as a tract of wild or desolate land'. For the line-ending *rura habitata colonis*, see George Buchanan, *De sphaera* 3.557; closer to the atmosphere of this passage is Andrew Melville, *Scotiae topographia* 623, on the isle of Scarba: *culta parum raroque suis habitata colonis* ('little cultivated and scantily inhabited by its farmers'). See also Claudian, *In Rufinum* 2.40.

22–3 See also *Grameid* 2.223: *flumina adhuc glacie ... concreta rigebant* ('the rivers were still frozen stiff with ice').

23 A strongly alliterative line; the effect is presumably to suggest the gusts of the wind (Drummond's translation [see Introduction] has: 'With warring winds and storms the air is toss'd'). *gelu* elides into *assiduis* (emphatic by position: the freezing winds *never stop*), and *algetque* into *aquilonibus*. *āēr* scans as two syllables. For the line-ending see [Ovid], *Nux* 64 and Lucan 6.104; later examples at Vida, *Bombyx* 2.74 and Fracastoro, *Syphilis* 2.86.

24 It is curious to find here an entire line reproduced verbatim from Theodore Beza's *Sylva* 4 (poetic preface to Psalm 51): see *Theodori Bezae Vezelii poematum editio secunda, ab eo recognita*, Geneva 1569: 59 (the volume also includes excerpts from George Buchanan). For the association of the French Protestant reformer Beza (1519–1605) with the Scottish humanist Andrew Melville, see E. R. Holloway III, *Andrew Melville and Humanism in Renaissance Scotland 1545–1622*, Leiden 2011: 136–46. The lines from Beza are probably based on Virgil, *Aen.* 9.381–2: *silva fuit late dumis atque ilice nigra | horrida, quam densi complerant undique sentes* ('There was a wood, bristling far and wide with brambles and dark ilex, which thick briars had filled on every side'). The imperfect *horrebant* sits rather uncomfortably with the present *dominantur* in the following line. NLS MS 100 has *ante* ('before them') for *late* ('far and wide').

25 Beza continues with *dumique tribulique*. In the rest of the line Philp moves away from Beza and turns to Virgil's *Georgics*: for *tribuli . . . dominantur* ('thistles hold sway') see *Geo.* 1.152–4, and for *in arvis* ('in the fields'), 1.151. *incultis* is emphatically placed, reinforcing the atmosphere of barrenness and neglect (and the elision over the usual main caesura perhaps serves to corroborate the impression of untended nature running out of control).

26 For the line-opening *Vestit erica solum* ('Heather cloaks the soil') – naturally appropriate in a description of a Scottish landscape – see Henry Anderson's *Musarum querimonia*, line 189, in *Delitiae poetarum Scotorum huius aevi illustrium*, 2 vols, Amsterdam 1637: 1.24–33. Once again, there is an awkward change of tense from present *vestit* to imperfect *tegebat*, then back again to present *concrescunt*.

27 Philp's virtuoso performance concludes with a 'Golden Line' (adjective A, adjective B, verb, noun A, noun B) and alliterative patterning f c [more cs] f c. The slowing of the rivers' course can be heard in the long syllables of *ferratis concrescunt*. The description ultimately goes back to Virgil, *Georgics* 3.360–1: *concrescunt subitae currenti in flumine crustae, | undaque iam tergo ferratos sustinet orbis . . .* ('sudden shells congeal on the running river, and the wave now supports on its back wheels shod with iron': has Philp misunderstood the meaning of *ferratos . . . orbis* here?). The exact formulation *concrescunt*

flumina crustis is found, however, in an elegy by Tarquinio Galluzzi, SJ: see *Elegiae* 2.1.31, in *Tarquinii Gallutii Sabini e Societate Iesu carminum libri tres*, Rome 1611: 150. It is not necessary to suppose that Philp was perusing the poetry of the Italian Jesuit as he wrote his poem, or even that the parallels with Virgil's *Georgics* are the result of first-hand engagement; for both the Virgilian passage and the lines by Galluzzi are cited in the section entitled 'Hyems' (winter) in J. B. Gandutius [Giovanni Battista Ganducci], *Descriptiones poeticae ex probatioribus poetis excerptae*, 3rd edn, Venice 1676: 81–2. It is therefore likely that our poet was using a compositional aid such as Ganducci's to compile his picture of the wintry landscape, consulting the entries relevant to his subject-matter. It is important to keep in mind the prevalence of this kind of authorial practice when attempting to determine the significance of allusions to earlier literature in the work of Neo-Latin poets.

18

Thomas Gray Prophesies Space Travel

Thomas Gray (1716–1771),
Luna habitabilis 51–72, 78–95

L. B. T. Houghton

Introduction

The eighteenth-century poet Thomas Gray (1716–1771) is best-known for his 'Elegy Written in a Country Churchyard', which has often been translated into Latin (see Gibson *et al.* 2008). Gray was a friend of Horace Walpole and played a pioneering part in the study of medieval Gothic architecture. In addition to his more celebrated English poetry, he also produced a quantity of classicizing Latin verse. The self-critical poet, who published little during his lifetime and declined the position of Poet Laureate, was educated at Eton (another of his famous pieces in English is the 'Ode on a Distant Prospect of Eton College') and at Peterhouse, Cambridge, where he composed the poem *Luna habitabilis* ('The Habitable Moon' / 'The Moon [is] habitable'). This was written as a submission for the Tripos Verses (a Latin composition requested by the Moderator on a prescribed topic) of 1737 and was later printed in the poetic compilation *Musae Etonenses* in 1755.

In this poem of ninety-five Latin hexameters, the narrator appeals to his Muse to reveal to him the wonders of space, whereupon the Muse invites him to scrutinize the moon by means of a telescope (entertainingly described in Latin verse in lines 25–9 of the original poem, not included here). The poet presents the physical characteristics of the moon before proceeding to imagine its inhabitants, who are pictured gazing at the earth in the same way that terrestrial astronomers contemplate their celestial world. The work ends with a prediction of future dealings between earth and the moon (the second of the extracts given here), anticipating inter-planetary commerce and colonization and concluding on a triumphalistic note with a vision of the expansion of the British Empire, which already rules the waves, into the realm of space.

Like much of Gray's Latin poetry, the verse is heavily dependent on classical tags (some particularly blatant examples can be seen in these lines), but the poem is of considerable interest for its subject matter, which looks ahead to the later genre of science fiction. Lines from the closing section of the poem, foretelling England's mastery of the air, enjoyed some celebrity around the time of the Battle of Britain (see 'Gray's Prophecy', *The Spectator*, 1 January 1943, pp. 11–12, and J. Levine, *Forgotten Voices of the Blitz and the Battle for Britain*, London 2006: 304).

Metre: dactylic hexameter

Bibliography

Baldwin, B. (1994), 'On Some Greek and Latin Poems by Thomas Gray', *International Journal of the Classical Tradition*, 1: 71–88.

Baldwin, B. (2015), 'Fifty (-47) Shades of Gray', *Vates: The Journal of New Latin Poetry*, 11: 24–37.

Bradner, L. (1940), *Musae Anglicanae: A History of Anglo-Latin Poetry, 1500–1925*, New York and London [241–4, 279, 289].

Gibson, D., P. Wilkinson and S. Freeth (eds) (2008), *Thomas Gray: Elegy in a Country Churchyard: Translations into Latin 1762–2001*, Orpington.

Haan, E. (2000), *Thomas Gray's Latin Poetry: Some Classical, Neo-Latin and Vernacular Contexts*, Brussels [esp. 35–50 (the fullest and best discussion of *Luna habitabilis*) with 168–73].

Haan, E. (2015), 'The British Isles', in S. Knight and S. Tilg (eds), *The Oxford Handbook of Neo-Latin*, 427–43, Oxford.

Starr, H. W. and J. R. Hendrickson (eds) (1966), *The Complete Poems of Thomas Gray: English, Latin and Greek*, Oxford.

Source of the Latin text

The Latin text has been taken from Starr and Hendrickson 1966: 130–1, checked against *Musae Etonenses: sive Poematia in duos tomos distributa*, London 1755: 2.109–12.

Latin text

(51) Et dubitas tantum certis cultoribus orbem
      destitui? exercent agros, sua moenia condunt
      hi quoque, vel Martem invadunt, curantque triumphos
      victores: sunt hic etiam sua praemia laudi;
5 (55) his metus, atque amor, et mentem mortalia tangunt.
        Quin, uti nos oculis iam nunc iuvat ire per arva,
      lucentesque plagas lunae, pontumque profundum:
      idem illos etiam ardor agit, cum se aureus effert
      sub sudum globus et terrarum ingentior orbis;
10 (60) scilicet omne aequor tum lustrant, scilicet omnem
      tellurem, gentesque polo sub utroque iacentes:
      et quidam aestivi indefessus ad aetheris ignes
      pervigilat, noctem exercens, coelumque fatigat;
      iam Galli apparent, iam se Germania late
15 (65) tollit, et albescens pater Apenninus ad auras:
      iam tandem in Borean, en! parvulus Anglia naevus
      (quanquam aliis longe fulgentior) extulit oras:
      formosum extemplo lumen, maculamque nitentem
      invisunt crebri proceres, serumque tuendo
20 (70) haerent, certatimque suo cognomine signant:
      forsitan et lunae longinquus in orbe tyrannus
      se dominum vocat, et nostra se iactat in aula.

      . . .

(78)   Non tamen has proprias laudes, nec facta silebo
      iampridem in fatis, patriaeque oracula famae.
25 (80) Tempus erit, sursum totos contendere coetus
      quo cernes longo excursu, primosque colonos
      migrare in lunam, et notos mutare penates:
      dum stupet obtutu tacito vetus incola, longeque
      insolitas explorat aves, classemque volantem.
30 (85)   Ut quondam ignotum marmor, camposque natantes
      tranavit Zephyros visens, nova regna, Columbus;
      litora mirantur circum, mirantur et undae
      inclusas acies ferro, turmasque biformes,
      monstraque foeta armis, et non imitabile fulmen.
35 (90) Foedera mox icta, et gemini commercia mundi,

English translation

And can you be unsure as to whether so great a world lacks fixed inhabitants? These too work their fields and found their own city walls, or they rush into warfare and arrange triumphs when they are victorious: here too glory has its own rewards; for these people, fear and love and mortal things touch the   5 mind.

Furthermore, just as at this moment it gives us pleasure to go over with our eyes the fields and shining stretches of the moon, and its deep sea, so the same enthusiasm drives them too, when the golden ball and the vaster globe of the earth presents itself in the cloudless sky. Then undoubtedly they survey   10 every ocean, undoubtedly every land, and the peoples lying under either pole; and some unwearied watcher stays awake by the fires of the summer sky, wearing out the night, and tires the heaven. Now the Gauls appear, now Germany raises herself up far and wide, and white-tipped father Apenninus   15 rises into the air; and now at last, to the north – see! – that tiny spot, England (though far brighter than the others), lifts up her shores. At once the leaders come in a throng to see the gorgeous light and gleaming dot, and are rooted to the spot, gazing long into the night; and they compete to designate it, each   20 with his own name. And perhaps, too, a distant tyrant in the world of the moon calls himself master [of the earth], and throws himself around in *our* palace.

[*Five lines follow, in which the speaker (the poet's Muse) declares that she can tell of other lands too, but her sister is now starting to sing.*]

Even so, I shall not keep silent about these glories of our own, nor about the deeds long since fated and the oracles of our country's fame. A time will   25 come, when you will see whole crowds reaching for the skies on a long outward flight, and the first colonists emigrating to the moon and changing their familiar household gods, while the old inhabitant is struck dumb in silent gazing and examines from afar birds never before seen and the flying fleet.

Just as once Columbus sailed over an unknown ocean and the watery   30 plains, seeking new kingdoms in the West, the shores around marvel and the waves marvel at the columns enclosed in iron, and the two-formed squadrons,

agminaque assueto glomerata sub aethere cerno.
Anglia, quae pelagi iamdudum torquet habenas,
exercetque frequens ventos, atque imperat undae;
aëris attollet fasces, veteresque triumphos
40 (95)   huc etiam feret, et victis dominabitur auris.

and the monsters pregnant with weapons, and the inimitable lightning. Soon 35
I see treaties struck and commerce between the twin worlds, and columns of
people gathered together beneath a sky which they have grown used to.
England, which for long has controlled the reins of the sea, and in great
numbers has put the winds to service and commanded the wave, will take on
power over the sky, and here too will she bring her long-running triumphs, 40
and rule over the conquered air.

Commentary

1 For the line-ending *cultoribus orbem*, see Virgil, *Georgics* 2.114, and for the pattern of a rhetorical question introduced by *et* and a form of *dubitare* see Virgil, *Aeneid* 6.806–7. *tantum* is emphatic by its position and separation from *orbem*: the implication is that the moon is *so great* that it *must* be inhabited.

2 *destitui* ('lacks') receives emphasis from being enjambed (running over on to the next line). The activities pursued by the inhabitants of the moon mirror human pursuits on earth, as reflected in the poetry of Virgil (though no herding is mentioned here, to correspond to the *Eclogues*). At *Georgics* 1.99 Virgil has *exercet . . . tellurem* (the farmer 'works the land') and at *Geo.* 2.356 *exercere solum* ('to work the soil'); for *moenia condunt* at the end of the hexameter, see Virgil, *Aeneid* 12.361 (also *Mavortia condet | moenia, Aen.* 1.276–7: Romulus 'will found the city walls of Mars').

3 *hi quoque* ('these too'): like those on earth. The translation of *Martem invadunt* offered here ('they rush into warfare') follows the parallel expression at Virgil, *Aen.* 12.712: *invadunt Martem clypeis* ('they rush into battle with their shields'); but is it possible that in this astronomical context there might also be a suggestion that the moon-dwellers quite literally 'invade Mars' (i.e. the planet)? For the expression *curare triumphos* see Virgil, *Georgics* 1.504 (the envious heaven complains that Augustus 'cares for the triumphs' of humankind).

4 With the exception of the first word, the entire line is taken verbatim from Virgil, *Aen.* 1.461, where viewing the temple of Juno at Carthage leads Aeneas to infer that the Carthaginians are a civilized people who give merit its due reward. The Virgilian passage is picked up again in the second half of the following line: as Carthage is presented in the *Aeneid* as the twin of Rome, so here the moon is cast as the twin of earth.

5 The inhabitants of the moon not only engage in human activities and reward merit, but are subject to recognizable and relatable human emotions: for fear and love (and grief and joy) as representative of human emotions, see Virgil, *Aen.* 6.733: *hinc metuunt cupiuntque, dolent gaudentque* ('hence they fear and desire, they grieve and rejoice'). The second half of the line reproduces that of *Aen.* 1.462 (of which the first half is the famous assertion *sunt lacrimae rerum*, '[here] there are tears for things'), following on from the quotation of the immediately preceding line from Virgil in the previous verse. The Virgilian component is integrated into the structure of Gray's line by making *metus* and *amor*, as well as *mortalia*, the subjects of *tangunt* (unless we

understand *est* with the first two elements and leave *mortalia* as sole subject of *tangunt*: 'these experience fear and love; and mortal things touch [their] mind').

6 Gray continues the parallel between lunar and earthly civilizations, imagining the existence of astronomers on the moon, who behave like their terrestrial equivalents. The characterization of the human astronomers' activity fittingly echoes the Roman poet Manilius, who wrote a five-book hexameter poem entitled *Astronomica*: see Manilius 1.13–15: ***iuvat ire per ipsum*** | *aëra et immenso spatiantem vivere caelo* | *signaque et adversos stellarum noscere cursus* ('it is pleasing to go through the air itself and pass one's life walking about in the boundless heaven, and to get to know the constellations and the contrary courses of the stars'). See also the lines from Ovid's speech of Pythagoras at *Metamorphoses* 15.147–9: ***iuvat ire per*** *alta* | *astra, iuvat terris et inerti sede relicta* | *nube vehi . . .* ('it is pleasing to go through the stars on high; it is pleasing to travel on a cloud, leaving behind the earth and one's fixed abode . . .').

7 Note the marked alliteration of this line: l p l p p. The final two feet perhaps recall Virgil, *Eclogues* 4.51, also cosmic in its subject matter: *terrasque tractusque maris cael**umque profundum*** ('the earth and the expanses of sea and the deep heaven'). The Virgilian line has already been evoked earlier in the poem, at *Luna habitabilis* 42–3: *Hinc longos videas tractus, terrasque iacentes* | *ordine candenti . . .* ('from here you may see long tracts, and the lands lying in a gleaming row . . .').

8 There are three elisions in this line: *idem* into *illos*, *etiam* into *ardor*, and *se* into *aureus*. Take *aureus* with *globus* in the following line. Another possible source for *ardor agit* is suggested in the note to line 27 below, but the expression may come from Virgil, *Aen.* 7.392–3, on the Latin women driven to Bacchic frenzy: *furiisque accensas pectore matres* | *idem omnes simul **ardor agit** nova quaerere tecta* ('and the same passion drives all the matrons at once, their hearts fired by frenzy, to seek new dwellings').

9 The postponement of *globus* builds up tension and perhaps suggests the waiting for its appearance on the part of the lunar astronomers. For *sudum* as the clear sky, see e.g. Virgil, *Aen.* 8.528–9.

10 The anaphora (initial repetition) of *scilicet* ('undoubtedly') is emphatic: *of course* this is what happens. The repetition *omne/omnem* ('every . . . every') conveys the vast prospect over the earth afforded to viewers on the moon. Both *omne aequor* and *omnem tellurem* are objects of *lustrant* (as is *gentes . . . iacentes*).

11 *gentesque . . . iacentes* completes the tricolon (series of three elements) of terrestrial features surveyed by the lunar astronomers: the tripartite division of sea, land and peoples perhaps serves to reinforce the suggestion in *omne/ omnem* that they see *everything*.

12 *Musae Etonenses* (1755: 2.110) has *ab*, corrected to *ad* in Starr and Hendrickson (1966: 131) and other editions. The model for this line and the next is Virgil, *Geo.* 1.291–2: *et quidam seros hiberni ad luminis ignis | pervigilat ferroque faces inspicat acuto* ('and someone stays awake by the late fire of the winter lamp and whittles torches to a point with sharp steel'). The long syllables of the first half of the line may evoke the long-drawn-out vigil of the astronomer (the Virgilian original is even more spondaic); *quidam* elides into *aestivi*, and *aestivi* into *indefessus*, enhancing the impression of uninterrupted contemplation by elision over the main caesura (principal metrical break in the middle of the line). For the line-ending *aetheris ignes*, see Lucretius, *De rerum natura* 1.1034, 5.448 and 5.585.

13 The run-on of *pervigilat* from the previous line possibly reinforces the idea of continuous vigil, while *noctem exercens* presents another elision over the usual position of the main caesura in the third foot. For *caelumque fatigat* ('and tires the heaven') see Virgil, *Aen.* 1.280 (Juno 'tires sea, earth and sky' with fear).

14 The line is wholly spondaic (i.e. consisting of long syllables) apart from the fifth foot, as the astronomer's gaze moves slowly over the surface of the earth, tracing the contours of Europe. The anaphora of *iam* ('now') marks out the different stages of the sequence of viewing: first France (*Galli*, 'the Gauls'), then Germany.

15 The verb *se . . . tollit* must be understood with both *Germania* in the previous line and *pater Apenninus* in this line. The verse is largely a direct quotation from Virgil, *Aen.* 12.702–3: *gaudetque nivali | vertice se attollens pater Appenninus ad auras* ('and father Appenninus rejoices in his snowy peak, raising himself into the air': part of a simile comparing Aeneas to various mountains). The reference to the Apennines (here personified, as in Virgil) represents Italy: the gaze of the lunar astronomer has moved east from France to Germany before heading south.

16 The course of the astronomer's eye changes direction and finally (*tandem*) moves north. The excited exclamation *en!* creates expectation, maintained by the late position of *Anglia*. The diminutive *parvulus* emphasizes the miniature appearance of England as seen from space, perhaps with a note of irony. *naevus* is literally a wart or mole on the skin; Starr and Hendrickson (1966:

133) translate as 'no bigger than a beauty spot'. *parvulus* ... *naevus* is in apposition to (i.e. describes, presenting further information, and agrees grammatically with) *Anglia*.

17 *quanquam* for *quamquam*. The parenthesis seeks to make amends for the less than flattering description in the previous line. Might *aliis longe fulgentior* ('far brighter than the others') hint at one proposed etymology of Albion ('white'), the traditional name for Britain, as well as sounding a patriotic note?

18 Note the symmetrical distribution of adjectives and nouns: *formosum* ... *lumen, maculam* ... *nitentem*. Both *lumen* ('light') and *nitentem* ('gleaming') continue the theme of shining from *fulgentior* ('brighter').

19 Virgil twice uses *tuendo* (ablative gerund from *tueor*) at the end of the line in contexts relating to a gaze that cannot be satisfied (*Aen.* 1.713; 8.265): so here the lunar luminaries never grow tired of contemplating the radiance of England.

20 The enjambed position of *haerent* lends it emphasis: the princes of the moon are utterly rooted to the spot with wondering admiration. Like earthly leaders and discoverers, they compete to give their names to this distant land.

21 *longinquus* ('distant') is emphasized by its position and separation from its noun *tyrannus*. Both terms, together with the next line, seem to imply that this presumptuous figure has little right to lay claim to the remote earthly territory of Britain – but is there really so much difference, on an ethical level, between this and the envisaged addition of the moon to the British Empire later in the poem? Perhaps it is primarily the unsubstantiated nature of the lunar despot's pretensions to mastery which is here deprecated, whereas the British actually will go on to annex the moon; even so, given that Gray has consistently presented the inhabitants of the moon as a mirror of those of earth, there remains room for ambiguity.

22 The second half of the line comes from Virgil, *Aen.* 1.140, *illa se iactet in aula* ('let [Aeolus] throw himself around in *that* palace'), uttered by Neptune as he sends the winds packing and quells the storm raised by Aeolus at Juno's command. The tone in the Virgilian passage is undoubtedly dismissive, which reinforces the pejorative suggestion of the previous line. Here *nostra* ('our') is emphatically placed, immediately after the main caesura and ahead of its noun *aula*: the lunar *tyrannus* can vaunt all he likes, but the sparkling glory of miniature Britain is *ours*. The repeated *se* (prominently placed at the start of the line) adds to the impression that the monarch of the moon is lord of *Anglia* only by his own say-so.

As observed in the previous note, however, the close parallels between the civilizations, activities and sentiments of the terrestrial and lunar worlds make this picture of the moon-ruler sit a little uncomfortably with the imperialism of the closing lines: after all, presumably he has his earthly counterpart(s), just as the other moon-dwellers do.

23 On the formula *neque te silebo* ('nor shall I keep silent about you') as a conventional motif of Latin panegyrical poetry, see K. M. Coleman (ed.), *Martial: Liber Spectaculorum*, Oxford 2006: 6, citing Horace, *Odes* 1.12.21–2 and Virgil, *Aen.* 10.792–3.

24 As in line 22, Gray's Muse identifies with a British perspective: the *patria* ('country') is the poet's own. Like the expansion of the Roman Empire in Virgil, the encroachment of the British Empire into space is fated. For the expression *in fatis* (literally 'in the fates'), see Ovid, *Metamorphoses* 1.256, *Fasti* 1.481, *Tristia* 3.2.1 and *Epistulae ex Ponto* 1.7.56.

25 For *tempus erit quo/cum* ('a time will come when …') as a formula for introducing prophetic pronouncements, see Ovid, *Fasti* 1.529, with S. J. Green (ed.), *Ovid, Fasti I: A Commentary*, Leiden and Boston 2004: 243 ('such phrases often form part of solemn prophetic diction'); *Ars amatoria* 3.69. *totos* is emphasized by its position: there will be no gradual trickle of settlers, but a vast, organized movement.

26 The sequence of long syllables (the line is entirely spondaic apart from the fifth foot) reflects the meaning of *longo excursu* ('on a long outward flight'), perhaps reinforced by the elision of *longo* into *excursu* across the expected interruption of the main caesura. *contendere coetus* and *colonos migrare … et … mutare* are both accusatives and infinitives dependent on *cernes*.

27 Travel to the moon had been envisaged by Johannes Kepler in his *Somnium* (1634), which has been called 'the first work of science fiction' (see C. Neagu, 'East-Central Europe', in S. Knight and S. Tilg (eds), *The Oxford Handbook of Neo-Latin*, 509–24, Oxford 2015, at 521). For a translation of Kepler's story, see E. Rosen, *Kepler's Somnium: The Dream, or Posthumous Work on Lunar Astronomy*, Madison 1967. The line-ending *mutare penates* is found in Marco Girolamo Vida's Latin poem of 1527 on the silk worm (Vida, *Bombyx* 1.317: *atque novis priscos cupiunt mutare penates* ['and they desire to change their old household gods for new ones']). A few lines earlier in Vida's poem appears the phrase *nova quaerere regna | ardor agit* ('an enthusiasm drives them to seek new kingdoms', *Bombyx* 1.313–14), which parallels both Gray's *ardor agit* in line 8 above and his *nova regna* in line 31 below.

28 The verse is partly modelled on Virgil, *Aen.* 1.495: *dum stupet obtutuque haeret defixus in uno* ('while he is amazed and is rooted to the spot, fixed in a single gaze': Aeneas surveys the scenes depicted on the temple of Juno at Carthage); for *obtutu tacito* ('in silent gazing') see also Virgil, *Aen.* 12.666. The line is hypermetric: the final syllable of *longeque* must be elided into *insolitas*, the first word of the next line.

29 The 'birds' (*aves*) refer to space rockets, which the lunar inhabitant examines (*explorat*) from afar – just as the travellers from earth are themselves 'exploring' something unknown and far off. *classis volans* ('the flying fleet') would be a credible expression in classical Latin, denoting swift sea-travel; but here the fleet is quite literally 'flying' through space.

30 The future expedition to the moon is compared in a simile to Columbus' voyage to America (1492), traditionally seen as the discovery of the New World. The line is wholly spondaic apart from the fifth foot, perhaps implying a long and arduous voyage. For the line-ending *camposque natantes* (literally 'the floating plains') see Lucretius, *De rerum natura* 5.488 and 6.405; also Virgil, *Geo.* 3.198.

31 The text and translation given here take *Zephyros* as object of *visens*, with the phrase *nova regna* in apposition to it (literally 'the west winds, new kingdoms'). For *nova regna* used of the 'New World' in relation to Columbus, see Ubertino Carrara's Latin epic poem *Columbus* (1715) 1.479 (*Zephyrus* appears three lines earlier, and *migrantes* [cf. *migrare*, line 27 here] in the following line).

32 The amazement of the landscape at unfamiliar intruders is emphasized by the repetition of *mirantur* ('they marvel'). Both the situation and the language closely recall Virgil's description of the journey of Aeneas' ships up the Tiber at *Aen.* 8.91–3 (with repetition of the same verb): **mirantur et undae,** | *miratur nemus insuetum fulgentia longe* | *scuta virum fluvio pictasque innare carinas* ('the waves marvel, the unaccustomed wood marvels at men's shields shining far off and at painted keels floating on the river'). The effect in both texts is to suggest an unprecedented voyage into previously unnavigated territory, similar to the voyage of the Argo (the first ship) narrated at the start of Catullus 64 and sometimes seen as the end of the pristine Golden Age.

33 The expedition comes prepared for war. *turmas . . . biformis* ('two-formed squadrons') seems to indicate cavalry, composed of man and horse: possibly there is a suggestion that in the eyes of the moon-dwellers – or of their landscape – there is something monstrous about these troops (Virgil uses

biformis of the Minotaur at *Aen.* 6.25–6 and of Scyllas at *Aen.* 6.286), reinforced by *monstra* in the following line.

34 At *Aen.* 2.237–8 Virgil calls the Trojan Horse *machina . . . feta armis* ('the device pregnant with weapons'); once again, the classical parallel does not reflect entirely favourably on the expeditionary force, suggesting treacherous intent. The second half of the line is taken directly from *Aen.* 6.590, where the sinner Salmoneus is said to have counterfeited Jupiter's 'inimitable lightning' with bronze and the clatter of horses' hooves: here it presumably refers to some kind of firearm. It may be relevant that the Virgilian tag was quoted by Francis Bacon in his discussion of advances in cosmography in *The Advancement of Learning* (1605; ed. M. Kiernan, Oxford 2000: 71): 'But to circle the Earth, as the heauenly Bodies doe, was not done, nor enterprised, till these later times: And therefore these times may iustly beare in their word, not onely *Plus vltrà* in precedence of the ancient *Non vltra*, and *Imitabile fulmen*, in precedence of the ancient: *Non imitabile fulmen,* | *Demens qui nymbos et non imitabile fulmen, &c.* But likewise, – *Imitabile Cœlum*: in respect of the many memorable voyages after the manner of heauen, about the globe of the earth'. Kiernan (2000: 272) relates *Imitabile fulmen* here to the invention of artillery.

35 Both *foedera* and *commercia* are objects of *cerno*, as is *agmina* in the following line. Any initial conflict is swiftly passed over with *mox* ('soon'), giving way to treaties and trade (if that is what *commercia* means here, rather than just 'dealings'). For *gemini commercia mundi* ('commerce between the twin worlds') see Corippus (or Gorippus), *In laudem Iustini Augusti minoris* 1.111 (also Claudian, *De raptu Proserpinae* 1.91: *geminoque facis commercia mundo* ['and you establish dealings between the twin worlds'], addressed to Mercury).

36 Gray does not spell out clearly what these people are doing. Virgil once has *agmina . . . glomerant* ('they gather their columns', *Aen.* 4.155–6), used of deer in flight. *agmina* need not refer to a military formation, though it very commonly does; likewise *glomero* is regularly used in the context of fighting (see e.g. Virgil, *Aen.* 2.315; 9.440; 9.689). In the previous line, however, we have heard of peaceful activities: treaties and commerce. If this line is not meant to signify war, it is remarkably ambiguous, and if it is supposed to signal fresh hostilities, leading to the triumphs with which the poem ends, Gray is surprisingly reticent. A twenty-first-century sensibility is probably not needed to detect a noticeable ambivalence in the poet's attitude towards the imagined lunar expedition. For *cerno* ('I see') as a marker of prophecy, see e.g. Virgil, *Aen.* 6.86–7 (an anticipation of war).

37–8 In view of the expression of these lines, it may come as a surprise that Gray's poem predates by three years Thomas Arne's song *Rule, Britannia* (1740), with words by James Thomson. Evidently the idea of British (in Gray, English) naval supremacy was prevalent in expressions of patriotic feeling around this time. For 'empire over the sea' (suggested in *imperat undae*), see Virgil, *Aen.* 1.138 (*imperium pelagi*).

39 With *fasces* and *triumphos* Gray appropriates for England ancient Roman symbols of political and military dominance. *fasces* are literally the 'rods' of office carried before Roman magistrates as a sign of their authority. We have moved here rather quickly, and by an unclear sequence (see preceding notes), from the agreements and commerce of line 35 to full imperial possession.

40 *huc etiam* ('here too' or 'even here'): in addition to all the other places where British power has now extended. That conquest has been involved is clear from *triumphos* in the previous line, but especially from *victis* ('conquered'), emphatic by its position, and juxtaposed *dominabitur* ('will rule'). The model here is Virgil, *Aen.* 1.285, where Jupiter prophesies that in time to come 'the house of Assaracus' (i.e. the Romans) *victis dominabitur Argis* ('will rule conquered Argos', i.e. the Greeks). Gray's speaker has said very little, however, about the process by which this supremacy will be accomplished, and although the final four lines are ostensibly celebratory, various details earlier in the poem arguably serve to adumbrate a perspective somewhat less one-sided than the nationalistic fervour of this conclusion (which Haan 2000: 40 sees as satirical).

Index of Names

This index includes the names of early modern (and other) authors mentioned as well as the ancient authors and biblical books referred to as inspirations and precedents in the introductions and commentaries in this volume.